IDITAROD SILVER

TEXT BY LEW FREEDMAN ❧ PHOTOGRAPHY BY JEFF SCHULTZ

EPICENTER PRESS

•

FAIRBANKS   SEATTLE

25 YEARS OF THE IDITAROD TRAIL SLED DOG RACE

Next to God, my family, and my photography, the Iditarod has been one of the biggest parts of my life,
and I dedicate this book to my wife Joan, children Ben and Hannah, and to the countless volunteers who have made
the Iditarod happen each year. I am blessed to be a part of this great event.
—J. S.

Library of Congress Cataloging-in-Publication Data
Freedman, Lewis.
     Iditarod silver / text by Lew Freedman : photography by Jeff Schultz.
     p. cm.
     Includes index.
     ISBN 0-945397-57-7 (hardbound : alk. paper). — ISBN 0-945397-56-9 (softbound : alk. paper)
     1. Iditarod Trail Sled Dog Race, Alaska—History. 2. Sled dog racing—Alaska—History. I. Schultz, Jeff. II. Title.
SF440. 15.F74 1997
798' .8—dc20

96-41043
CIP

Editor: *Tricia Brown*
Photo Editor: *Jeff Schultz*
Proofreader: *Lois Kelly*
Mapmaker: *Penny Panlener*
Cover and text design, typesetting: *Elizabeth Watson*
Prepress and printing: *Print Vision*
Production coordinator: *Nancy Deahl*

To order single copies of the trade paperback edition of *Iditarod Silver,* mail $29.95 (Washington residents add $2.46 for state sales tax) plus $5 for first-class mailing to: Epicenter Press, Box 82368, Kenmore, WA 98028.

Booksellers: Retail discounts are available from our trade distributor, Graphic Arts Center Publishing™, Box 10306, Portland, OR 97210, Phone 800-452-3032. This and other Epicenter Press titles also are available from major wholesalers

Printed in Hong Kong

First printing, December, 1996

10 9 8 7 6 5 4 3 2 1

Page 3 (opposite): Diana Dronenburg winds along Pass Creek shortly after cresting the summit of Rainy Pass in the 1989 race. Rainy Pass is the highest point on the Iditarod trail cutting through the Alaska Range. The trail in this area is very narrow and winding.

Pages 4-5 and front cover: Andy Sterns and his team are dwarfed by the spectacular Alaska Range as they approach the Rainy Pass summit, 1995.

Page 6: View from the bottom. Booties on the dogs' feet help protect their pads when the trail is icy and coarse.

Pages 8-9: Bill Cotter exits frozen Golovin Bay as he heads for shore and the village of Golovin in the 1994 race.

THE IDITAROD SPIRIT

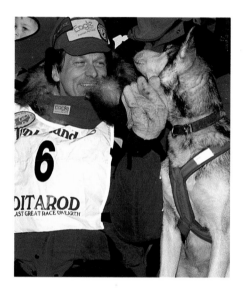

WHY WOULD ANYBODY willingly embark on a journey with an unpredictable outcome, and do it more than once?

Dog mushers, veterinarians and countless volunteers alike sign up to be a part of the annual spectacle, the Iditarod, the world's longest sled dog race. The start is on the first Saturday in March, but work on making the next Iditarod possible starts as soon as the trail-weary mushers are being dragged across the finish line by their incredibly dedicated dogs.

Working with the staff of the Iditarod Trail Committee are hundreds of volunteers and silent supporters who labor behind the scenes. For every mile of trail, someone is helping with a task. The obvious supporters are the sponsors of the race and of the competitors; however, there are many more tasks performed that largely go unnoticed. The trail is laid down and marked every year by Iditarod trail breakers as well as local volunteers working on sections near their villages. Often their only memory is a successful passage of the race, and worn out or broken snowmachines and chain saws.

An enthusiastic crowd of behind-the-scenes supporters also helps with the sixty to hundred tons of trail supplies, straw for the dogs, tents, fuel and food for the checkpoints. Every item is handled many times, from initial pick-up to final delivery in some of the most remote places in Alaska. Several thousand dog exams are performed, from the pre-race at headquarters, to team checks along the trial, to the final health exam after the finish line.

Everyone involved with the race finds himself or herself challenged to the utmost. Some of the volunteers come back year after year; some work the race only once. Just like the mushers and the dogs. The once-in-a-lifetime experience often turns into an annual trip to the Iditarod, and in some cases, leads mushers into a lifestyle where "The Race" becomes the main focus of their working and playing life.

The challenges are great and varied, whether one lifts a seventy-pound food-drop bag for the first time, enters the race for the first and only time, or returns as a champion looking for another win.

It is remarkable that all these people are working together, communicating, flying, driving, shoveling, and calculating for one common cause: the dogs. These are the true athletes, the canine racers, bred and trained for the ultimate sled dog journey, the dedicated, fast, hard-working huskies working together in a team.

I think the dogs are the ultimate reason for all of us getting together. The mutual need between "man" and dog is never more obvious than during long-distance journeys. The commitment and hard work to be part of the Iditarod experience, vicariously or real, is almost beyond description.

Thanks to all who are part of "The Iditarod Spirit."

Happy Trails,

Martin Buser

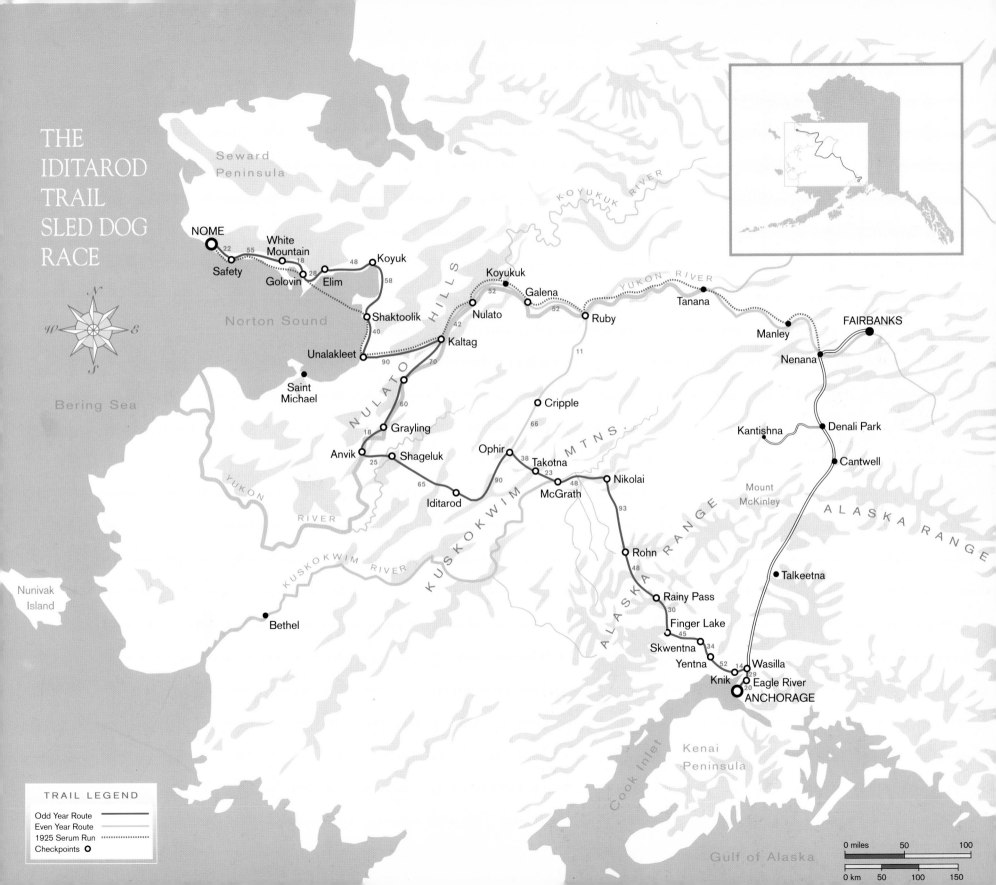

1970s

A PIONEERING RACE IS BORN

Mush dog teams a thousand miles across the Last Frontier?
In 1973, some said it couldn't be done.

 A letter is posted above an entryway in the Nome music store that belongs to former Iditarod Trail Committee President Leo Rasmussen. It was written by Joe Redington, Sr., and is addressed to local musher Howard Farley. "Dear Howard," the salutation reads, "I thought you might be interested in this race."

The letter, dated December 9, 1972, and asking for organizing help, represents the understated beginnings of The Last Great Race on Earth, the low-key origins of the 1973 adventure that was the first 1,100-mile mush along the historic mail trail between Anchorage and Nome.

This organizing letter is to the Iditarod what the Magna Carta is to democracy, the underpinning of unforeseen, unanticipated wildfire growth, the foundation of something very special.

Musher Charlie Harrington photographed this view from the runners as he crossed the highest point on the Iditarod Trail: Rainy Pass. CHARLIE HARRINGTON

The first Iditarod Trail Sled Dog Race began a few months later, inaugurating a tradition that on the first Saturday in March each year Alaska remembers a simpler, more rustic time when the only way across this frigid and unforgiving frontier was by dog sled. The Iditarod boasted proud origins, recognizing the pioneering efforts of grizzled mushers who linked the state's small settlements by driving the mail through sleet and storm. And, more specifically, the race honors the bold mushers and dogs of the 1925 serum run that hurriedly delivered life-saving medicine to Nome to subdue a dangerous diphtheria epidemic.

However, what in a quarter-century has presented the world such famed mushing champions as Rick Swenson and Susan Butcher, such esteemed lead dogs as Andy and Granite, and uncounted tales of adventure, was at first an iffy proposition. As the race picks up speed, as the athletic dogs become more proficient and the mushers more efficient, memory recedes. Few recall that in the beginning most Alaskans doubted whether such a race was even possible.

Could dogs race more than a thousand miles? Would the mushers even make it to Nome? Those were legitimate, unanswered questions when the Iditarod began.

The one true believer always was Joe Redington, Sr., a small, leathery-faced sourdough who over the years has evolved into an Alaska icon. The man known as the "Father of the Iditarod" earned his title.

Nearly fifty years ago, Redington, who was born in Pennsylvania and grew up in Oklahoma, crossed the border from Canada into Alaska with his family. During a rest stop, someone offered the couple a puppy. That dog became the first in the renowned Redington kennel in Knik, Alaska, which at its peak in 1988 harbored 527 dogs and even now holds 250, probably the greatest concentration of huskies in the world.

Redington has long ago lost track of how many miles he's traveled standing on sled runners as loping dogs bound across pristine terrain under moonlit nights, but it is well into six figures, perhaps even a quarter-million miles. His love of long-distance rides and of the animals themselves, so well-endowed with stamina and the born instinct to run, helped motivate him when he saw dogs' roles in Alaska villages reduced by the snowmachine.

By the early 1970s, it seemed, the only racing dogs around were huskies entered in the annual Fur Rendezvous World Championship sprint races. Redington set out to restore the respect of the long-distance husky and revive interest in the dormant Iditarod trail.

In 1967, the hundredth anniversary of Alaska's purchase from Russia, a Wasilla woman named Dorothy Page promoted the idea of holding a dog sled race as part of the celebration. The race was held on the old Iditarod trail, but was just twenty-eight miles long.

"That was Dorothy's idea for the

▲ Joe Redington, Sr., and Roamer, the primary sire of the Redington kennel. In this 1974 photo, Roamer was fourteen years old and lived for another year. He is the grandfather of Obie and Andy, who led Rick Swenson to win four Iditarods; the grandfather of Granite, who led Susan Butcher's team to victory; and the great-grandfather of Dugan and Axle, lead dogs for Libby Riddles when she finished first in 1985. A profile of Roamer shows an unusually deep, muscular chest, a superb quality for a distance dog. RICHARD BURMEISTER

◄ The Iditarod Trail Sled Dog Race was the brainchild of Joe Redington, Sr., but raising money for the first year's purse kept him out of the race. Here, Redington trots along with his dogs as he approaches the 1974 finish line. RICHARD BURMEISTER

I-did-a-what?

"Iditarod" is a Shageluk Indian word meaning *clear water,* used in the name of the Iditarod River. So says one definition. But that's not the last word. Another source claims that it's an Ingalik Indian word, "Haiditarod," meaning *distant place.*
And yet another version comes from Professor James Kari of the University of Alaska Native Language Center: "The name 'Iditarod' came from an Ingalik and Holikachuk word, 'hidedhod,' for the Iditarod River. This name means *distant* or *distant place.*" In 1979, Kari claimed the word was still known by elders in the villages of Shageluk, Anvik, Grayling, and Holy Cross.

Lucky Number Five

Joe Redington, Sr., finished in fifth place in 1975, 1977, and 1978.

▲ His face encrusted with frost, Rick Mackey celebrates after finishing the 1975 race. Rick and his father, Dick Mackey, were the first and only father-son pair to win the Iditarod, Dick in 1978 and Rick in 1983. Both men wore the number thirteen in their winning races. RICHARD BURMEISTER

▲ ▶ Dorothy Page set up shop at Nome in 1989, selling Iditarod souvenirs including the annual that she edited and published since 1974. Page, who is remembered as the "Mother of the Iditarod," died later that year.

▶ Dick Mackey relaxes with friends and dignitaries in Nome after the 1974 race. From left is Mayor Bob Renshaw, Julie Farley, and Howard Farley.

RICHARD BURMEISTER

▶ ▶ Joe Redington, Sr., brought along his camera almost every year. Here he captures a scene on the Bering Sea near Elim. JOE REDINGTON, SR.

centennial race," said Redington. "I want to give Dorothy all the credit in the world for the centennial race."

The short race that preceded the full-length Iditarod was a big hit, though the organizers struggled to come up with the promised $25,000 in prize money, Redington recalled.

Page became renowned for her devotion to the Iditarod as it developed, from its seed in that centennial race until her death at age sixty-eight in 1989. A long-time journalist, she took responsibility for publishing the annual yearbook of mushers' biographies. Today she is remembered as the "Mother of the Iditarod."

But it was Redington who was the Iditarod's creative force. Redington was determined to show the world these Alaska dogs were capable of incredible feats. Along with Susan Butcher in 1979, Redington would actually take a dog team to the summit of 20,320-foot Mount McKinley, the tallest mountain in North America, demonstrating his own implicit faith in huskies.

Originally, for 1973, Redington proposed a mush from Anchorage to Iditarod, the mining ghost town some five hundred miles down the trail. Dick Mackey, then an Anchorage sprint musher, was one of the most enthused of those who listened to Redington and saw the possibilities for excitement in a long-distance event.

Mackey remembered the general reaction among those who even thought it could

MONTANA MUSHER TERRY ADKINS COMES A LONG WAY TO GO A LONG WAY

The military shipped Adkins to Montana, but that didn't stop him from returning each year for the Iditarod.

TERRY ADKINS made himself a popular fixture in the Iditarod Trail Sled Dog Race by traveling more miles than anyone else. Not by dog sled. By truck.

Adkins got himself involved in the first Iditarod in 1973 and didn't extricate himself for twenty-one years. What set Adkins apart, besides his longevity, was that unlike most of the mushers who competed in the 1,100-mile race year after year, Adkins didn't live in Alaska.

It wasn't unusual for a handful of mushers from the Lower Forty-eight states, Europe, or Japan to contest the Iditarod each year, but generally, those visitors from outside Alaska were drop-ins, people who wished to mush the Iditarod once to say they had done it. Rarely would those mushers plan a return engagement, and even more rarely would they become regulars. Adkins was the only entrant living outside Alaska who competed year after year.

An Air Force officer stationed in Anchorage when the Iditarod was created in 1973, Adkins served as the race's first chief veterinarian. However, Adkins was then shipped out, eventually settling in Sand Coulee, Montana, near Great Falls. Wherever he was, he made time to race the Iditarod, and he competed twenty times between 1974 and 1994.

Beginning in 1983, Adkins regularly drove the twenty-five hundred miles from his Montana home just to get to the starting line in Anchorage. He earned his share of official finishers' belt buckles, too, placing among the top twenty slots twelve times with a best placing of eighth in 1984.

Raised on a farm outside Greenville, Kentucky, population two thousand, Adkins retains a slight southern drawl, and when he's not decked out in heavy-duty winter gear, he looks more like a cowboy than a musher. He is prone to wearing blue jeans, cowboy hats, cowboy boots, and jackets with fringe.

A year on the trail as a vet during the first Iditarod whetted Adkins' appetite to give the race a try in 1974. Racing was less sophisticated then, and Adkins pulled together a team from the

Terry Adkins served as chief veterinarian for the first Iditarod, and he was hooked. For the next twenty years, Adkins made the trip to Nome as a musher. BILL DEVINE

Anchorage dog pound. His team of refugees consisted of twelve dogs, and they all made it all the way to Nome.

"I had 429 miles on the team, mostly from short races," said Adkins. "The dogs aren't different these days, they've just been fine-tuned. They're bred for stamina and to have tough feet."

Adkins witnessed many other changes as the Iditarod grew up and evolved. Lightweight sleds and sled runners were developed. Mushers learned about animal nutrition, and premium dog foods were invented. And even booties, the little sock-like pouches designed to protect dogs' feet as they trot along icy trails, saw improvement. Or rather the method of holding them in place advanced. Mushers used to tape the booties tight with such utensils as black electrical tape, said Adkins. Then along came Velcro, and they could be snapped on.

"It made it a lot quicker to put them on," said Adkins, resulting in checkpoint efficiency. "In the old days, I remember getting down on my knees and taking off booties with my teeth."

Over the years, the jovial Adkins developed a reputation as a man who could be counted on out on the trail. He won the Most Inspirational Musher award in 1986 and twice won the Iditarod Sportsmanship Award. Once, Adkins mushed most of the last thousand miles with a broken right hand suffered in a crash. He just wrapped it up and mushed on. Another time Adkins stopped his own race to care for a dog belonging to competitor Jerry Austin. The dog had been kicked by a drunk in a village. Another time Adkins stopped racing to pick up fellow musher Robin Jacobson, who had lost his sled.

"I just think when someone gets in trouble, the race ends," said Adkins. "Because it is just a race."

In 1991, Adkins thought he had his best chance ever to win the race. He was coming off a victory in Minnesota's five-hundred-mile John Beargrease Sled Dog Marathon and was brimming with confidence. He dressed his dogs accordingly— in pink scarves and pink booties.

Adkins pushed to the lead early, but his race was wrecked by the broken hand and a series of snowstorms that slowed down the pace. Adkins had plenty of time that year to indulge one of his pastimes with other mushers stuck in checkpoints—playing poker.

"I enjoyed the challenge of the race, the people along the trail, and just running dogs," said Adkins, who stepped away from the Iditarod at age fifty in 1994 to nurse an arthritic back. "And there's always the chance you have the [winning] team."

At the finish line of Adkins' last Iditarod, checker Leo Rasmussen made a brief presentation. He said a collection had been taken to buy the Montanan an appropriate gift, but that the small amount gathered permitted purchase of only a small present. Then Rasmussen handed Adkins a roll of toilet paper.

Joke or not, Adkins felt he deserved a different reward. Parked under the finish arch on Front Street, Adkins reached into his sled bag, pulled out a bottle of Canadian whiskey and took a celebratory gulp.

If Adkins thought retirement would be easier than coaxing a team of hustling huskies through the Alaska wilderness and fending off frostbite, he was mistaken. One day within a year of his last Iditarod, Adkins was quietly sitting in his living room when he heard his dogs howling. He got up and went to the window and looked out, but saw nothing suspicious. He sat down again. Once more the dogs went berserk. This time, Adkins, in his stocking feet, threw open the front door and stepped out on the porch.

He promptly was bitten by a rattlesnake. And the snake held on, fangs gripping his ankle tightly. Stunned, Adkins tried to throw it off, but couldn't. The only weapon within reach was a shovel. Adkins grabbed it and was able to beat the snake off.

Before he phoned for emergency assistance, Adkins took off his belt and turned it into a tourniquet. And when the cinch was good and tight on his leg, Adkins tied it off with an Iditarod finishers' belt buckle.

All those years of racing the Iditarod finally paid off in a big way. 🐾

◄▲ B.A. McAlpine is poised at the 1973 starting line. Note the absence of a sled bag, and that McAlpine's provisions are held in place by ropes. At far left is "Muktuk" Marston, famous leader of Alaska's Eskimo Scouts during World War II. Marston donated $10,000 toward the first race's $50,000 purse. ANCHORAGE MUSEUM OF HISTORY AND ART

▲ Dick Wilmarth waits for the signal at the starting line of the 1973 Iditarod. His handlers will keep the dogs under control until the countdown to "Go!" The starting line was Tudor Track, now known as Tozier Track in memory of Dick Tozier, a long-time supporter of both sprint and distance dog mushing. ANCHORAGE MUSEUM OF HISTORY AND ART

◄ In the 1970s, mushers already knew that proper care of the dogs' feet was critical to performance. Dan Seavey tends to a team member's paws. ANCHORAGE MUSEUM OF HISTORY AND ART

be done: "No one's heard of Iditarod. Why don't you run to Nome?" Done.

These days, the Iditarod is operated with an almost military-like efficiency. A trail committee and executive offices are in place year-round. The purse is $300,000 or more. The race is manned by some fifteen hundred volunteers at the start, finish and checkpoints along the trail; approximately thirty snowmachine drivers who mark the trail with stakes and smooth it with their tread; about thirty veterinarians who oversee dog care amongst the world's greatest canine athletes; and a few dozen pilots who fly up and down the trail delivering dog food and supplies, as well as key officials to checkpoints, and who constitute the heralded Iditarod air force.

The Iditarod is both splashy sporting event and big business now, but in 1973 it was an infant struggling to walk—and to gain credibility. Redington worked with Tom Johnson and Gleo Huyck to incorporate the Iditarod, but when Redington guaranteed a purse of $50,000 at the finish line, he astounded the mushing community. At the time, said Howard Farley, also an initial organizer, there wasn't $50,000 in prize money for all the dog races in the world combined. No wonder people thought Redington was nuts.

"When I guaranteed a purse of $50,000, we didn't have a dime," said Redington. His pledge became a reality only through a combination of the largest of old World War II Eskimo Scouts leader Col. "Muktuk" Marston, who donated $10,000, and the Bank of the North, which approved the cosigning of a $30,000 loan for Redington by local businessman Bruce Kendall. Redington had to put up his Knik homestead as collateral, though, and the frantic fund-raising effort kept him from entering the race he created.

Redington's salesmanship had whipped up enough interest to bring thirty-four dog teams to the Anchorage starting line at the then-called Tudor Track sprint complex.

The Iditarod is seen as one of the last true solitary wilderness pursuits in the world, but that first year racers were allowed to mush in duets. Only a few double-driver teams participated, and brothers Robert and Owen Ivan placed 16th, the only double mushers to finish.

When the mushers gathered in Alaska's largest city for departure, the real issue was whether anyone at all would finish. A feeling of excitement pervaded the mushers, a feeling of being in on the ground floor of something new, perhaps a once-in-a-lifetime race.

"We were explorers, man," said Mackey, who became one of the Iditarod's most effusive early supporters. "We were all walking ten feet tall. It was a big deal."

No one had raced huskies a thousand or more miles.

At the turn of the century, Nome gained worldwide fame as the hub of one of the great gold rushes. Some 20,000 people flooded its beaches searching for riches. Wyatt Earp, the Old West marshal, was among those who drifted north to make

▲ Dick Wilmarth at the start of the first Iditarod in 1973. He would go on to win the race, but never entered again. ANCHORAGE MUSEUM OF HISTORY AND ART

▲ Robert and Owen Ivan set out for Nome in 1973, the only year in which double-driver teams were allowed. ANCHORAGE DAILY NEWS PHOTO

Birth of a Slogan

Ian Wooldridge, a sports reporter for the *London Daily Mail*, followed the race in 1977. He first called the Iditarod "The World's Last Great Adventure."

▲ A musher passes through Farley's Camp outside Nome on his way to the 1973 finish line. ANCHORAGE DAILY NEWS PHOTO

▶ Veterinarian Tony Funk examines Rick Swenson's lead dogs, Obie and Andy. BILL DEVINE

a mark. But when gold fever subsided in the early years of the twentieth century, Nome became a mecca for something quite different—the longest, most challenging dog sled races.

The All-Alaska Sweepstakes was created in 1908, and while the 408 mile race from Nome to Council and back was contested just ten times before World War I interrupted, its heroes became enduring legends in Alaska lore. Scotty Allan and Leonhard Seppala, who also played a key role in the serum run, were three-time champions, and John "Iron Man" Johnson was a two-time winner and the lasting record-holder.

Growing up in rural Minnesota, a young boy studying survival skills who had a keen appreciation of adventure, read stories of the early mushers and became a fan. That boy was Rick Swenson, who in the modern era emulated his heroes and became the Iditarod's winningest champion with five titles.

But even those early Sweepstakes champions who introduced Siberian huskies into the Alaska breeding mix never attempted a race so long. At the first Iditarod's pre-race banquet, George Attla of North Pole, the ten-time world sprint mushing champion, announced he had conferred with Athabaskan elders for an estimate of how long it should take the dogs to run to Nome. The race, proclaimed Attla, would take ten days.

"George Attla was the first to predict a ten-day race," said Bill Cotter, the veteran

ANDY: AN INTERNATIONAL STAR, AN OLD FRIEND

THE TRUE STARS of the Iditarod Trail Sled Dog Race are the huskies that pull the sleds. And the superstars among them are the lead dogs, those with special abilities not only to pull, but to make astute choices in the wilderness with a sense that makes them seem almost human.

Andy, the leader on all four of Rick Swenson's 1970s and 1980s championships, was the top dog of the Iditarod's first decade, the Michael Jordan-magnitude star among all other hard-working dogs. In a tough breed, he stood out as the toughest.

During the dog's prime racing years nearly twenty years ago, not only was Andy the best leader—the king of the Iditarod—but while on loan to Swenson's friend Sonny Lindner, he led

Andy was with Swenson for four championships. He also led Swenson to top finishes in the Knik 120, the Kuskokwim 300, and the All-Alaska Sweepstakes. When Swenson loaned him out to friend Sonny Lindner for the 1984 Yukon Quest, Andy led yet another team to a first-place finish.

a team to victory in the thousand-mile Yukon Quest between Fairbanks and Whitehorse, Yukon Territory. Later, Andy also played a part in the European Alpirod stage race championship won by Kathy Swenson, at the time Swenson's wife.

Several mushers have described the best leader in their kennel and on the trail as a "once-in-a-lifetime dog." Certainly, Swenson felt that sort of admiration and affection for Andy. Swenson has never been viewed as the most sentimental of men, but he is unabashed when it comes to revealing his emotions about the dog that meant so much to him. The Two Rivers, Alaska, musher felt such a special kinship for the husky that when his son was born he named the boy Andy after the dog. The dog always will have a special place in Swenson's heart.

"He's probably the most personable dog I ever had," said Swenson.

In 1988, when Andy was retired and no longer part of Swenson's team, someone asked the musher if he missed his old leader. "I think about him almost every day," he said. "Hardly a day goes by that I don't think about Andy." 🐾

▲ George Attla was an established sprint mushing champion when he decided to enter the 1973 Iditarod. His team came in fourth in the first distance race. ANCHORAGE MUSEUM OF HISTORY AND ART

▶ Bill Cotter served as a checker at the first checkpoint in the first Iditarod. Then he decided to run it for himself. Here he is, frosted over, in the 1975 race. Cotter has run the race eleven times.

RICHARD BURMEISTER

musher from Nenana who was a volunteer checkpoint checker for the first Iditarod. The elders and Attla eventually were proven correct. Eventually. It took most of two decades for the Iditarod to evolve into a ten-day event. The first ten-day Iditarod winning time was recorded in 1992, when Martin Buser of Big Lake notched his first victory. The mushers of 1973 truly headed off into the unknown. Lavon Barve says it was like being Lewis and Clark.

In fact, unlike most sports in which distances are measured precisely, the exact distance of the Iditarod remains unclear. At first the Iditarod was figured to be 1,049 miles long. Redington said it was at least a thousand miles from Anchorage to Nome by dog team and then he added in the forty-nine-mile bonus representing Alaska's status as the nation's forty-ninth state. Gradually, it became apparent the distance was about a hundred miles longer. Changing weather and shifting ground conditions each year mean the trail is never the same from year to year, so the distance is rounded off to eleven hundred miles.

Similarly, over time, checkpoints have changed, and the Iditarod now shifts between a northern route and southern route in even and odd years, so as not to terribly tax the hospitality of some small villages. But when the first mushers gathered, they were more concerned with getting from point to point than how.

"The sense was this was going to be a great adventure," said Farley, one of the initial organizers. "'This is going to be great.'"

These days, Iditarod racers mush sturdy, short lightweight sleds and carry minimal gear. There is much required equipment, including sleeping bag, ax and stove (for protection against sudden, life-threatening storms), and, symbolically, Iditarod mail. The autographed packets of cachets the mushers take are used for race fund-raising, but also represent the link with the past, when the postman traversed the trail.

Technological advancements coupled with experience mean the mushers are propelling just a hundred and fifty pounds of weight. However, the early Iditarod racers like Farley, Attla, and Mackey drove huge wooden freight sleds designed for transportation, not racing, and given the uncertainty of the challenge facing them, loaded up on food and equipment.

Farley, who has raised touring dogs in Nome since the early 1960s, said his sled was more than thirteen feet long, compared to today's more streamlined six-foot-plus models.

"We took two of everything," he said. "Tents. Porcelain cook pots. Overall, the sled had to weigh five hundred pounds."

Farley, who was forty-three at the time, remembers the first Iditarod was an old man's race. No one had huskies specifically trained for a long-distance event because there was no long-distance event around. Mostly, the men—and it was all men the first year—who owned dogs came from Alaska's small, isolated, off-the-road-system

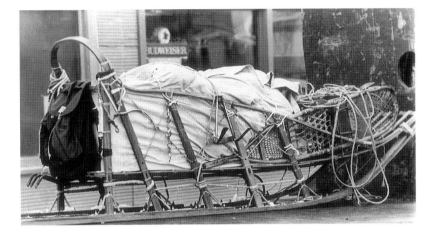

No Odometer on This Sled

The Iditarod Trail Sled Dog Race is billed as "The Last Great Race on Earth," a 1,049-mile course that travels from Anchorage to Nome, crossing two mountain ranges, two great rivers, and the sea ice of Norton Sound. It's actually about 1,100 miles long.

◄ ▲ A 1974 finisher's sled at the end of the trail is still packed to the hilt. RICHARD BURMEISTER

◄ George Attla (left) and Herbie Nayokpuk competed in the 1973 race. They remain racing legends in Alaska; Attla, for his reputation as a champion sprint musher, and Nayokpuk for his incredible speed, lending him the nickname "Shishmaref Cannonball." ANCHORAGE DAILY NEWS PHOTO

▲ Participants in the 1973 race wore wool, down, and heavy boots against the deep cold. The white vapor barrier boots known as "bunny boots" have become part of a cold weather uniform commonly seen throughout Alaska. ANCHORAGE DAILY NEWS PHOTO

Athabaskan Indian or Eskimo villages of the Interior. The dogs had been raised as reliable work dogs that earned their keep by transporting firewood or working trap lines for people who were rooted in a subsistence living style. The people depended on fishing, hunting, and trapping for existence, and the dogs were partners in the endeavors. These same dogs made the daring journey to Anchorage for the Fur Rondy sprint championship, or to Fairbanks for the North American.

Typically, in the smallest villages, residents donated their top dogs to the best musher who carried the banner of the community in the big competitions, as those left behind at home glued themselves to radios to listen.

By the early 1970s, some of the most prominent racers, like Attla, had developed their own breeding programs and were raising dogs purely for racing, but overall, the work-race dog represented the history of the Native mushers' teams. Many of the village entrants like Herbie Nayokpuk, known as the "Shishmaref Cannonball," Bobby Vent, Isaac Okleasik, and Ken Chase, were regarded as owners of the toughest, best dogs.

The tiny town of Knik is located about fifty miles north of Anchorage. In the first Iditarod, it was the first checkpoint. Bill Cotter, who later would become a champion of the thousand-mile Yukon Quest race and a perennial Iditarod contender, was the first checker at the first checkpoint. And the first mushers he checked in on a dark night

▲ Crowds and cameras lined the race course in the first-ever Iditarod as mushers sped through Anchorage on their way to Nome. ANCHORAGE DAILY NEWS PHOTO

► Editor of *The Nome Nugget,* Albro Gregory was among the first newspapermen to get the story into print, proof that men and dogs could endure more than a thousand miles across Bush Alaska in the dead of winter. ANCHORAGE DAILY NEWS PHOTO

Olympian Musher

In 1932, Col. Norman Vaughan competed for the United States in the single time that dog mushing has been featured in the Olympics.

were Attla and Oklesik of Teller, two old, cagey rivals who had placed a $1,000 bet on who'd be first to the checkpoint. Oklesik beat Attla and claimed their personal prize. Attla lamented the loss. Since he wasn't sure the prizes would truly be there when the racers hit Nome, he said he figured he'd lost out on his only chance to make money on the race.

The front of the pack consisted of a miner named Dick Wilmarth, Vent, Dan Seavey, Attla, Nayokpuk, and Oklesik. The Native mushers had loaded their sleds with fish they'd caught. Many other mushers actually bought supplies as they went. The pace was slow compared to current standards. Rather than race through the night, mushers who had little experience in night travel raced during daylight hours, then made camp. Hence, the notion that the first Iditarods were just long camping trips. That idea underestimated the mushers' pride, professionalism, and commitment to chasing the $12,000 first prize. The mushers did go hard, but their equipment, the weight they were carrying, and their experimental feeding patterns meant they weren't prepared to mush as long a period at a stretch.

It would be some time before scientific study revealed dogs running the Iditarod needed to ingest seven thousand calories a day. In 1973, dogs and mushers all were feeling their way. The chief veterinarian that year was Terry Adkins, an Air Force captain stationed at Elmendorf Air Force Base in Anchorage. Adkins, who mushed the race

◀ In the first running of the Iditarod, with no speed record to challenge, front-runner Dick Wilmarth rests his dogs outside Nome. No one was able to overtake him before he crossed the finish line in 20 days, 49 minutes. ANCHORAGE DAILY NEWS PHOTO

◀▼ Dick Mackey's team at the start of the 1978 race. BILL DEVINE

"You can never duplicate the feeling [of the 1973 Iditarod] because when we left down there from the track, half the family was there, but the mothers and daughters and so forth were all crying. And it was tough on them because they thought they're never going to see you again, and you're going off in the middle of nowhere. And I suspect a great many of us wondered if, in fact, we would make it.

"I went on the assumption that if anyone made it, it was going to be me."
—Dick Mackey,
who finished in the top ten of
every race from 1973 to 1978,
when at last he took the title.

BUSH HOSPITALITY: GOOD EATS AND WARM WELCOMES ALONG THE TRAIL

IT IS OFTEN SAID that Anchorage is the biggest village in Alaska, and from the standpoint of the Iditarod Trail Sled Dog Race that certainly is true. Anchorage is a city of 250,000 people, by far the largest community in the forty-ninth state, and where the 1,100-mile race begins.

Every year on the first Saturday in March, thousands of fans line Fourth

Villagers roll out the welcome mat when the mushers move through their towns. Kaltag is the last village on the Yukon River and separates the Indians of the Interior from the Eskimos on the coast at Unalakleet.

Avenue to send the waving and grinning mushers off into the wilderness. A festive atmosphere prevails, with vendors selling souvenirs and snacks.

Some ten days later, the weary, sometimes frostbitten mushers drive their dog teams into the old Gold Rush town of Nome along the Bering Sea coast.

Anchorage and Nome are two of the best-known communities in Alaska, but it is the villages that give the Iditarod a special flavor. Small and far-flung, the Athabaskan and Eskimo villages serve as checkpoints and havens for mushers.

Some of the checkpoints are simply solitary cabins in the woods. Some are thriving communities. Joe Delia, who has a landmark cabin in Skwentna, has been involved with the Iditarod for years. Other communities have gained a special fame in modern-day Alaskans' minds because of their Iditarod relationship.

The checkpoints have changed during the Iditarod's first twenty-five years. Even now there is a northern route and southern route so several villages can swap participation in alternating years to relieve them from

the overwhelming commitment of catering to the horde of mushers, officials, and followers who pass through as the race speeds along.

The Iditarod race begins in Anchorage, passes through Eagle River on the outskirts of the city twenty miles away, and then a day later goes through an official re-start in Wasilla in the Matanuska-Susitna Valley some fifty miles north of Anchorage. Linking up directly with the original Iditarod trail, the race passes through Knik, Yentna Station, and Skwentna, all sparsely populated. Next the trail takes mushers to Finger Lake and Rainy Pass, the highest elevation on the trail at more than three thousand feet, and Rohn Roadhouse, as the dogs and drivers head through the Alaska Range. From there mushers begin their visits to the Native villages, checking in at Nikolai, population 109.

Next on the route is McGrath and Takotna, where checkpoint supervisor Jan Newton is on hand as she has been for twenty years. In a village of seventy people, said Newton, the March excitement provided by the race is the antidote to cabin fever.

Takotna has developed several traditions over the years, including a meal of Kodiak king crab—and moose stew and chili for all the mushers. High school students lend a hand by hauling the dog food and straw to the mushers' camping area.

"Come in and have a bite to eat and sit and visit," is the theme, said Newton. "We pamper the mushers who come in."

Depending on the pace of the race, mushers stay for just a short while and then race on quickly, or they hunker down and take their mandatory twenty-four-hour rest that must be declared somewhere along the trail.

Takotna is more than four hundred miles into the race, and as race strategy has changed and the race itself has speeded up, more and more mushers choose to spend an entire day in the community. The residents love it.

"It's less hectic than when they just buzz in and out or stay for three or four hours," said Newton. "Mushers know they pay for their food with autographs."

Leaving Takotna, the next stop is Ophir, population zero, a tent stop near a cabin that's owned by Dick and Audra Forsgren, and an official checkpoint since

1974. The couple don't live there year-round, but fly in annually to host the checkpoint during the Iditarod. Ophir is followed on the southern route by Iditarod itself, the old, abandoned mining town. Once a community of ten thousand people, Iditarod, the official halfway mark on the journey to Nome, is now a ghost town.

After the halfway point, the race stops in Shageluk, then turns to the Yukon River, passing through the communities along the vast frozen river: Anvik, Grayling, and Eagle Island on the southern route; Cripple, Ruby, Galena, and Nulato on the northern route.

Kaltag is the first village checkpoint on both courses, marking the home stretch and the area where storms are routine, often determining the final finishing places.

Unalakleet, with a population of more than seven hundred people, is the major hub of the area. In Native language it is known as the place "where the east wind blows." And the wind does indeed blow strongly there. From Unalakleet, the first checkpoint on the Bering Sea coast, mushers go on through Shaktoolik, Koyuk, Elim, Golovin, White Mountain, and at last, Safety, the roadhouse pass-through just twenty-two

miles from Nome, and the finish line.

Nome features the polished burled arch on Front Street with its memorable sign that reads "End of the Iditarod Dog Race." Typically, whatever time of day it is, daylight or middle of the night, the street is jammed with revelers. A siren sounds to alert spectators that a musher is on the way. The siren blasts for the first musher and for every musher thereafter, so those sleeping can be awakened and come out to cheer on every finisher.

It is a celebratory scene in Nome. Fans bundle up and ignore snowstorms, frigid temperatures, or howling winds when the winner approaches.

Although the biggest party of them all takes place in Nome, similar but smaller festive scenes greet the mushers in every village when the whole town may turn out to say hello and applaud.

"I don't think the villages get enough credit," said former Iditarod Trail Committee President Leo Rasmussen. "There's no way you can put a value on what they do."

Sometimes the Iditarod ships out hot dogs, coffee, and other food for thank-you parties, and once, said Rasmussen, the race organization distributed Iditarod commemorative

pins. Volunteers along the trail generally receive certificates acknowledging their participation, as well.

The Iditarod official who maintains the closest connections to the villages is race manager Jack Niggemyer. A burly man with a bird's nest of a dark beard, and thick, brown flowing hair that he sometimes gathers into a pony-tail, Niggemyer is the man who handles race logistics. As the Iditarod's ambassador to

the villages, he makes regular off-season visits to the isolated communities that are off the road system, reachable only by small prop planes.

His goal to make sure the villages feel like a true part of the Iditarod.

"It's politics," Niggemyer said. "But it's doing it with people I enjoy being with. If I get a week off, and it's a choice of going to Hawaii or Unalakleet, it's almost always Unalakleet." 🐾

Tim Osmar makes a late-night arrival at the Takotna checkpoint. The checkpoint is famous for its friendly atmosphere and for feeding a home-cooked meal to every musher who passes through their town hall, shown in the background here. They also provide hot water for the mushers to use to cook their dog food. In the mid-1990s, many mushers chose to take the mandatory twenty-four-hour layover here because of the hospitality and quiet this small village offers.

Rick Mackey, in camp at the Rohn River, sets about feeding his dogs. In the late 1970s, many mushers fed their dogs a fish stew supplemented with commercial dog food. JIM BROWN

the next year and became an Iditarod mainstay over the next two decades, joked, "I was the only sucker they could find to go that year." His first impression of the Iditarod, traveling by small plane, was that it looked kind of easy. But dogs and people on the ground found the going hazardous.

"I think I sewed up some mushers as well as dogs that year," said Adkins.

One characteristic emerged in the first Iditarod and has persisted throughout its existence. The race, it soon became apparent, was for everybody, the fast and the slow. There was something special about driving a dog team through the wilderness, over harsh terrain, battling the elements. The spirit of adventure, enthusiasm, and wonder struck top contenders and back-of-the-pack mushers equally. For many, the most coveted prize of all was just earning a finisher's Iditarod belt buckle.

"It sounds corny, but it's just a dream," said seventeen-time competitor John Barron of Sheep Creek, whose first Iditarod was in 1979. "The Iditarod doesn't make sense financially. I love my dogs. It's like a rancher with a ranch or a farmer with a farm. It's in my blood."

Barron's perspective is pervasive. The special bonding with the dogs and the land continues to make the Iditarod a great lure.

"Some of it is the mystique of Alaska," said Bobby Lee, a former musher and longtime race marshal. "It's the fact you can be out there under the full moon and the northern lights, and hear the wolf howling."

Winner Dick Wilmarth, who never competed again, finished the debut Iditarod in 20 days, 49 minutes. Vent was second, Seavey third, Attla fourth. They were the fast guys. The mushers like Farley were hundreds of miles back along the trail listening to the radio when the top group finished.

"I didn't think I'd be up front," said Farley, who remembers loving every minute of being on the trail. "The trail conditions were beautiful. We didn't know where we were much of the time. You'd just run between cabins."

Of the thirty-four teams that started, twenty-two completed the run to Nome. John Schultz finished in 32 days, 5 hours, nearly two weeks behind Wilmarth. Schultz was the first recipient of a special prize that is still awarded—he won the initial red lantern, awarded to the final finisher in each year's race.

"They figured the last guy ought to get something," said Farley. "We just kind of made it up as we went along."

Farley, in twentieth place, finished in 31 days, 11 hours. But he was mushing home along the Bering Sea coast. From Unalakleet on, the last 280 miles, he and his dogs were in familiar territory. And when he mushed across the finish line, he was given a hero's welcome by enthusiastic cheering neighbors.

Race organizers had promised a party for everyone who got to Nome, and they came through. Thus began the tradition of a post-race banquet. At the get-together,

▲ Joe Redington, Sr., (left) the "Father of the Iditarod," and Orville Lake (right) present 1973 winner Dick Wilmarth with a trophy and a check for $12,000 at the Nome Awards Banquet.
ANCHORAGE DAILY NEWS PHOTO

◄ Nome musher and race organizer Howard Farley (behind the sled) is rested and ready at the start of the first Iditarod in 1973. ANCHORAGE MUSEUM OF HISTORY AND ART

LEO RASMUSSEN: THE MAN MUSHERS CAN'T WAIT TO MEET

LEO RASMUSSEN is Mr. Iditarod.

The bearded, enthusiastic, fifty-five-year-old former mayor of Nome was there for the first Iditarod in 1973, and he's been there for every one since.

"There is really nothing like it in the world that's unmotorized," said Rasmussen.

Rasmussen has been the president of the Iditarod Trail Committee, a high-visibility leadership position in the organization. But almost equally visible for mushers, he's been the man who greeted them when they got to Nome at the end of their 1,100-mile run across the state.

For about eighty percent of all the mushers who finished the first twenty-four Iditarods, Rasmussen was the first one to shake their hands and congratulate them. Although he doesn't work around the clock these days, for one stretch of fifteen out of seventeen years, Rasmussen met every single Iditarod finisher, no matter what time of day it was, no matter how cold it was, no matter how far behind the next musher was.

And since 1975, Rasmussen has been the chairman of the mail committee. Each year, mushers are required to carry commemorative cachets in their sleds as they move along the trail from Anchorage to Nome. The toting of the mail is symbolic of the old days when the Iditarod Trail was used mainly to transport letters by dog team. The racers ultimately autograph each envelope they carry and then the "mail" is sold as a fund-raising tool for the race.

Clearly, given the amount of time he devotes to it, the Iditarod has a special hold on Rasmussen.

"I felt a commitment to carrying forward that historical thing we were doing," he said. "It's something that has depth to it. This is a piece of the past dealing with the present, moving into the future."

Rasmussen has seen it all in Nome, drama and comedy, and a mix of the two. He recalled one last-place finisher staggering to the podium at the break-up banquet and succinctly summing up his race: "I came to Nome to get drunk and I'm drunk." And then the musher fell over.

Two early landmark events dramatically increased consciousness about the Iditarod, Rasmussen is

Mayor Leo Rasmussen, center, follows the progress of the 1979 race with volunteers in the Nome headquarters. ANCHORAGE MUSEUM OF HISTORY AND ART

convinced: Dick Mackey's one-second victory over Rick Swenson in 1978, a result so stunning that it became a lifetime conversation piece, and Libby Riddles's 1985 triumph.

Riddles became the first woman to win the race by boldly facing a storm head on from the Bering Sea when the male mushers behind her chose to wait it out. Riddles's victory earned worldwide attention and the rarity of a woman defeating men on equal turf turned many women into fans of the race.

"That was a goddarned wonderful thing that happened to us," said Rasmussen. "And she masterfully handled the job of being champion for someone who had absolutely no experience at what she was getting into."

Looking back over the last twenty-five years, the same might be said of Rasmussen. 🐾

Redington, who indeed somehow had raised the promised purse, asked if they should do it all again the next year. A mighty roar went up. The Iditarod was established.

Farley never raced the Iditarod again, but he spent the next eighteen years as a race official on the Nome end. And twenty-five years after the Iditarod's somewhat chaotic beginnings, Farley believes the allure of mushing dogs across vast expanses of open country has spread from Alaskans to those who live in even the biggest cities elsewhere in the world.

"It's that old adventure thing," said Farley. "It's romantic. The Iditarod reminds people that there's things left to do. The essence of the Iditarod is that you've done something that's still pretty limited in this world. The guy from New York and the guy from New Orleans who says, 'I'd really like to try that' . . . it's that guy's dream that helps the race keep going."

In 1974, the Iditarod title was captured by Carl Huntington, who remains the only musher ever to win the premier long-distance race, the Fur Rendezvous World Championship, and the North American Sled Dog Championship sprint races. But it still took the winner a monumental 20 days, 15 hours to reach Nome.

Women made their debut in the second Iditarod, and Mary Shields and Lolly Medley attained the distinction of the first females to complete the race. Shields finished 23rd and Medley 24th, only a half hour behind. In the ensuing years, Shields

▲▲ **Nome turns out to greet local musher Howard Farley in the 1973 finish. At center is Farley's wife Julie and her mother.** HOWARD FARLEY COLLECTION

▲ **First-place finisher Carl Huntington poses with his trophy at the Nome banquet honoring the 1974 mushers.** HOWARD FARLEY COLLECTION

Ever the Trail Breaker

"I was intrigued that the dog teams could make it over land and that we still couldn't do it by car. The trail hadn't been used in over fifty years. It was just there, and nothing had been done about it. You see, dog mushing went right into aviation . . . there wasn't any in between! When [aviator] Eielson took over delivering the mail from the dog team mail drivers, that was it.

"When we started opening the trail out of Knik, people said it was impossible, that it couldn't be done. Why, that was the wrong thing to tell me! I guess it wasn't the thing to tell Joe Redington, Sr., either."

—*Dorothy Page*
"Mother of the Iditarod"

▲▲ Fatigue lining her face, Lolly Medley takes a break in the 1974 race. Medley and Mary Shields were the first women to complete the Iditarod. RICHARD BURMEISTER

▲ Susan Butcher prepares to set up her bulky cookstove in the 1978 race. Later, she would cross the finish line at 19th, making her the first woman to place in the money. Following her was Varona Thompson, who came in 20th. BILL DEVINE

▲ Pilot Larry Thompson is a key person in the 1976 Iditarod air force, delivering dog food and other supplies to checkpoints along the race route. Thompson was one of the first volunteer pilots for Iditarod. ANCHORAGE MUSEUM OF HISTORY AND ART

▶ It was a father-daughter year in 1978. Iditarod air force pilot Larry Thompson tips his wings in salute to his daughter, Varona, who was on her way to Nome and a place in the history books. That year, she and Susan Butcher were the first women to place in the money. BILL DEVINE

has retained close ties with dog mushing. She has written a book about her dog sled experiences and each summer provides dog mushing demonstrations for tourists.

Shields well remembers one thing that motivated her in that first race: the disparaging comments of an anonymous male fan near the Anchorage starting line. "You'd better turn around now," the man shouted. "You'll never make it to Nome!" It took Shields more than twenty-eight days to do so, but she did make Nome, though she never raced in the Iditarod again. Still, her irrefutable pioneering status is entrenched in Iditarod history. Meanwhile, until her death in 1996, Medley preserved her connections to the Iditarod in the most generous of ways, each year presenting the Golden Harness Award to the lead dog making the most significant contribution to the race.

The emergence of Emmitt Peters as champion in the 1975 race marked a significant demarcation point in the Iditarod's evolution. Peters is from Ruby, the first checkpoint on the Iditarod northern route along the Yukon River, a primarily Athabaskan village of two-hundred-plus people. Peters's winning performance, just ahead of Jerry Riley and Joee Redington, Jr., the race founder's son, showed that the Iditarod was indeed a sport for fast dogs who exhibited remarkable stamina. The thrilling close race pitted the three men against each other over the final eighty miles, and Peters prevailed with a time that shaved nearly a week off the previous best finish. His

RICHARD BURMEISTER: SOUL OF A POET, HEART OF A VOLUNTEER

The Musher's Prayer

O Lord give my dogs
the strength to continue on
and me the knowledge to survive

For we are out in your wonders
moving slowly along the trail
Matching wits with your nature

O Lord give my leader the wisdom
of the trail that lies ahead
and prevent us from losing the trail

And finally O Lord
lead us to our final destination
and the end of the trail

—Richard Burmeister

In 1996, Richard Burmeister was elected to a three-year term on the Iditarod Trail Committee's Board of Directors.

CALL RICHARD BURMEISTER the Iditarod poet. The Nome educator mushed the Iditarod in 1979 and 1982, but that barely touches upon his involvement with the race that has so rooted itself in his soul.

Since 1974, when he moved to Nome, Burmeister not only has raced the event, he's published a book of poetry about the Iditarod; served as an official photographer, dog handler, operator of the finish-line dog lot; worked at the Nome headquarters; helped put the trail in by snowmachine between the Topkok Hills and Nome; and in recent years served as an Iditarod pilot. He's even inspired his son Aaron to compete in the Iditarod twice.

"There's just a glory to the whole thing," said Burmeister. "I think dog mushing is a fantastic sport." So fantastic that Burmeister retired as a junior high principal at age fifty in June of 1996 with hopes of once more pulling together a dog team to compete in the twenty-fifth annual Iditarod.

Burmeister was one of the mushers whose joy was simply being on the trail rather than competing seriously for the cash prizes offered for the top twenty finishers. Mushing the Iditarod was a fulfilling experience, he said, recalling details of his 1979 debut with astounding clarity.

"It was a chance to do a lot of thinking on my own," said Burmeister. "I love being on my own. At Finger Lake, the northern lights were dancing up there from one edge of the mountains to the other and reflecting off the snow."

At one point during the race, with the panting of his dogs and the hiss of sled runners as his main accompanying sounds, Burmeister realized he and his dogs were surrounded by a pack of wolves.

"I was scared by wolves coming out of Grayling," he said of the the Yukon River village. "There were twelve sets of yellow eyes staring down at you. They'd come right up and nudge me on the back of the legs. They'd follow three to five feet from the dogs."

When Burmeister camped at the Old Woman cabin between Kaltag and Unalakleet, a huge she-wolf weighing perhaps seventy-five pounds and standing three feet at the shoulders, stared for long minutes as Burmeister and fellow musher Jon Van Zyle built a fire.

"I can still see her standing there," he said. The wolves did no harm to either Burmeister or his dogs, and he understands now that there was never much chance they would, but at the time he was frightened to his core. More frightened of the wolves than the weather, which had an infinitely greater capacity to do damage.

"I was a lot younger," said Burmeister, laughing. "I never remember being cold." Not even in Nikolai, where the windchill factor was likely one hundred degrees below zero.

"I believe a lot of stuff is mind over matter," said Burmeister. "You just go out and do it because you have to do it. The first time I got home from the

Iditarod, I couldn't sleep in the house. It was too hot. After three hours, I took the sleeping bag out on the porch."

And then he couldn't sleep there either—too restless. So he hitched up his dog team and mushed to Safety and back, a bonus of forty-four miles added to his Iditarod.

In the 1982 Iditarod, the mushers faced humbling storms. Burmeister said he got stuck at Kaltag, both trying to get there and trying to leave.

"I remember snowshoeing about thirty miles coming out of Kaltag," he said.

Although he was not able to race the Iditarod again over the years, Burmeister chose poetry as an art form to try to describe the emotional way the race grabbed him. He worked on his poems between 1979 and 1987 before the slender volume was released.

The poems, he said, are meant not only to represent his own trail experiences, but those of all Iditarod mushers and the men who came before them on the old mail trail.

"You think about the old miners and those who were delivering mail and those who were in the [diphtheria] serum run," said Burmeister.

And those who might come later, too. 🐾

May It Last Forever

The day was
cold
And the trail
well marked
As sixteen dogs and I
move along

The trees standing so
tall
With the mountains
reaching the sky
As we swiftly move along
the trail

The marvels I see will
always be with me
And maybe some day my
sons
may also see this

For the beauty is
there
And hopefully it will
always be there.

— *Richard Burmeister*

▲ ▲ Friends and competitors, a group of 1974 mushers gather to share stories at Nome. From left, Rudy Demoski, Ken Chase, Warner Vent, and Dan Seavey. RICHARD BURMEISTER

▲ Long-time HAM radio volunteer Orville Lake (left) interviews 1974 champion Carl Huntington. At right is press member Slim Randles. RICHARD BURMEISTER

▲▲ A crowd of supporters turned out for the 1975 Iditarod start at Mulcahy Stadium in midtown Anchorage. ANCHORAGE MUSEUM OF HISTORY AND ART

▲ In 1975, the Rohn cabin was a bustling spot for mushers, their dogs, checkers, and other volunteers. Twenty years later, it still looks the same. ANCHORAGE MUSEUM OF HISTORY AND ART

Racing in 1975, Herbie Nayokpuk checks his standing with Iditarod HAM radio operator Orville Lake, center, and an unidentified village volunteer. ANCHORAGE MUSEUM OF HISTORY AND ART

winning time of 14 days, 14 hours and 43 minutes beat Riley by twenty-six minutes.

Peters, thirty-five years old at the time, was always around dogs growing up. His classic village upbringing involved using dogs for help in hauling water to the family home, in gathering firewood, and for transportation to other villages. His dad and uncles raised the dogs, and Peters competed in the world championship sprint races of 1973 and 1974. There he encountered Dr. Roland Lombard, the eight-time victor second only to Attla in legendary status. Lombard examined his dogs and said, "You're in the wrong race." So Peters entered the next year's Iditarod. Fortunately for him, it traversed the northern route and hence led through his hometown.

In those days it was within the rules for villagers to help take care of the dogs. While Peters rested in his own bed in Ruby—his natural choice for taking his mandatory twenty-four-hour layover—friends and family pampered his dogs. This rejuvenated him and allowed him to haul in the leaders on the Bering Sea coast.

Relying on Nugget, the lead dog that took Carl Huntington to the championship the year before, Peters negotiated this new territory and finally took the lead in Solomon, some thirty miles from Nome. It was there, as Peters passed Riley, that Orville Lake, a prominent sprint mushing figure, broadcast the news all over the state: "Ladies and gentlemen, we have a new leader. The Yukon Fox is in the lead." The

Yukon Fox. Nice ring to it. "That's how I got the nickname and it stuck to me ever since," said Peters.

Peters's close win turned Front Street into the wild, celebratory scene it always is now when the winner approaches the finish line.

"It was just like watching the Super Bowl crowd," Peters recalled. "Everybody is yelling and screaming and you're the hero."

If Peters's 1975 race set a new standard for speed, the 1978 race set an impossible-to-match standard for closeness. In an astounding finish, after eleven hundred miles of racing, the championship between Dick Mackey and Rick Swenson was decided by one second.

Leo Rasmussen, whose involvement as an Iditarod checker spans all twenty-five years of its existence, calls the Mackey-Swenson finish one of the most important events in Iditarod history. It was so exciting, said Rasmussen, that many new Iditarod fans were generated.

Mackey, then forty-five, had been involved in the Iditarod since its inception, but his organizational duties often detracted from his training. In the winter of 1977-78, he felt he had his strongest dog team ever, and he wanted to do it justice. He trained better than ever. By Unalakleet, less than three hundred miles from the end, it was apparent to Mackey that he and Swenson, who was then the defending champion after his first triumph in 1977, had the best dogs, even though Emmitt Peters hovered close

▲ Herbie Nayokpuk at the Farewell Lake checkpoint, 1975. ANCHORAGE MUSEUM OF HISTORY AND ART

▲ ▲ Emmitt Peters of Ruby stepped up the pace of the Iditarod in 1975, shaving nearly a week off the previous best finish. He crossed the Nome finish line after 14 days, 14 hours, and 43 minutes on the trail. ANCHORAGE MUSEUM OF HISTORY AND ART

▲ Weary Iditarod dogs curl up and rest while they can. ANCHORAGE MUSEUM OF HISTORY AND ART

Last-place winners gain special notoriety in winning the Red Lantern Award. Joel Kottke and Red "Fox" Olson shared the honor as they moved across the 1974 finish line. RICHARD BURMEISTER

> "It's Mackey! It's Swenson!
> It's Mackey! It's Swenson,
> it's, it's, it's . . ."
> — *Tom Busch, KNOM radio
> announcer at the 1978 finish line*

by. As the race turned toward Nome, the two mushers pushed hard, but also played psychological games with each other.

"Swenson expected he was going to win," said Mackey. "I wasn't sure whether I could or not." Most of the time Swenson led. Mackey felt Swenson's dogs were faster, his own stronger. Mackey would periodically downplay his chances, trying to give Swenson a false sense of security. When Swenson was leading, he'd periodically boast that things were going fine, "Stay right where you are, and we've got it made, one-two."

They were a tandem, sometimes mushing through blowing snow, trying to ignore nasty winds. A few miles out of town they paused for coffee. When word came that Peters was closing, they made ready for their last push.

Fans turned out by the thousands to pack the road, and as both men mushed towards the finish line their excited dogs sometimes veered off into the crush. Over the final hundreds of yards, the mushers were sprinting down the street by their dogs, going all out.

The finish line is marked by a burled arch, a spectacular detailed carving from a spruce tree that bears the statement "End of the Iditarod Dog Race." The smooth, shiny wood, carved by Red Olson, is impressive in its immensity. The crossbar is well over the head of any man, and the thickness of its legs and cross beam make it seem as if it is anchored. The arch also is called "the monument" by some in Nome. While it looms

HE'S HAPPY TO HELP, BUT DON'T ASK JON BROBST TO MUSH

ONE OF THE MOST remarkable things about the Iditarod Trail Sled Dog Race is its capacity to provoke some fifteen-hundred volunteers into putting their lives on hold for weeks at a time each March just so they can be part of the sprawling-across-Alaska event.

In a sense, Jon Brobst is a symbol of many who invest so much time and effort in the race for free. They caught the fever long ago, and they stick with it no matter where they go or what happens in their personal lives.

Brobst is a big man in his forties who stands over six feet and weighs

Jon Brobst says he'll never run the Iditarod, but as a volunteer, he's worked at both ends of the race and many checkpoints in between. Brobst is shown here in Anchorage using a portable microphone to move spectators away from the start line.

more than two hundred pounds. For most of the last two decades, even when he's lived in places that don't get very cold, he's kept his thick parka ready for his annual Iditarod adventure. For Brobst, the Iditarod has been a constant, even when he's moved his residence from Missouri to Alaska and back to Washington state.

Brobst was living in St. Louis when he first learned about the race. He traveled to Alaska for some salmon fishing in the summer of 1977 and met musher Bill Cotter. Until then, he'd never even heard of the event. Curiosity piqued, he flew to Alaska for the 1978 race, and in minus-fifteen degrees Brobst hitchhiked from the Anchorage airport to Knik, more than fifty miles north. He volunteered to answer phones and helped park dog trucks at the re-start, which then was held on Big Lake.

A year later he was back and

helping out at the Lake Lucille re-start. He watched in amazement as Alaska played one of its many weather tricks on mushers. The wind gusts roared to forty miles an hour, and dogs had trouble keeping their footing on the ice.

"Teams were going across Lake Lucille sideways," said Brobst. "It was just madness."

Unlike many volunteers who dream of competing in the Iditarod, Brobst has never mushed and never expects he will tackle the trail. Instead, he's devoted his time to working as start coordinator in Anchorage, at the re-start in the Mat-Su Valley, at the finish line in Nome, and many checkpoints in-between such as Rainy Pass, McGrath, Cripple, Skwentna, and Kaltag. He has checked off names as mushers came into the communities, he's been a chute worker as they've finished, and he's worked the phones in Nome as inquiries come in from all over the world.

One of Brobst's Iditarod highlights was working as start coordinator for the 1983 race. It was observed at the time, he said, "the start coordinator has butterflies the size of bald eagles in his belly."

Another highlight for Brobst didn't even occur during the race. He was scouring antique shops in Oregon and stumbled upon a trunk of old Alaska maps, including an ancient map of the Iditarod trail. It was marked as the "Haiditarod" trail, using the old Indian name meaning "distant place."

They were surveyors' maps. Brobst bought the maps and donated them about ten years ago to the Iditarod Trail Committee in the name of "Father of the Iditarod" Joe Redington, Sr., Cotter, and Dorothy Page, affectionately known as the "Mother of the Iditarod."

For a man who runs a travel agency in Washington, it seems Brobst could vacation anywhere he chooses. But Brobst is still in love with the Iditarod and has no qualms about taking his vacations in the wild.

"I think it's just absolutely a wonderful commitment of man and animal against nature," he said of why he is so enamored of the Iditarod. "Your number one adversary is Mother Nature. Your number one ally is your team. These mushers are my heroes. This is something I would never do, could never do." 🐾

large over people standing at the finish and spans much of Front Street, in a crowd it can be an obscured speck of a target. And a crowd had gathered that day.

"It was a mob," said Rasmussen, who said it was tough to keep the straining viewers from blocking the finish line altogether.

Mackey and Swenson ran and drove their teams side-by-side under the arch, creating pandemonium. Rasmussen dropped to his knees.

"I was looking through legs and knees," said Rasmussen. "I didn't know which team had won, but I knew which side the lead dog was on." Swenson pushed his dogs over the line and declared himself the winner. Mackey believed he had the title.

"There was such a crowd, you couldn't go any further if you wanted to," said Mackey. "I went to flop on my sled, and I missed it. I just slumped down on the ground. I knew I'd won. No doubt in my mind."

Al Crane, another race official, pushed his way over to Rasmussen and asked, "Who won?" Rasmussen said, "I knew it [the winning team] was on the south side of the monument." Farley, who was race marshal, conferred with other officials. Mackey was right. He had won.

"I called it on the nose of the dog," said Farley. As has often jokingly been recalled by way of comparison, horse races aren't determined by which rear end of the animal crosses the finish.

How close was the difference in the closest of all Iditarods? "Maybe eight inches," said Rasmussen. "I still see it in my mind."

◄ Competitors, yet still friends, Rick Swenson and Dick Mackey share a laugh moments after the official announcement that Swenson had lost the 1978 title to Mackey by one second. BILL DEVINE

▼ Champion Rick Swenson is all smiles in his 1979 finish, which made him a two-time winner. Swenson would claim three more championships before calling an end to his Iditarod career.

ANCHORAGE MUSEUM OF HISTORY AND ART

◄ ◄ In perhaps the most thrilling moment in Iditarod history, Dick Mackey finds a burst of strength for a final charge down the 1978 finish chute. One second behind him, Rick Swenson was giving it all he had. ROB STAPLETON

JON VAN ZYLE: EXPRESSING THE ART OF THE IDITAROD

Van Zyle's posters have become popular Iditarod collectibles.

Musher and artist Jon Van Zyle ran the race for the second time in 1979. He continues to imbue his series of Iditarod paintings with the beauty and mystique he saw on the trail firsthand. BILL DEVINE

JON VAN ZYLE mushed his first Iditarod in 1976—and fell in love. His journey down the trail was as much a spiritual as physical experience, and when he returned to his Anchorage home, the artist painted a series of twenty works on the Iditarod and held an exhibition.

Now one of Alaska's best-known painters, Van Zyle was just establishing himself two decades ago, but he donated one of his dog mushing works to become a fund-raising poster for the 1,100-mile race.

The poster was a hit, and what began as a one-shot item has evolved into an Iditarod institution. In 1996, Van Zyle, now in his fifties, released his 20th Iditarod commemorative poster.

The Iditarod itself wasn't nearly as well known in 1976 as it is today, and Van Zyle came off the trail from the first of his two Iditarod races determined to show the world this special event.

"I wanted people to know what it was," said Van Zyle. "It [the poster] became for all intents and purposes the first merchandise for Iditarod. It was only going to be a one-time thing. That's why I didn't put a date on it. They came back to me the next year and I did it again."

Van Zyle's paintings are evocative of both his appreciation for the race and the huskies who run it, but also represent many of the obstacles mushers face along the trail. Some of the paintings are ghostly in nature, featuring hovering shadowy faces that almost seem like guardian angels watching over hard-working dog drivers. Some show

Van Zyle's favorite medium is acrylic.

"The main thing was running just to travel with my dogs," said Van Zyle. "That to me was the whole thing. Our lives get so hectic and so demanded upon, that whole aspect of being turned loose with a bunch of dogs out there, it keeps me centered."

Van Zyle's work is exhibited all over the United States and he even makes appearances overseas. In Alaska, his prints and posters are valued among Iditarod collectibles, and the Anchorage Museum of Art and History accepted a donation of a collection of the first eighteen Iditarod posters.

Erosion of the strength in his knees means Van Zyle cannot consider entering the Iditarod again, but his vivid memories repeatedly show up on canvas.

"It keeps me remembering what I think the race is about," said Van Zyle. "The race still has a mystique about it."

That mystique has such a hold on him that the man who lives to make bold brush strokes said he often wishes he could mush the Iditarod again, to absorb both its hardships and its pleasures.

"There are times I'd rather be out there than painting," said Van Zyle. 🐾

mushers and their dog teams as small specks against a backdrop of intimidating Alaska wilderness, or confronting breaks in the ice that might swallow them up. And still others show the solitude of the trail and the bond formed between mushers and dogs.

Van Zyle entered the race again in 1979, and although he was always a back-of-the-pack musher, his experience of simply finishing the Iditarod gave him credibility among other mushers. More so, it forever touched him with the romance of being alone in the silent snow with his dogs.

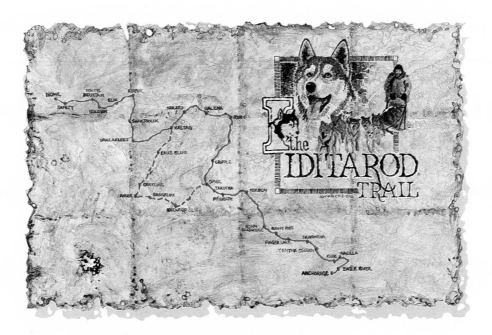

1980s

WHEN MEN WERE MEN AND WOMEN WON THE IDITAROD

As the race transforms from a two-week camping

trip to an intensely competitive sport for both genders,

the Iditarod is the great equalizer.

Alaskans enjoy cozying up to their heroes and frequently in conversation an eavesdropper might hear the names "Rick," "Susan," and "Libby" being dropped as if they are members of the family.

Family, no. Familiar, yes. Rick Swenson's triumphs and rivalry with Susan Butcher, plus the breakthrough, enervating, and heart-stopping victory by Libby Riddles defined the 1980s for the Iditarod Trail Sled Dog Race.

As the decade changed, Swenson had emerged as the one true giant of long-distance dog mushing. He captured his first title in 1977 and second in 1979 after losing the 1978 race by a mere second.

Terry Adkins mushes on glare ice down the South Fork of the Kuskokwim outside the 1986 Rohn checkpoint.

Others contended, others even won, but Swenson always hovered, a threat that made all other mushers glance over their shoulders wherever they were on the trail. No one who raced the Iditarod discounted Swenson's chances. Ever. Swenson solidified his reputation by winning the 1981 and 1982 races, giving him four championships at a time when no one else had even won two.

"Rick was the race's first great figure," said former Iditarod Trail Committee President Leo Rasmussen.

A distinguishing characteristic of all Swenson's victories: He had the same lead dog, Andy. The huskies who become lead dogs in the Iditarod are special animals. They are renowned for their heart, their stamina, and their smarts. Many times it is the dog who makes the decision in the darkness, in the storm, that carries the team and the musher to safety. Good leaders not only develop an instinctive sense about the trail, they have a special bond with the musher.

Andy was a winner and Swenson stayed one during the race's first decade. Rasmussen carries a mental picture of a joyful Swenson after his first victory, sitting at Nome City Hall, talking a mile a minute to anyone who happened by.

A tall, sturdily built man, Swenson grew up in rural Minnesota. As a youngster, he was fascinated by outdoor survival and pumped the trapper who lived next door for advice. Taken with the young man's earnestness, the man gave Swenson books to read. Many of them were Jack London stories,

◄ By 1980, Rick Swenson already was a two-time champion and had missed his third by a mere second.

BILL DEVINE

◄ ◄ Swenson, ever scientific and precise, checks his watch to gauge his speed as he nears Shaktoolik in the 1989 race.

Seeing It Live

A first for the Iditarod in 1980:
The Front Street finish was broadcast live
through Alascom's facilities.
The satellite earth station at Nome
carried the signal to the satellite for
distribution to the entire state.

JOANNE POTTS: AFTER ALL THESE YEARS, SHE'S STILL NOT DOGGED OUT

A former teacher, Potts helped put the Iditarod on the World Wide Web with race updates and online chat.

JOANNE POTTS was a public school math teacher when she became fascinated by the Iditarod in 1977. What began as an enthusiastic hobby as a volunteer in the 1970s evolved into a full-time occupation in the 1980s, and by the 1990s made Potts one of the most visible of Iditarod officials.

Potts is now the Iditarod's full-time race director, based at the event's Wasilla, Alaska, headquarters. She plays a highly public role speaking for the race, representing the race, and participating in administrative decisions. Which was not what she envisioned some two decades ago. The Iditarod was a thrilling race that captured her attention and energized her, but she never expected to leave the teaching profession when she first became a volunteer in the late 1970s.

In May 1982, after several years of volunteer work in a variety of capacities, Potts went to work at race headquarters. The job was supposed to last a month, and after two years of part-time work, she became a full-time Iditarod employee.

"The most fun thing is the people," said Potts. "Mushers, they're all like my kids. I try to take care of them. When you work for something like the Iditarod, you meet people from all over the world."

The scope of the Iditarod has expanded dramatically during Potts's years of involvement with the race, from an Alaska event to one that receives worldwide notice. The changes are boggling to her, especially since she remembers the small-timey aspects of the race in the 1970s.

When Potts joined up, the Iditarod's Anchorage headquarters was a small room at the Hilton Hotel. It housed one table and one chair. Two volunteers worked the room during the race giving out information to the public while keeping one telephone line free for calls with standings updates from the trail.

Things are far more sophisticated these days at the Regal Alaskan Hotel, the current Anchorage headquarters. The hotel is the focal point of Iditarod fever once the race begins in the city's downtown and wends its way along the trail to the Bering Sea coast. Once the mushers have covered two-thirds of the trail, the focus shifts to Nome headquarters, but the Regal remains a clearinghouse of information and updates, and those telephone calls pour in from all over.

"At the Regal," said Potts, "it's twenty people working around the clock."

Where once upon a time all information was recorded with paper and pencil, now, of course, everything is computerized.

As an insider, Potts is no less impressed with the way the Iditarod has grown in public awareness and spread its reputation beyond the state's borders. In her mind, one of the earliest developments to expand notoriety was a nationally televised appearance by multiple winner Susan Butcher on the show "20-20" about fifteen years ago.

"That was the first time the Iditarod was in prime time," said Potts. "That was pretty widely watched. That created national interest. The next summer when people came to Alaska, they would ask about the Iditarod."

The focus on the finish has given rise to even more interest in the Iditarod. Not only do television cameras bring the conclusion to the world. Nome has become a party destination for revelers who want to witness the finish in person. A festival atmosphere prevails as people fly into town from all over Alaska and elsewhere, and thousands of people line the streets waiting for the champion's arrival.

There is live music in the bars, and the saloons themselves are filled to overflowing as fans stay up all night waiting for the winners, the contenders, and their favorites to complete The Last Great Race.

Potts never tires of the scene and gets caught up in the finish events every year, even after nearly twenty years of watching.

"It's just as exciting to me," she said. "The high's still there. The tears start to come to my eyes. I get thrilled for whoever it is and for all of them as they finish. I try to get out there to watch for as many of them as I can."

But planning to go to Nome and getting there are two different things.

In 1991, Potts cut her planned arrival time in Nome close as she worked supervising the Anchorage operation. As a result, her plane was diverted to Kotzebue, above the Arctic Circle, and forced to land because of a snowstorm. Potts and her fellow passengers were frustratingly stuck in Kotzebue for fourteen hours.

When Rick Swenson completed his milestone fifth victory, coming into Nome at roughly 1:30 A.M. after battling and overcoming a vicious storm, Potts was listening on the radio instead of standing under the finish line arch on Front Street where she normally is. The storm let up sufficiently to get the plane in the air and by 3:45 A.M., when

second-placer Martin Buser came in, Potts was there to greet him.

This actually made the second year in a row Potts missed the winner, however, and by comparison, it was for a tame reason.

A year earlier, Potts innocently found herself under arrest when she sought to leave Anchorage for Nome. Part of her carry-on baggage, entrusted to her by Iditarod officials, contained some raffle prizes in sealed boxes. She was told they were worth $5,000 and not to let them out of her sight. Potts was diligent, and forgot what the packages contained. Unfortunately for her, one of the prizes was a commemorative Iditarod handgun, and when she tried to pass through security to board her plane, things went a tad haywire.

"My stuff doesn't come out of the X-ray machine," is the way Potts remembers the first signal that things might not be running smoothly.

Then a security agent calmly asked her, "Would you come with me?" Then she was asked, "What's in this bag?"

That is when it dawned on Potts that what was in the bag was contraband. Uh, oh.

"I know what's wrong now," she

thought. But when Potts tried to explain, she was rebuffed. Federal Aviation Administration officials were alerted. The FBI was called. Four security agents massed around Potts, a smallish woman with graying hair who more resembles a grandmotherly figure than an international terrorist.

The agents began talking very sternly to Potts, saying things like, "Were you aware this was a $10,000 fine and ten years in jail?"

That's when she began crying. Potts ultimately was rescued by an Alaska Airlines vice president. Alaska Airlines is one of the race sponsors, and Potts was able to reach one of the airline's top officials, Bill MacKay, who vouched for her as a respectable citizen.

"I was released into the custody of Bill MacKay," said Potts. And that's how Potts came to be sitting at Anchorage International Airport nursing a well-deserved Bloody Mary and snacking on a bagel and cream cheese when Susan Butcher crossed the finish line for her fourth win.

"That was such an empty feeling those two years," said Potts of her two missed winners.

If Potts has seen just about everything in the past, she's also

on board as the Iditarod looks to the future.

Beginning in 1989, the Iditarod began to concentrate on making fans out of children. An in-classroom education program began, and by 1996 it had grown to reach two thousand classrooms a year.

Just after Jeff King won the 1996 race, Potts was joined by two-time champion Martin Buser, who'd just finished third, and his wife Kathy Chapoton, for an hour-long online Internet chat open to kids. Potts said she wouldn't be surprised if overall that year, some 200,000 schoolchildren followed the race.

"Ten questions would come before I could get one answered," she said. The kids' excitement rubs off on Potts. She can envision the day when all of the Iditarod classroom work pays off for the race.

"Those kids who are enthusiastic today are going to be the mushers, the sponsors, the fans in the future," said Potts. "I hope I still work for the Iditarod when the first kid comes in to mush who's grown up and says, 'I got your packet when I was in the third grade.'"

It is an image worth preserving.

▲ Kazuo Kojima camps at the Rainy Pass checkpoint in 1985. The sight of a bona fide tent on the Iditarod is rare.

▲ ► After leaving the Rohn checkpoint in 1983, Roger Legaard of Norway struggles to get his dogs turned around. The dogs were confused because of the lack of snow on the South Fork of the Kuskokwim, which is nearly always snow-free due to constant winds. Steering is almost impossible with no snow on the trail.

► As part of a military exercise in 1984, the Air National Guard stepped in to help with a food drop at Finger Lake, but the well-meaning experiment flopped. They missed their target at Finger Lake by a few hundred yards, and caretaker/checker Gene Leonard had to go into the trees to recover the drop.

and other tales of Alaska and the Far North.

Swenson dreamed of becoming a dog musher. He moved north, to Interior Alaska, and in his first Iditarod in 1976, Swenson placed 10th. For the next nineteen Iditarods, Swenson was a fixture in the top ten, a record never approached.

Often Swenson thrived on the trail when the going was the roughest, when storms battered the mushers, when hard conditions slowed up the race. He prided himself on being a savvy woodsman who would never be intimidated by the weather.

"This is the challenge of the Iditarod," he said. "To go out in forty degrees with a packed trail, you can do that in Anchorage in the Fur Rendezvous. To me it's the challenge of the unknown. The race isn't always to the swiftest."

No, Swenson was certainly not an in-town musher racing the Fur Rondy World Championship sprint race. He made his name as a grizzled man of few words who spoke his mind with a bluntness that sometimes made others wince when he did start talking.

Swenson was never one to sugarcoat his feelings. If he was mad at you, you knew it. If he thought you'd done a great job, you'd hear that. He didn't believe in excuses and if someone faltered and peppered their explanations with if-onlys, he wouldn't let it pass. The measure of the musher was the performance.

By dint of both his stature through top finishes, and his personality, Swenson established a reputation as a man's man, the symbol of rugged Alaskan manhood.

From its founding in 1973, through the early 1980s, the Iditarod was very much a male domain. Not only was Swenson preeminent, but even in the years that Swenson didn't own the race outright, experienced men who had grown up with dogs took over.

In the 1983 race, Swenson placed fifth, his domination interrupted by a milestone performance by Rick Mackey. For the first time, a son following in the footsteps of his father won the Iditarod. Dick Mackey won the 1978 race and now twenty-nine-year-old Rick claimed the title.

Not without difficulty. Following his best-ever winter of training, Mackey left Fourth Avenue with fifteen top-notch dogs. The year before he placed 11th, but in the interim he moved his kennel from Wasilla, where the barking dogs drove neighbors crazy, to more remote Trapper Creek. Mackey and his family lived in an old cabin with no stove, no heater and had an outhouse for a bathroom.

"We were really committed," said Mackey. And that commitment paid off. For much of the race, the front pack consisted of Swenson, Herbie Nayokpuk, Larry "Cowboy" Smith, Eep Anderson, and Mackey. Over the final stretch, though, it became a race to Nome between Mackey and Anderson.

Anderson had a two-hour lead on Mackey leaving White Mountain, which is seventy-seven miles from the finish, but only a ten-minute lead coming out of Safety, fifty-five miles later.

▲ Helping his father Lavon Barve in the 1983 race, dog handler Lance Barve works with a lead dog that's never seen a tunnel, like this one on the Anchorage bike trail. Handlers ride along while teams pass through Anchorage for surprises like this.

◄ Rick Mackey opts for a quick snooze inside Rich and Vi Burnham's Kaltag home in the 1988 race. Usually mushers can sleep anywhere, anytime, no matter how much noise or disturbance because of exhaustion and lack of sleep. They can and do try to take even ten- or twenty-minute naps at any opportunity.

▲ Musher Babe Anderson adds his name to the autographed ceiling at the Cripple checkpoint during a stop in the 1982 race. The first official Iditarod artist, Bill Devine, drew the famous dog-head logo on the ceiling here in 1978. Devine created the logo, which is still used today, in 1974. Originally it was to be used as the U.S. Postal Service cancellation stamp for the mail cachets that each musher carries over the trail.

▲ Power napping at Gene Leonard's cabin, Finger Lake, 1986.

► Roger Nordlum and Herbie Nayokpuk enjoy the warmth of a campfire as dawn breaks at the Rainy Pass checkpoint in 1985.

►► A cold, windy day finds Sonny Lindner, Vern Halter, Lavon Barve, and Tim Moerlein crossing Norton Bay in 1985. The spruce trees, set in the ice by local villagers, are the only trail markers on this desolate stretch between Shaktoolik and Koyuk.

"Then I knew I could catch him," said Mackey. "I was pumping and running. My dogs just about ran up the back of him."

Mackey finally passed Anderson with less than twenty miles to go, and even though he lengthened his lead to an hour and forty minutes at the finish, he never felt confident until he passed under the burled arch in downtown Nome.

"It wasn't a photo finish, but it was a real race," said Mackey. "We were jockeying back and forth for the last couple hundred miles. It felt like every inch of the way he was two minutes behind me. It takes a while to absorb what it really means [to win]. It probably makes it more special looking back because it's hard to win it again. I sure hope I do get a chance to win it again someday."

In 1984 the champion was Clam Gulch commercial fisherman Dean Osmar, who put to rest the superstition that the leader at the halfway mark couldn't hold his team together and win the race. Osmar promptly retired, but was soon followed into Iditarod racing by son Tim, who has been a regular top ten finisher ever since.

Although no woman had become champion, by 1985 it was apparent to all that the sex barrier would soon be broken. Susan Butcher, a musher who spent her youth in Cambridge, Massachusetts, and worked her way north as a young woman, placed second in 1982 and 1984. It was no longer a question of if, but when.

Many say that the 1985 race was the Iditarod's defining moment, that its result

FLOYD TETPON: A CAPTAIN IN THE IDITAROD AIR FORCE

Floyd Tetpon prefers to view the trail from aloft in his Super Cub, rather than from sled runners.

FLOYD TETPON became part of the Iditarod air force as a fallback position. In 1982, Tetpon flew the Iditarod Trail out of curiosity, scouting the terrain because he was considering entering the race as a musher. He flew the route again the next year and a third time as well. Studied the heck out of hills, valleys, and mountains.

"It looked like the ultimate challenge," said Tetpon, who grew up in the mostly Native village of Shaktoolik, one of the checkpoints along the Iditarod Trail. Such a challenge that

Tetpon eventually decided that flying the Iditarod was more practical than mushing it.

"I found out it's just a lot of work," he said. "I didn't have the time to devote to it, and I found out it was expensive. You try to encourage Native mushers to do it and they say, 'Do you have $15,000 to hand me?'"

But if his original dream was thwarted, Tetpon displayed his adaptability.

"The pilots looked like they were having fun," he said.

One thing that makes the Iditarod go each year is the work of the pilots who devote up to three weeks of their time flying supplies to drop-off points along the trail before the race begins, and who fly officials up and down the trail once it starts.

Race manager Jack Niggemyer said he looks for pilots to volunteer a week of their time each March during the race, but that a half-dozen or so of the twenty-five to thirty pilots on board annually put in three weeks of flying on behalf of the race.

Tetpon, in his mid-fifties and living in Anchorage, is one of the regulars

now. A short, dark-haired man with glasses and a wry sense of humor, Tetpon's first official Iditarod flying took place during the 1985 race. He's been part of every one since except for the 1987 competition.

"It's been great getting to know the mushers and the people who support the race," he said.

Tetpon flies a Super Cub that weighs about a thousand pounds. Which means he can safely carry about six hundred pounds, the equivalent of three good-sized men. He jokes that of the comfortable volume he hauls, "one hundred and forty of it is the pilot."

The airplane is light enough that any wind gusts that exceed thirty miles an hour can be bothersome, and that type of velocity is common in Interior Alaska in March.

"The conditions are the challenge—and trying to stay with the race schedule," said Tetpon.

Perhaps Tetpon's greatest public service along the trail was participating in the rescue of musher Mike Madden in a remote area during the 1989 race. Madden had collapsed along the side of the trail and was being tended by fellow mushers. Some mushers went for help and Tetpon said he flew the doctor to the site. Madden ended up in the hospital with salmonella poisoning, but quickly regained his health.

"I thought that was great being able to help," said Tetpon.

In recent years, it's been Tetpon's assigned task to fly the race marshal along the trail. The race marshal must have the flexibility to be where the action is if something's happening. That means Tetpon isn't always flying ahead to later checkpoints, but sometimes flies back to checkpoints the lead mushers have passed through.

"You're always planning one day ahead," said Tetpon. "No one can fly the Iditarod Trail year after year in the winter without running into unplanned adventures."

Once, Tetpon was flying into the village of Golovin along the Bering Sea Coast in whiteout conditions. The snow was swirling, the wind was blowing, and the sky was a dense gray. Hardly ideal for touch down. Tetpon could barely see.

"I could see the tree line," he said. "That saved my butt. It is scary having to make a landing and feel for it."

There have been crashes along the trail, and Tetpon has had his share of

The Iditarod airmen of 1987. Officials, volunteers and especially the mushers count on these volunteer pilots to keep the Iditarod in motion.

close calls. He classifies "bad visibility" as a view of three miles and "real bad" as a half mile or mile. Flying that way is no picnic.

"I don't care to do it," he said simply.

Perhaps Tetpon's scariest experience occurred a few years ago when he was flying then-race marshal Jim Kershner from Ophir to Iditarod. The snow was blowing around and

visibility was terrible, but Tetpon got them out of the predicament safely.

"I got turned around in there trying to find the trail," said Tetpon. "For ten minutes I didn't know where I was. That's spooky. You have to fly a bigger and bigger circle."

Once in a very great while the weather is so bad that a prudent pilot simply won't take off. Tetpon said he's

been marooned on the trail for a couple of days at a time.

"It's too big an area where it's all white," he said.

Alaska can get like that in the winter, for sure. Only Tetpon will never experience that on the back of a dog team. He's perfectly content to fly overhead.

"I tell the mushers they're all a bunch of masochists." 🐾

▲▲ Musher Ron Robbins at forty below at the Grayling checkpoint, 1986.

▲ The 1975 champion, Emmitt Peters, crosses Norton Bay where a day earlier Libby Riddles had spent the night in a blizzard before going on to win the 1985 race.

► Dewey Halverson hits the trail on the Bering Sea shortly after leaving the Elim checkpoint in 1982.

You're Joking, Right, Doc?

In 1979, Emmitt Peters was diagnosed with a severe allergy . . . to his dogs. With medication he was fit to run again.

was the most important ever. But it was a result that fooled everyone. A woman won, spawning teasing T-shirts that read, "Alaska, Where Men Are Men and Women Win the Iditarod." But it was not Butcher who became the victor. Instead, comparatively unheralded Libby Riddles claimed the spoils.

This was supposed to be Butcher's year. She was confident she had her best team ever. However, early in the race, where the trees are still thick and the brush is rough, she found herself confronted by a vicious moose. Butcher had chosen not to carry a gun for protection, as most mushers do, and was helpless to dissuade the nasty moose from tearing into her dogs, killing or injuring several. It took the arrival of fellow musher Dewey Halverson, who shot the moose, to rescue her. But the damage was too great, and Butcher had to scratch from the race.

It was Riddles who emerged from the pack of mushers farther down the trail to triumph. And she did so in such daring style that it endeared her to women the world over.

At the time, Riddles was a twenty-eight-year-old transplanted midwesterner living in the Bering Sea coast village of Teller with her partner Joe Garnie, another musher. They pooled resources raising dogs and alternated years in which they raced the Iditarod. Garnie was third in 1984, but 1985 was Riddles's turn.

Riddles mushed with the other leaders past the halfway mark, on to the village of Unalakleet. There she made a fateful choice. While all of the other leaders stayed put in the face of bad weather, Riddles chose to mush out of town and into the void. When a tremendous storm blew up, Riddles huddled her dogs together, zipped herself into her sled bag, and waited it out, worrying and shivering in the fifty-two-below-zero temperatures.

Although the others might have endured the storm in more comfort, the distance Riddles put between herself and the pack by this single move proved decisive.

"I was in that race to do my damned best and that storm was not going to get in my way," she said. "I was mentally prepared to do anything within the realm of sanity to keep moving forward."

Her bold maneuver—which was roughly interpreted as meaning that the woman showed guts when the men turned tail—galvanized the public and eventually took on mythic proportions.

"The thing that made it so noteworthy at the time was that it was done in such a brave manner," said musher DeeDee Jonrowe of Willow, who later became a top competitor.

When the storm cleared, Riddles pushed on to Shaktoolik and then to Nome. The men behind her frenziedly tried to close the gap. Halverson, who so gallantly saved Butcher, couldn't catch Riddles. He got within two and a half hours at the finish. But it was Riddles who pocketed the $50,000 first prize by finishing in just a smidgen over eighteen days.

The entire world took notice. The Women's Sports Foundation selected her its Professional Athlete of the Year. The photo-

◄ Trailbreakers and racers alike must be wary of open water. Here John Cooper mushes on the glare ice of the Kuskokwim's South Fork outside the Rohn checkpoint in 1985.

Last Place With Honors

In 1982, Ralph Bradley was the first black man ever to complete the 1,049 miles to Nome, and he didn't go home empty-handed. He gladly accepted the Red Lantern Award.

genic, blonde Riddles was featured in national magazines, some of which dressed her up in types of fancy clothes completely foreign to the Alaska Bush. She wrote a book about her race, and was transformed from being a little-known, somewhat shy woman, accepting jobs training dog teams for movies, doing television commentary, and writing children's books.

Riddles's win clearly was one of the most significant developments in Iditarod history. It made her a role model, albeit somewhat grudgingly, and made her at least regionally famous. And it did the same for the Iditarod. Once of marginal interest to the everyday sports fan, a rare event in which men and women competed on equal footing captured the imagination of the public and sponsors.

"How she did it is far more important to the race than that she was the first woman," said Leo Rasmussen. "Was Libby's win important? To tell you that it wasn't would be telling you the greatest lie on earth."

A few years after her win, when much of the furor had died down and Riddles had moved away from Teller, she reflected on the changes her dramatic victory wrought.

"It's pretty amazing," she said. "I still don't know what to make of it. Overall, it's been wonderful. Ninety-nine-point-nine percent wonderful."

Jonrowe, who became a frequent top-five finisher herself, later said that one of the more significant meanings of Riddles's triumph was that it showed the world that

▲ Even mushers DeeDee Jonrowe and John Cooper helped the checkers at Rainy Pass during the first ever "freeze" of the race. They created lath markers to help mark trail near Rainy Pass in 1985.

◄ Riddles, the first woman to win the Iditarod, poses with leaders Axle and Dugan at the 1985 finish line. Like so many other Iditarod leaders, these two were descendants of Joe Redington, Sr.'s, sire, Roamer.

◄ ◄ Libby Riddles leaves Kaltag through freeze-dried laundry.

Good Money, If You Can Get It

By the 10th running of the Iditarod, in 1982, organizers were able to offer a $100,000 purse, doubling that of the first race.

▲ Susan Butcher beams in the limelight shortly after crossing the 1988 finish line. Husband Dave Monson is in the background.

▶ Enthusiastic villagers Gloria Semaken and Renee Wiseman welcome Susan Butcher to Kaltag in the 1989 race.

Susan Butcher wasn't the only woman in the race.

But the Iditarod soon enough became Butcher's private domain. If Riddles beat her to the glory of becoming the first female victor in the Iditarod, Butcher made up for that loss in a hurry.

Butcher rebounded with a vengeance. In 1986, she recorded her first win and set a race record by winning in 11 days, 15 hours, 6 minutes. Second place went to Riddles's still-partner Joe Garnie, just under an hour behind.

For Butcher, the brown-haired, braided musher who ran an efficient, huge kennel in a remote area of the Interior, this was joy and vindication. Her turn had at last come. A year later she joined Swenson as the only musher with more than one Iditarod title, again setting a record, and finally, in 1988, she won her third straight championship. All of the teams were led by her legendary lead dog Granite, and by this time, even if people around the United States didn't know her name, they referred to the Iditarod as "That race in Alaska that woman always wins."

A medium-sized woman with gargantuan drive and a tunnel-vision focus, Butcher thrashed all contenders. Butcher's emergence and Swenson's continued status racing close to the front—he was second in 1988—divided Iditarod fans. Women rooted for Butcher, men for Swenson, and for some it was hard to see how the twain would ever meet.

Ironically, the two had been close friends and neighbors in their little corner of

GRANITE: THE THROW-AWAY DOG THAT MADE GOOD

Susan Butcher poses with lead dog Granite at the Nome finish of 1986.

I⊤ SHOULD come as no surprise that as Susan Butcher ascended into Iditarod supremacy in the late 1980s, she was aided and abetted by a stable dog team in its prime, led by the indomitable Granite.

Granite became the most famous dog in Alaska as the Iditarod grew in popularity by living up to his name as a constant, a reliable block of granite for Butcher as she recorded victories in 1986, 1987, 1988, and 1990.

Granite proves the old adage about not judging a book by its cover. Not all beautiful puppies are suited to the rigors of the Iditarod, and not all scrawny pups should be rejected out of hand. Dogs can be late bloomers, as well as people, and Granite fits into that category.

Butcher and Joe Redington, Sr., the founder of the Iditarod, trained together for a while in the 1970s and exchanged several dogs. One day, as it happened, Redington owed Butcher a dog, and she took a fancy to a two-year-old hanging around the lot, despite its scroungy looks.

"There was this dog, his hair had all fallen out," she said much later. "He had some skin disease. He was hairless, he was skinny, he was terrible."

Redington suggested Butcher take the dog off his hands, which she did. And that dog became the great Granite.

Initially, Granite was low in self-esteem, said Butcher, but his confidence built, and he became her greatest ever Iditarod performer, leading the team in her first three triumphs.

"He's very mellow, never fights, and is friends with all the dogs," she said. And pretty good pals with her, too. When an inquiry was made about the aging Granite's status for the 1990 team, Butcher said he would be there contributing his power and consistency to the team.

"He's my best friend," said Butcher. "It's nice to have your best friend on the trail. I want to make him a four-time champion."

And Granite did share in that final championship, working in the team for about half of the race before being sent home. At nine he was just a little bit too old to keep up for all 1,100 miles.

Still, that April when Butcher was invited to the White House to visit President George Bush, who did she bring with her? Her best friend. 🐾

▲ An unidentified HAM radio operator at Elim, 1987. In the early years and through the late 1980s, the volunteer HAMs were indispensable for passing news and information to the outside world on the whereabouts of mushers. With the coming of new technology, only a few HAMs remain at checkpoints where other communication methods are difficult, such as Rohn and Finger Lake. Portable satellite telephones and fax machines are now used even at remote checkpoints like Cripple.

▲ ▲ Mushers line up for food rations at Rainy Pass during the first ever "freeze" of the race in 1985. Bad weather on the Rohn side of the Alaska Range prevented pilots from flying in with supplies. So race marshal and former musher Donna Gentry put a halt to the race at Rainy Pass. Within days, mushers began to run out of dog food and rationing became necessary. Mercy planes loaded with food arrived later from Anchorage, and soon the weather cleared enough for the race to continue.

▲ Meager accommodations for volunteers in the 1987 race. Here, vets wait on teams at the Shageluk checkpoint.

the world in Manley, far north of Fairbanks. When Butcher married another musher, David Monson, Swenson was an honored guest at the wedding.

However, as Butcher's triumphs mounted, tension seemed to as well. It was never really clear just how much the two's rivalry spilled over to the personal level, but it surely made good copy for writers and broadcasters within Alaska, and fans seemed to love choosing sides between Rick and Susan, as they were usually referred to. One year to kick off the Iditarod, *Alaska* magazine put out a creative issue—if you held the magazine one way, Swenson was on the cover, but if you turned it over, Butcher was on the cover. Swenson did not gain fame as a diplomat. His bluntness is both legendary and sometimes incendiary.

At the height of the rivalry, when Butcher was poised to equal his four titles, Swenson occasionally came off as a grumpy old man.

"Basically, I'm just tired of hearing how great Susan is," he said. "I think we're all getting tired of it. A lot of people are just as good."

It is often said in sport that true greatness is only brought out in a champion by a truly great rival. Muhammad Ali had Joe Frazier as foil, and Chris Evert was tested by Martina Navratilova. Similarly, Butcher's wins were magnified because she beat the best—Swenson.

With the eyes of the world on the Iditarod and strong personalities garnering tremendous attention, this was definitely one of the Iditarod's most glorious periods.

The rise of Butcher helped the popularity of the Iditarod because there were more contenders. Bobby Lee, who raced twice in the 1980s and eventually became the Iditarod's race marshal, marveled at the growth.

"What got me was how it unified the people of Alaska about one subject that wasn't world war," said Lee. "It combined the history of the state and the life off the road system. You see the kids coming for autographs. The race cast a spell over Alaskans."

Part of that spell was the difficulty of the challenge. Lee was a musher, yet recognized that being a very good musher set certain competitors apart.

"It was terrifying," he said of being out in the wilderness in winter, pushing on by himself. "I was in awe of anyone who would do it twice."

In fact, what Lee learned and others who attempted the Iditarod did, too, was that anyone who completed the course was seen as heroic. And mushers who succeeded in getting themselves to the end of the trail appreciated what they'd done as well.

"People do think you're tough," said DeeDee Jonrowe. "And I am tough in the head, if not the body. You know what you do. It brings with it a certain level of accomplishment and confidence that helps you in life. I know that I can pick it up and keep going if there's trouble, because I have."

Butcher made further impact by pushing the outside of the speed envelope. The

▲ Members of the Iditarod air force fly in formation above Nome at the end of the 1987 race. The airplanes range in size from a two-seat, single engine Super Cub to a twin-engine Baron. Race organizers rely heavily on the volunteer pilots who donate their time and airplanes and fly countless hours to make food drops, supply runs, return dropped dogs, and ferry officials all along the race route. Without the volunteer pilots, the Iditarod would be difficult, if not impossible, to run.

◄ The checker at Skwentna since the first race in 1973, Joe Delia checks in his neighbor from nearby Shell Lake, Gordon Brinker, during the 1987 race. A spectator airplane approaches to land on the Skwentna River among the teams. The practice of landing on the river during the Iditarod was ended by the Federal Aviation Administration in the early 1990s due to safety concerns.

NORMAN VAUGHAN: DREAMING BIG IN THE BIGGEST STATE

Col. Norman Vaughan—explorer, mountain climber, Iditarod musher—continues to shoot down stereotypes on aging. BILL DEVINE

IF THE IDITAROD Trail Sled Dog Race is a one-of-a-kind adventure, then Norman Vaughan is a one-of-a-kind hero.

No one else is really like the world's oldest dog musher. Many mushers have won admiration for their performances, but Vaughan has carved out a special place in Alaskans' hearts.

Vaughan was a long-time figure on the periphery of sprint mushing, mostly working as a handler, when he decided

he must give the Iditarod a try. He was seventy-six years old. He didn't finish his first attempt, or his second, but undaunted in 1983, Vaughan placed 52nd.

"I went in the first one because I'd be associated with and be among the best drivers in the world," said Vaughan, who grew up in the small Boston North Shore community of Hamilton. "I went out the second time and got lost. The third time I made it to Nome."

In the ensuing years, Vaughan entered the Iditarod many times. Sometimes he dropped out, sometimes he finished. Always he was applauded for his spirit and determination. His last finish was in 1990, when he was eighty-four. He was 60th out of sixty-one mushers.

White-haired and white-bearded, Vaughan became Alaska's favorite grandpa, eschewing retirement, refusing to go docilely to a rocking chair. Instead, he planned even bolder adventures.

Vaughan's mushing career began in the late 1920s, when he abandoned a Harvard education to travel to Antarctica with Admiral Richard Byrd. The explorations led to Byrd naming a mountain for him. The 10,320-foot peak was called Mount Vaughan.

In 1932, when dog mushing was a demonstration sport in the Winter Olympics, Vaughan was a participant. During World War II, as a colonel, Vaughan led an expedition to rescue men in downed planes, then in a separate operation he recovered a highly sensitive bomb site from one of the planes.

Never intimidated by age, Vaughan received a new lease on life through his

Iditarod experiences. He met his current wife, Carolyn Muegge-Vaughan, on a trip east when he told some tales of the trail and always has considered it a thrill simply to be involved in the race.

"You go on the trails only buffalo go on," said Vaughan. "We're gonna be a long time dead, we might as well do what we can when we can."

Although he never harbored ambitions of winning or finishing in the top twenty, Vaughan inspired many Iditarod fans with his perseverance. He travels around Anchorage and southcentral Alaska driving a truck emblazoned with a bumper sticker reading, "Norm To Nome." And people honk in support as they drive by.

"He's such a wonderfully positive example for people who are afraid of getting old," said Carol Phillips, an Anchorage writer who first met Vaughan at a dog sled race in 1964.

Vaughan has become a symbol to many as the man who, despite many of the usual infirmities of old age, never truly ages. Late in life, Vaughan decided that he must make a return visit to Antarctica to climb the mountain named after him. It was his goal to

With a handler's glove still caught up in the line, Col. Norman Vaughan leaves the Anchorage starting chute in the 1987 race.

reach the summit of the lofty peak for his eighty-eighth birthday in 1993, and he assembled a team of top mountaineers who knew him from his Iditarod exploits.

"I want to learn to be that motivated and have dreams of that scope," said Vernon Tejas, an Anchorage mountaineer who made the first solo winter ascent of Mount McKinley. "Norman is the biggest cheerleader I've ever met."

Only Vaughan could dream bigger than the Iditarod. The $1 million expedition was unsuccessful the first time, but a year later, on a scaled-down trip, Vaughan made his dream come true. He was just turning eighty-nine.

The zeal that sustained Vaughan as he braved the storms and whims of the challenging Iditarod Trail is encapsulated in the credo he adopted for his assault on Mount Vaughan. When he signs autographs, Vaughan's typical inscription is "Dream Big and Dare to Fail."

Vaughan dreamed big when he tackled the Iditarod. And he hasn't for a moment stopped dreaming since he crossed the finish line that first time in Nome.

▲ ▲ Posted at a Rainy Pass checker's cabin.

▲ Nikolai residents put their messages where they won't be missed.

▶ Volunteer Kent Sheets weighs a food-drop bag at an Anchorage warehouse in 1989. Two weeks before the start, mushers must bring their food and supply bags to Anchorage. The food is then sorted according to checkpoint, weighed and postage applied, or it is set aside for Iditarod pilots. Village checkpoints with post offices get the food via the U.S. Postal Service, and their "by-pass" mail. Checkpoints without mail delivery are supplied by the Iditarod's volunteer air force. The bags are weighed so a pilot can properly load his airplane. A musher sends out a variety of dog food to a checkpoint because as the dogs work, often they get fickle about what they will eat. Mushers also send food for themselves and extra supplies such as headlamp batteries, dog booties, gloves, sled runners, socks, boot liners, and other necessities.

▲ Alaska Governor Steve Cowper was among the volunteer army in 1989. Here he helps check in a musher with another volunteer checker at Nikolai.

Iditarod had changed dramatically, from a slow, race-during-the-day trudge across the state, to a race in which every second counted around-the-clock. Butcher was the queen of checkpoint efficiency. She was well aware that time could be gained by swift feeding of dogs, and she was renowned for her ability to work quickly. A musher, it turned out, could shave hours off the clock without going any faster on the trail.

The first Iditarod was a twenty-day race. That was a feeling-it-out year. Mushers didn't even know for sure if dogs could race a thousand miles. But within two years the winning time dropped to the fourteen-day mark. It took until 1981 for another quantum jump in speed to be recorded. Swenson's twelve-day winning time accounted for the next large drop in the record.

How fast could the dogs go? No one really knew. But mushers grew wiser in the way they packed their sleds, gained savvy in how they fed their dogs. Manufacturers invented lighter weight equipment that was just as sturdy as the old, bulky, clunky gear. And dog food companies invented calorie-packed, high-protein goodies that dogs lapped up. There was no more just tossing a dog a fish and figuring that would do. The mushers who learned more about nutrition left behind those who refused to change.

Long-time musher John Barron of Sheep Creek marvels at all of the changes he's seen in two decades of Iditarod racing: "Technology has made things a lot nicer."

Whereas once sleds were all made of

wood and were stiff and rigid, now they are mostly made of plastic and are flexible, he said, with aluminum runners. Whereas once they weighed sixty pounds, now they might weigh thirty. Lighter weights translated into less resistance being hauled by the dogs. Alcohol cookers replaced Coleman stoves. Pocket hand warmers were invented. Warmer, but lighter clothing was developed.

Butcher really was the first, not only to adopt the new style of blitzing checkpoints, but she also was responsible for speeding up the race again. It took five years for Swenson's twelve-day, eight-hour record to be broken, but Butcher shattered it. She introduced the eleven-day race. After three straight wins at roughly that speed, it became an issue of who could keep up with Susan.

Anyone who wanted to likely would have to adapt to a fiercely demanding schedule. Once the Iditarod represented a seasonal occupation. Or perhaps a demanding hobby. Butcher's success heralded the era of full-time, year-round mushers. She worked with her dogs seven days a week, fifteen hours a day, and she didn't believe in vacations.

Long-time competitor Jerry Austin of St. Michael was perhaps the first to understand the implications of her hard work.

"I believe what we see Susan doing is what should be happening," said Austin. "We're seeing the person who's putting in the most effort have the work rewarded. I think what we have to realize here with Susan Butcher is that it's her job, and she views it as a job. Just about

▲ ▲ Jerry Austin cooks dog food over a campfire at Rohn in 1982. Mushers no longer bother to build a fire because it slows them down.

▲ Tim Moerlein's meal heats up after his dogs have eaten, 1988.

▲ ▶ Mushers used to use various kinds of stoves in the 1980s, such as Bill Yankee's single-burner gas stove. The goal: fast and hot.

Reward of a Full Stomach

As the first man to the Yukon River in 1982, Emmitt Peters was wined and dined by the Bristol Bay Native Corp. and the Anchorage Westward Hilton. He enjoyed a steak dinner, complete with vintage spirits, shrimp cocktail, and to top the evening off, baked Alaska.

WHEN THE RACE TOOK SECOND PLACE TO A MAN'S LIFE

DESPITE THE hardships and dangers of the Iditarod Trail, no musher has ever died on the trek between Anchorage and Nome. But no one scared the people of Alaska as much as Mike Madden.

The rescue of Mike Madden during the 1989 Iditarod was one of the most dramatic episodes in the history of the demanding sled dog race. Without the help of fellow competitors who put aside their own aspirations in the event, the North Pole carpenter, then twenty-seven, might well have perished.

The leaders in the 17th annual

Iditarod were long gone, headed to Nome's bright lights and glorious rewards. Madden was one of several mushers set on placing in the top twenty and reaping a comparatively minor cash reward.

But the first reward for a rookie musher like Madden was to finish. As determined as he was, he found it difficult to will his weary body on and cajole his dog team to trot down the trail.

It's not unusual for mushers to become fatigued during the Iditarod. Makes perfect sense. They hardly get

the chance to sleep for more than a few hours at a stretch, so eager are they to save every minute or hour on the trail in their rush to reach the finish line.

Madden was mushing with Jamie Nelson of Togo, Minnesota, and roughly halfway into the race when he felt ill. At various spots along the trail the mushers drop into populated areas where doctors may reside. This was not such a place. Rather Madden's misfortune was compounded by the simple fact that he was mushing along the most remote piece of trail in the whole race. The barren area between Ophir and the tent checkpoint in the old mining town of Iditarod is the big empty. If not for the Iditarod Trail, it might be weeks between travelers in the area.

Madden is about six feet tall and is constructed with sinewy muscle. In his lucid moments, he thought it peculiar he should feel so weak. Perhaps, he thought, he was weakened by a three-stitch cut he'd received when he slashed himself with an ax in McGrath. But that didn't seem to be of sufficient gravity.

In early evening he stopped for a rest and to feed his dogs. He could barely muster the energy to feed the dogs, a paramount task on the trail, but one that isn't that physically demanding. Nelson stopped with him. What struck Madden was how lightly attired Nelson was compared to him—and he was freezing.

"She was wearing just a vest and a wool shirt and commenting how beautiful it was out," said Madden much later. "I had on parkas, goose down, pile. I was just chattering my teeth, and my head was real rummy."

Madden felt an urgency to reach a checkpoint where he could get medical attention. Nelson told him she would follow him.

It was a cold night filled with stars, gorgeous for mushing, but Madden could not enjoy the scene. Gradually, his body was weakening. His muscles weakened, his head was swimming, and his vision was blurring. He fought against his weariness and his aches, trying to push the dogs onward. He convinced himself help was ahead. If he could only make it to Iditarod.

But then the dizziness overtook

Mike Madden prepares to spread ointment on his dogs' feet at the Rohn checkpoint.

him, and he knew he must stop to rest. He pulled his dog team to a halt and jammed in his snow hook to park his sled. Devoid of energy, failing by the minute, he rolled off his sled onto the snow and lay alongside the trail.

About twenty minutes later, Nelson caught up to Madden and was shocked to see him sprawled helplessly on the ground. Nelson couldn't tell if Madden was sleeping or ill, but she was worried. She pulled her sled off the trail and immediately tried to help him, working the musher into additional layers of clothes and a sleeping bag.

"I realized there was something wrong, but I didn't realize how bad it was," said Nelson.

It is the law of the wilderness that no one in trouble gets passed by. The Iditarod may be the most prestigious sporting event in Alaska with high stakes and much personal pride involved in individual races, but compared to the risk of a man's health, even the Iditarod gets put on hold.

Soon after Nelson built a makeshift camp in the wild, reinforcements arrived. Kathy Halverson, Linwood Fiedler, Mitch Brazin, and Nelson were all rookies, yet they acted like seasoned pros. They were joined by Iditarod

Mike Madden passes through downtown Unalakleet in a whiteout storm. The winds always blow in the coastal village.

veteran Jerry Austin of St. Michael, who's often a contender, but was having an off-year farther back in the pack. Halverson was on the scene when the next group mushed up, suspicious of a middle-of-the-nowhere parking lot.

"We have a little problem here," said Halverson. The problem was pretty big at that point, actually. While none of the mushers were doctors or medical professionals, they were wily outdoorsmen with survival skills. A fire was built, water was boiled, and Madden was forced to ingest liquids. He was kept wrapped layers of clothing and sleeping bags, and was closely watched in teams.

"We just had to use a bit of common sense," said Brazin.

Madden's condition was frightening. It was obvious he was running a fever. He alternately sweated and shivered, and drifted in and out of consciousness. Of all the mushers, Austin was the most experienced, and he examined Madden trying to determine what ailed him. Blood poisoning from his cut, and hypothermia from a combination of exhaustion and the chilling weather were two guesses.

But they were only guesses.

Not only was this not the place to be sick, it was not the environment. As the group huddled together seeking a solution to Madden's woes, the temperature dipped to twenty-five degrees below zero. Clearly, Madden must be evacuated, but how? Eventually, word would reach Iditarod officials about the cluster of mushers alongside the trail, but could they wait for help to work its way to them?

It did not seem practical to load Madden into a sled and carry him on to the checkpoint. That likely would be a bumpy ride, and it might not be best for his health anyway. The groups caucused and decided that since Fiedler and Austin had the freshest dog teams, they would make a pell mell dash to Iditarod, roughly thirty miles away, and alert officials.

Fiedler said the mushers had good cause to move swiftly once they'd spent time around Madden, who was periodically delirious and shouting nonsensical things.

"It really kind of put the fear of God in us," said Fiedler. "It makes you realize how quickly things can happen. It was definitely serious."

On the rushed mush to Iditarod, Fiedler couldn't help but be reminded of

the Iditarod's historical antecedent. The famed diphtheria serum run of six decades before was all about using dog teams to help sick people in Nome. And here were Fiedler and Austin mushing as fast as they could to help a sick man in the Iditarod Trail Sled Dog Race.

Austin and Fiedler mushed through the evening and on into the middle of the night before they reached the Iditarod checkpoint. There was a radio there and the call went out for a doctor. A helicopter was sent to the village of Grayling to pick up Dr. Dan Stevenson. Austin rode along and helped guide the pilot back to the spot on the trail where Madden lay.

Stevenson took Madden's temperature and found it elevated to 103.4. Madden was bleary-eyed and had difficulty answering simple questions. As Madden was flown to Humana Hospital in Anchorage, he sadly realized his dream of finishing the Iditarod was thwarted for the year, and he started crying.

On the ground, Austin mushed Madden's dog team on to Iditarod, covering the same territory again.

What scared the mushers the most were Stevenson's words: If another two hours had passed without medical help, Madden might have died.

At the hospital, doctors determined

that Madden was hyperthermic, overheated, and more significantly, suffering from salmonella poisoning. He could only guess how he'd contracted it—perhaps from contaminated dog food—but could never be sure.

Rarely has a major sporting event witnessed such selflessness by competitors. The group of mushers who stopped to aid Madden lost eighteen hours on the clock, dooming most of them to finishes outside the top twenty and therefore out of the money. The move also cost any of them the rookie-of-the-year prize. But no one cared.

"The competition was kind of stifled," said Brazin. "It didn't even seem like a race after that."

The mushers may have lost out on monetary payoffs, but the rest of the Iditarod community praised them. At

the closing banquet, Austin, Fiedler, Brazin, Halverson, and Nelson were applauded and given a special reward—the race's Sportsmanship Award.

As for Madden, he spent just one day in the hospital and then woozy, but game, flew to Nome to greet his rescuers one by one at the finish line. When Austin arrived, Madden met him with a gin-and-tonic in hand and toasted him.

"I feel real fortunate to have people on the trail like that," said Madden.

Madden was pleased to be alive and on his way back to good health. But he also had unfinished business. In 1990, Madden returned to the Iditarod and mushed home in 13th place. 🐾

The mushers who assisted Mike Madden were recognized with a special award by the Iditarod Trail Committee.

everyone else is a working stiff."

As she geared up for a try at four straight wins in 1989, Butcher gave no sign of backtracking from her mental and physical commitment.

"There is no problem with me being a workaholic still," she said. "I was born that way. I'm made that way. I enjoy it. I'm all-consumed by it, but it doesn't bother me. I don't miss anything else I could be doing with my time. I love dog mushing."

Even more revealing than the stories of Butcher sitting up all night holding a sick dog's paw were the stories of her attention to detail. When she brought dogs to the veterinarian, checkups that routinely lasted a half hour for other mushers lasted four hours because she wanted every toenail and tooth examined.

Going into the 1989 race, Butcher seemed unstoppable.

"We were all kind of hoping she'd get pregnant this summer," teased Austin before the race. Not so much of a joke really because Butcher said she would like to raise a family. But, as it turned out, Butcher was beatable, anyway.

This was one year Butcher's dogs were not capable of running away and hiding. In Unalakleet, there was a group of five—Butcher, Joe Runyan of Nenana, Jonrowe, Swenson, and Martin Buser of Big Lake—jockeying for the lead, and Lavon Barve of Wasilla was gaining. That was a pretty good crowd.

The competitors all eyed each other,

▲▲ Martin Buser pauses for minor repairs on his sled runners as Matt Desalernos passes him at the summit of Rainy Pass during the 1988 race.

▲ The 1988 Iditarod proves a special challenge for Dewey Halverson in Rainy Pass. A tree trunk hidden by deep snow overturned the sled, but Halverson hung on so he wouldn't lose his team.

but it was unclear who was hurting and who was healthy. Mushing with a group is a little bit like playing poker. Bluffs are common. A musher might well know a secret about the condition of his dogs, but it will never be revealed. The mushers push on, husbanding energy, studying the enemy, but never really knowing who has the most in reserve.

Rest and run, rest and run. The race continued, and space grew between the teams. Runyan moved ahead, Butcher tried to hang with him. Barve and Swenson fell back. Jonrowe plodded on. Until her nightmare.

In one of the most unfortunate of Iditarod finishes, Jonrowe suffered as her dogs staged a five-hour sit-down strike on the outskirts of Nome. Swenson steamed passed her, taking third place and relegating Jonrowe to a frustrating fourth.

Meanwhile, the lanky Runyan, a previous victor in the Yukon Quest and the French Alpirod, became the first to win the so-called Triple Crown of mushing and broke Butcher's stranglehold on the Iditarod.

Butcher said she realized coming out of White Mountain that there was no way she'd be able to catch Runyan. She pushed as hard as she could, but got no closer than Runyan's winning margin of an hour and four minutes.

For his part, Runyan raced in fear of being caught from behind. Butcher's mystique was so strong, he somehow imagined her closing with such a rush that she'd pass him in a blur. Even though this defied logic—it was clear his team was the strongest by

Joe Runyan endures thirty-mile-an-hour winds through the Ptarmigan Flats area of Rainy Pass on his way to a 1989 championship. The win marked Runyan as the only musher to have won the Triple Crown of mushing: Europe's Alpirod, the Yukon Quest, and the Iditarod.

this time—Runyan took nothing for granted as his dogs trotted down Front Street on a picturesque, sunny afternoon.

It must be said that Runyan put on a good show of calmness, however. He comes across as laconic in public, but even he admitted he was tenser than a high wire stretched between two buildings.

"I was having nervous breakdowns," said Runyan. "I didn't know where she was."

Emphasizing the point that mushers would likely be among the best posers at a card table, Butcher raced to Nome with the calculated belief that a champion is never dethroned until the race is over, but with the doubting knowledge that a team that started out so strong in Anchorage didn't have much left as it approached Nome.

Along the long route, Butcher's dogs twice came down with viruses. At times in checkpoints she felt like a full-time veterinarian. The last three hundred miles seemed endless, and when she reached the village of Koyuk the unfolding race had her concerned. Runyan seemed too tough to overtake.

"I was pretty worried," she remembers. With good cause. Runyan held on, and Butcher was glancing over her shoulder, too, because Swenson was right in the hunt, finishing third. Butcher was gracious in defeat, giving Runyan all the credit, but even at the finish line she was looking to the future.

"Joe's put out a challenge I've got to beat," she said.

For the moment, though, the forty-year-old Runyan was the new star of the

AT LAST: IT'S NOT OVER UNTIL THE RED LANTERN SWINGS

ONE OF THE great symbols of the Iditarod Trail Sled Dog Race is the Red Lantern, the award for finishing last.

Perhaps no musher better personifies the spirit of those bringing up the rear than Scott Cameron, a

Red Lantern winner Scott Cameron prepares to serve his dogs a well-deserved hot meal. He worked hard to come in last.

musher who competed in the Last Great Race in 1983, 1985, and 1986, and who finished last in 1983. An Anchorage dental laboratory operator, Cameron is proud to be the recipient of a Red Lantern, figuring that it is far better to complete the 1,100-mile race slowly than not to finish at all.

"Not everybody can go out and run a race like this," said Cameron.

The Red Lantern has been presented to the last finisher in every Iditarod, beginning with John Schultz in 1973, the slowest of the slow, who took more than thirty-two days to complete the route.

Why a red lantern? It's more or less a statement that those who passed that way before will leave a light burning for you.

Although he no longer races in the Iditarod, Cameron remains in demand by schools and public service organizations who revel in his slide show presentations that detail his mushing adventures.

"It's my way of sharing it," he said. "My way of saying thanks." Actually, Cameron might have suspected complications lay ahead when he entered his first Iditarod. He had all sorts of woes in the Montana Creek 200,

a preparatory race. The major disaster was being stomped by an ornery moose. If dull-appearing moose seem cuddly to the uninitiated surely mushers know better than anyone else what a dangerous nuisance they can be when they block the trail and take their frustrations out on yipping dogs.

Cameron was stopped by the trail changing leaders, with his shotgun stowed in his sled basket, when the angry moose knocked him down. As the moose laid waste to the team, he swatted it with the shotgun, breaking the stock over its butt. He hurt for several days after that confrontation.

Gradually, as the 1983 Iditarod unfolded, Cameron nursed his team's feet and fell farther and farther behind, though maintaining a loose link with a pack that included Ron Gould, Norm McAlpine, and Norman Vaughan.

Near Shaktoolik, mushing in the dark, with no lights from the village visible, Cameron was sure he was hallucinating. He heard bagpipes playing, so there really was no other explanation. Late in the race, Cameron had trouble keeping up with the other trio. On the way into Koyuk, Cameron

was mushing along when he was startled to see a Native man on a snowmachine waiting for him.

"He announced he was an angel from heaven come to save me," said Cameron. Another hallucination? "I thought I was seeing an apparition. He was real, though. It turned out Colonel Vaughan paid this guy to come out and find me with a Thermos of hot lemonade and soup."

Gould mushed away, but in Safety, the final checkpoint, twenty-two miles from Nome, Cameron once again caught Vaughan and McAlpine. At 3 A.M. they discussed pushing on, but then decided to wait till after daybreak.

"It was sort of, 'Who's going to come out in the middle of the night to see us?'" Vaughan volunteered to finish last, but Cameron told him to just mush on.

"I said, 'Whoa, Colonel, I worked hard here and deserve to come in last,'" said Cameron. "Who's going to remember second from last?"

Vaughan finished 52nd that year, McAlpine 53rd, and Cameron 54th and last, in a time of 21 days, 4 hours, 36 minutes, roughly two hours behind Vaughan. 🐾

Iditarod, the man who stopped Butcher's march. Everyone wanted to know how he did it, and when they found out, Runyan quickly was hailed as "the thinking man's musher" because of his meticulous, scientific preparation.

The old days and the old ways of the Iditarod were gone. No longer was it sufficient to begin training when the first snow fell. The Iditarod was becoming a logistical as well as physical challenge, and one that required year-round preparation.

For most of the year leading up to the 1989 Iditarod, Runyan had sat in his Nenana home studying Iditarod finishing times and the times the best mushers clocked between checkpoints during the first sixteen Iditarods. He made charts and he made plans. He studied everything from the number of dogs the winners had at the finish to how many they had at different spots along the way. And he studied their rest patterns.

Runyan came into that year's Iditarod determined to stick to his own plan, not to be swayed by what other frontrunners did. He carried a little black book with notes and plans, and he followed his own strategy. Generally, his approach can be summed up simply by saying he ran his dogs longer at a time than most competitors, then rested them longer than other mushers.

During the 1,100-mile race, the temptation to vary his plan was great. Mostly he ignored such temptations. However, sometimes failure to deviate from an etched-in-

▲ Bill Cotter mushes up "The Glacier" thirteen miles out of the Rohn checkpoint in 1989. The creek is so nicknamed because freezing overflow guarantees a ride on glare ice. Some years, mushers have had to crawl up this stretch of trail.

◄ Martin Buser kicks to assist his team as they travel along the Norton Bay shoreline. A tripod marks the approach to Shaktoolik.

stone focus can be costly. Late in the race Runyan realized this—that the abstract can spoil the reality—and he was flexible enough to make one adjustment. At a time his plan called for taking a rest, Butcher was moving. He was afraid she'd be moving away from him for good, so he took the gamble of skipping a rest and ended up leading Butcher by one minute heading into Unalakleet.

Runyan thought he had the Iditarod figured out, and it turned out he was right.

"I wanted to develop a nice rhythm the dogs would have confidence in," said Runyan. "I figured I had to understand what I was doing if I was going to run a record-setting race." Runyan didn't quite set a record, but he did claim a championship. He was satisfied with that.

As the 1980s turned to the 1990s, what no one could know for sure was whether the Butcher dynasty was ending and a new one beginning, or if Butcher would come back stronger than ever the next year.

Goodbye to a Great Lady

Dorothy G. Page, "Mother of the Iditarod" and editor of the *Iditarod Runner* magazine for many years, died unexpectedly at her Wasilla home on November 16, 1989. At the time of her death, she was treasurer of the Iditarod Trail Committee and was active in the Wasilla-Knik-Willow Creek Historical Society. She also served as curator of the Wasilla Museum.

▲ Checkers and HAM radio operators keep the oil burning at the 1988 Rohn checkpoint, ready to greet any incoming mushers. The Rohn checkpoint is a twelve-by-eighteen-foot trapper's log cabin and has served as the checkpoint each year. While it's not large, it has housed and slept many people at one time. Often people find a spot under a bunk or in a chair.

▲ ▶ Northern lights shine over the home of Richard and Vi Burnham at the Kaltag checkpoint in 1989. Their home served as the official checkpoint in Kaltag for many years until the 1992 corraling rule.

◀ ◀ Tim Moerlein at sunset near Unalakleet, 1988. Unalakleet is Yupik for "where the east wind blows," and it almost always does blow through the coastal village, where snowdrifts easily can reach fifteen feet.

1990s

FOCUS ON TRAINING, TECHNOLOGY, AND DOG CARE

While mushers draw peak performances

from their dogs and themselves, the question begs:

Can the Iditarod get any faster?

Suggestions of Susan Butcher's demise after her loss in the 1989 race were greatly exaggerated. Such thoughts may have been promoted by opponents' wishful thinking; however, they were totally unfounded.

In 1990, Butcher raced to Nome faster than ever, missing the first ten-day-plus Iditarod by just under two hours. She edged Runyan, returning the favor, by less than three hours.

And most importantly, she tied Rick Swenson for the most number of Iditarod championships with four. Swenson placed seventh in the race, prompting detractors to say he was slipping. The two famous mushers were at the height of their rivalry.

Roger Dahl mushes through a stand of hoarfrost-covered birch trees outside the Knik checkpoint.

Mushers drop their mandatory handler at Knik and from there proceed to Nome unassisted.

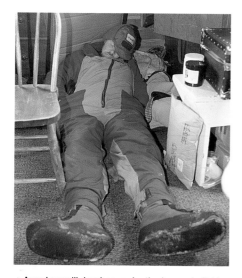

▲ Any place will do when you're tired enough. Robin Jacobson catches a nap at the Ophir checkpoint.

▲ ▶ The first Saturday in March marks the Iditarod start each year. Fourth Avenue is closed in the early hours of the morning to allow city crews to dump snow on the street for a trail. They also assemble the staging area and hoist the start banner. Recent rule changes have made the starting line in Alaska's largest city merely ceremonial. On the next day, the official re-start in Wasilla starts the race clock ticking.

▲ Ruby villagers enjoy a taste of urban entertainment provided by Anchorage celebrity Mr. Whitekeys. In the even-numbered years, Ruby is the location for the "First Musher to the Yukon" award offered by sponsor Regal Alaskan Hotel. In 1990 they not only brought in a chef for the meal, but also entertainer Mr. Whitekeys. Entertainment like this is rare in the villages and is most welcome by the youngsters.

This combination of circumstances—Butcher going for a record-breaking fifth victory, Swenson seeking to re-establish his primacy—served as the backdrop for the next Iditarod. The 1991 Iditarod proved to be one of the most dramatic in the race's history. It was a race that abruptly veered from the predictable to the astounding, producing unforeseen drama and results.

In the days leading up to the usual first Saturday in March departure, Butcher was supremely confident. This group of dogs might be her best team yet, she felt. These huskies were so talented she wasn't sure Granite, the primary lead dog in her first three victories, would even be able to make the team.

In the end, partially because of sentimentality, Butcher brought Granite along, though as a regular team member, not a leader, and ended up dropping him around five hundred miles into the race.

"I'm looking for a record," she said shortly before the race. "But I always do. In ten days, under eleven. Obviously, it's important to me to get this one."

Could anyone beat Butcher? It seemed preordained that Butcher would become the race's winningest driver, and during the early stages everything went smoothly for her. When the lead pack gradually sorted itself out, and the frontrunners began their push to the Bering Sea coast, Butcher was well-positioned.

And then in the critical miles between Unalakleet and White Mountain, as others faced difficulties, Butcher had smooth sailing. As Nome went to sleep ten days into the race, expecting a midday following day finish, Butcher was in command. Her fifth win was hers for the taking.

However, those who believe in sure things were reminded the next morning that especially in a long-distance endurance event, the race is never truly over until it's over. Too many things can go wrong. And in the middle of the night, while fans rested in warm beds, the leading mushers were bashed by a brutal storm of such severity that the race was stunningly altered.

The blizzard conditions of swiftly falling snow and high velocity wind effectively sealed off all communication on the trail between White Mountain and Safety. While the world waited for a winner, a news black-out descended.

Reports on just what was happening to mushers and dogs were at first confused. Then incomplete.

Eventually, the scene in White Mountain was patched together. Butcher, Swenson, Tim Osmar, and Joe Runyan left the check-point in the vicious storm, and quickly were swallowed by whiteout conditions. The weather was so bad that Butcher and Swenson worked together searching for signs of the proper trail. But soon they got separated.

Decision time. Butcher, Runyan, and Osmar turned their dog teams around and headed back to White Mountain. They thought Swenson was joining them. On the outskirts of White Mountain, Butcher

▲ Unalakleet residents greet Susan Butcher, the first one to arrive at the coast in the 1991 race.

▲▲ It's the middle of the night when a musher checks in at the Finger Lake checkpoint, but volunteers are ready, 1991.

▲ A weary DeeDee Jonrowe rests up in Canatser's cabin, Eagle Island checkpoint, 1991. In a year with seventy-five mushers at the starting line, Jonrowe placed seventh.

encountered Martin Buser going the other way. She warned him the trail was so rough the only prudent course was to turn back. He shouted, "Hey, you're going the wrong way, girl!" and chose to push on. The trio in White Mountain was surprised when Swenson didn't appear soon after. They felt Swenson and Buser were making a serious mistake by gambling with the weather and would be forced to camp by the trail and withstand battering by the wind while they reposed in comfort.

Word reached Nome that three of the best mushers in the world had turned around in the face of a nasty storm and that two other mushers were out on the trail somewhere.

As time passed, no one spotted either Swenson or Buser or could account for them at all. Speculation about their safety grew. Friends and relatives were worried. In such a storm, with almost no visibility, they could easily be sidetracked, could easily mush far out of their way. They might be lost, might be in extreme need of assistance. Or they might be camped, waiting out the storm much as Libby Riddles did in 1985.

No one really knew anything, and in an information vacuum, gossip and rumor spread. Hours passed. A whole day passed. The storm was relentless. Where was Swenson? Where was Buser?

Finally, in the early evening hours two nights later, came the electrifying news that Swenson was in Safety. He had made the run against the wind over the Topkok Hills, mushing fifty-five miles to the last check-point. He was alive. He was well. He was poised to become an Iditarod champion again, nine years after his last win.

Once again, Swenson proved that when things got tough, he was the toughest. It was wickedly uncomfortable even standing at the finish line waiting for Swenson's early morning arrival. With the wind blowing sideways and the thermometer dipping to less than twenty below, the chill factor was minus fifty. And that was in town.

When Swenson came down Front Street shortly past one-thirty in the morning, a shivering crowd of thousands gave him a celebratory welcome. Only narrow patches of skin on his face showed, and his mustache was coated with a thick layer of frost.

"If I was going to walk, I wasn't going to turn back," said Swenson, who indeed had been reduced to such slow movement. He frequently had to walk in front of his dogs, slowly seeking the trail.

"I'll never forget last night. It was a little scary, and it was stressful. It was not a pleasant night. As long as I stayed on the trail I wasn't going to die."

A fan yelled, "Five times, baby!"

Five championships. The race had begun with that goal a seemingly realistic one for Butcher. It ended with Swenson once more extending his own record.

Three hours behind Swenson came Buser. He, too, had braved the seemingly unconquerable storm. Only once during his long run in the snow did he have a clue of

▲ Paperwork is essential in keeping track of dropped dogs and seeing to their veterinary care. This paperwork is filled out by the musher and the attending vet, and stays with the dog until it is met by handlers.

◄ Volunteer checker Doug Katchatag meets musher Laird Barron for check-in at Unalakleet. Volunteers must be hardy souls and love their "jobs" to brave the elements and long hours during the Iditarod.

◄ ◄ Susan Butcher heads out along the coast near the Elim checkpoint in the 1991 race. In this windblown and icy region, should mushers need to hole up, there are three shelter cabins on the trail before Golovin.

High Hopes

The elevation of Rainy Pass is 3,160 feet, the highest point on the Iditarod Trail.

LAVON BARVE: LOST IN A WHITEOUT

ONLY THE COMBINATION of good fortune and mushers' preparedness has prevented tragedy along the trail. No man or woman driving dogs has been killed during the race, but there have been several close calls.

And one of the most experienced mushers of all ran one of the biggest risks of all.

The ordeal of veteran Lavon Barve began when his dogs drifted away from him in a whiteout during the 1991 Iditarod Trail Sled Dog Race. He stepped off the sled runners to find the right direction on the trail, and poof, they were gone.

For the next eighteen hours, the Wasilla musher wandered alone in a raging snowstorm seeking his team. He had no food or water and only the clothes he was wearing for protection as he trudged through the wilderness.

The wind roared and the snow fell heavily in this lonely area between the villages of Elim and Golovin, far along the trail toward Nome. Visibility shrunk to nearly zero, and what began as a likely swift search turned frightening in a hurry. Barve was lost. Lost because he could barely see.

Alone against the elements, the idea of trying to find his dogs was never very far from the forefront of Barve's thoughts, yet it quickly became apparent to him that the situation was dire, and he adopted another focus. "I was surviving," he said. "I lay down until I got cold, and then I walked again."

At the time, Barve was forty-seven, a solidly built man with a balding head and a thick, brown mustache. He was a respected competitor who'd made his mark in long-distance mushing by placing fifth in the 1989 event and third in 1990. This was a source of great satisfaction to him for many reasons, not the least of which was his need to work full-time at the print shop he ran in the Mat-Su Valley while others worked on their mushing careers year-round.

Also, Barve had gravitated to the Iditarod after his sprint mushing career fizzled. His somewhat self-deprecating explanation for how he happened to start long-distance racing was simple.

"I wasn't doing that well," he said of the sprint races. "And I always liked to go camping. I thought, 'Shoot, maybe I'll put the two hobbies together.'"

It had taken years of racing, but in

Lavon Barve has run the Iditarod Trail Sled Dog Race thirteen times.

1991, Barve was considered one of the Iditarod favorites, and when he ran into trouble he was mushing not far from the front of the pack in sixth place.

The trail connecting the two checkpoint villages is just twenty-eight miles long. Although the weather was bad and the hour late—after midnight—Barve had no hesitation about plunging ahead with his race. That was the way it had to be if one wanted to be a top finisher.

Barve's difficulties began when he realized he no longer could see the sticks with orange ribbons that mark the trail. The wind likely had blown them away, and the fresh snow piling up covered the tracks of mushers who'd passed through. The dogs couldn't see any better than he could, and they trotted off the trail, pulling the sled into an icy ravine, and tangling the gang lines in some alders. Barve had to hack his way out of the brush to turn the sled around in winds that howled at upwards of sixty miles an hour.

The next obstacle was getting the dogs and sled up over the hill and back where they'd come from, but even with Barve leading and pulling on the harnesses, the dogs resisted. Ultimately this tactic failed because the dogs' feet

Rather than waste time melting snow, Lavon Barve hauls water from an open lead on the South Fork of the Kuskokwim at the Rohn checkpoint.

slipped on the icy lip of the rise.

Barve gave up. Instead of retracing his path he planned to lead the dogs around the steepest, most slippery section to softer stuff. Only he made a mistake. Making the assumption that the dogs would follow closely as he bent into the wind, he didn't hang on to their harnesses.

After a few minutes of fighting through the snow, Barve turned around, and he was alone. No dogs.

Stunned, Barve didn't panic. He figured the dogs were nearby, so he began searching, walking in ever-widening circles.

"I figured I would find the team," he said. "How hard would that be?"

Harder than expected. He yelled for them, but heard no answering barks. Minutes became hours. Still no dogs. The temperature dipped well below zero. The snow kept coming down. The wind kept blasting. The blizzard was in control.

After a while, Barve became more cognizant of his predicament. He was chilled, burning up calories, and focused on putting one foot in front of the other headed toward Golovin. He hoped someone would find him, a snow-machiner, or another musher, but there was no one in sight. When he stumbled a few times, Barve became alarmed.

"I was not as sharp as you should be," he said later.

By sunup, Barve had been walking for about seven hours. Yet the dawn offered false hope. He didn't see his dogs, or anyone else, and he could still barely see at all because the snow continued to swirl. Barve pushed himself, forced himself onward, hour after hour.

It was about 6 P.M. when two snowmachiners discovered him trudging along the trail about seven miles from Golovin. Worried race officials had called asking for someone in the

community to see if Barve could be found. Weary and cold, Barve was carried into town and fed by rescuers, who thought he was in pretty good shape, but definitely in need of some warmth and eats.

"Those guys saved my bacon," he said. A small search was mounted for the dogs in the dark, but it wasn't until the next day, when a group of riders drove Barve back to the area where he started walking, that he was reunited with his team.

The dogs, it turned out, in contrast to the musher, hadn't wandered very far. They'd just hunkered down and made themselves as comfortable as possible resting in the snow and waiting for Barve to come back.

The harsh experience discouraged Barve because he thought he had a chance to win the race. But he also proved his hardiness and determination. He jumped back in the race and eventually placed 17th, still in the money.

And he understood he was a lucky man.

"If I hadn't had the right clothes on, I would have had frost-bitten extremities," said Barve. "The 17th place finish means a lot to me, just in that I was able to finish the race." 🐾

▲ A competitor in the 1990 race, Roy Monk carefully crosses open water on a makeshift bridge in the Farewell Burn.

► Having fed the dogs first, Macgill Adams of Big Lake cooks a meal for himself at his Rohn checkpoint camp, 1991.

Swenson's whereabouts. At the shelter cabin in the Topkok Hills forty miles from Nome, Buser saw a message that Swenson had carved on the wall proclaiming victory. At least he knew he'd been there. Buser continued his pursuit, but to no avail. He finished frostbitten and windburned, but proud of his effort.

"It was a long last day," Buser said. "I got pushed into submission for a few hours."

The others trickled in later in the day. Butcher was third, Osmar fourth, Runyan fifth. By huddling in White Mountain they thought they'd given themselves the best chance to win. They were wrong.

"It looked terrible," said Osmar. "You couldn't go anywhere."

But Swenson and Buser proved you could. Butcher was a disappointed but gracious loser, uttering a statement that might have surprised Iditarod fans who considered her and Swenson mortal enemies and were unaware of their history of friendship.

"As a friend watching a friend win, I feel terrific," said Butcher. "But as a four-time winner watching another four-time winner win a fifth—when in every other circumstance the race was mine—I don't feel good about it."

Swenson, naturally, felt great about it. He had reclaimed his supremacy. During this period in the early 1990s, the Iditarod's top purse of $350,000, with $50,000 going to the winner, was heavily supported by national sponsors. The event was televised nationally by ABC and seemed to be experiencing a growth spurt.

But then the Humane Society of the United States came to town.

The Washington, D.C.–based animal rights group sent a representative to Alaska to study the Iditarod, to follow the race along the trail, and ultimately to file a report so the organization could take a position on Iditarod dog care.

Iditarod lovers were suspicious of the HSUS's intentions, and those suspicions were only inflamed when that official, a vice president of the organization named David Wills, made a statement that implied the HSUS already had formed its opinion. He said that in a perfect world the Iditarod would not exist.

Fans of the race urged the Iditarod Trail Committee not to acknowledge the HSUS's existence and not to cooperate with the group. The Iditarod took a more conciliatory stance, though a four-year war of words ensued when the HSUS was highly critical of the Iditarod and threatened to organize boycotts of sponsors.

Although mushers' success is predicated on the health and performance of their dogs, who are the athletes in the race, periodically dogs die in harness. Sometimes, despite pre-race veterinary checks, they die of heart ailments. Other times the cause of death remains mysterious, and a seemingly healthy animal keels over. The HSUS declared that no dog death was acceptable and lobbied the Iditarod to change its rules to help prevent such occurrences.

Over a period of years, as Iditarod

▲ Lavon Barve takes a break from the 1991 race for a few winks in the closest soft spot he could find.

▲▲ Frank Teasley avoids a Native snowmachiner who's sharing the portage trail from Kaltag to Unalakleet in the 1991 race.

▲ Rick Mackey rests at the Grayling checkpoint during the 1991 race.

The entry fee in 1978 was $525. By the 1996 Iditarod, it was $1,750. The first day of 1996 sign-ups was June 24, 1995. Defending champion Doug Swingley traveled all the way from Simms, Montana, to be there. Swingley, along with mushers DeeDee Jonrowe, Lavon Barve, and Martin Buser, signed autographs and met their fans during the afternoon barbecue that says thank you to hundreds of volunteers.

officials and mushers protested that the dogs already were receiving the best care in the world, alterations were made to accommodate HSUS objections. Mandatory twenty-four-hour and six-hour rests already were encompassed in the rules. In some years additional rests were required, and the time when the six-hour rest could be taken was changed.

Penalties were instituted and tinkered with that called for disqualifying mushers in the case of dog deaths. Maximum team size was reduced from twenty to sixteen by 1996. And straw for individual dog beds at farflung checkpoints was required.

In addition, in 1993 the HSUS was given a seat on one of the Iditarod's policy-making committees, the animal care committee, and was given veto power over the hiring of a chief veterinarian.

At the same time, the Iditarod suffered a verbal backlash from its main constituency—Alaskans. Residents accused the race of turning its back on local supporters and of pandering to the HSUS. There is a well-known saying in the state that is emblematic of Alaskans' independence. The theme is that Alaskans don't care how people do things elsewhere, they will go their own way. And certainly that sentiment surfaced in this case.

All of this battling with the HSUS took a toll. While no company actually admitted its action was related to any HSUS adherents' complaints, one by one several of the Iditarod's key major sponsors dropped away,

▲ Aerial view of the Ophir checkpoint as a team arrives in the 1992 race. Even though they live near Wasilla, Dick and Audra Forsgren have flown out and hosted the Iditarod at their Ophir cabin since 1973. The atmosphere is warm, and homemade food always awaits the mushers. Ophir is now a ghost town left over from the early 1900s when a minor gold rush hit the area.

◄ Open water on the Kuskokwim's South Fork creates vapor at twenty below zero as Jon Terhune leaves the Rohn checkpoint in 1992.

letting their contracts run their course and then not renewing the affiliation. The Iditarod lost its national television contract and the backing of its flagship sponsor Timberland, the maker of outdoor gear.

In response to both the corporate withdrawals and Alaskan fans' concerns, Iditarod officials under the leadership of Executive Director Stan Hooley and Iditarod Trail Committee President Matt Desalernos, instituted a successful two-pronged campaign to raise money within the state and increase ITC membership.

In-state sponsors stepped forward and made up the financial losses felt when national corporations retreated from the race. A brochure was printed urging Alaskans to help the Iditarod. It featured the slogan "Join the Iditarod Team and Bring Your Friends." Grass roots membership grew from about twelve hundred to more than twenty-five hundred. A new wildly popular program was created auctioning off rides on mushers' sleds for the first few miles of the race. And merchandise sales were emphasized and increased.

"We feel very good about what we've been able to accomplish," said Hooley.

As another step towards financial independence from sponsors located outside of Alaska, the state Legislature gave the Iditarod permission to run its own lottery as a fund-raiser. The lottery was scheduled to begin in 1997.

"Alaskans love to gamble," said Matt Desalernos, a prime backer of the lottery

▲ Charlie Boulding cares for his dogs as dawn breaks over the Finger Lake checkpoint in 1992.

▲▲ Pausing at the Rohn checkpoint, Sonny Russell boots his dogs at twilight. Proper dog care is the number-one priority of a musher. The dogs are the mushers' best friends, and the only way to get to Nome is to take good care of their dogs. Later Russell would scratch from the 1992 race.

◄ Mike Williams passes through one of the narrowest stretches on the Iditarod shortly after cresting Rainy Pass.

"This year as every year, the United States Humane Society has sent outraged telegrams demanding that the Iditarod Trail [race] be canceled. If the huskies could read, they would fall about laughing. They are half-wolf and wild-eyed and run until their hearts give out, which is usually about a dozen years later around the age of eighteen.

"They are heroically mad, as are most of the forty-seven humans they pulled off the starting line in bright sunshine and at a temperature of twelve below. This, around here, is a balmy spring day.

" . . . There was only one hitch. Before one muffled figure was even a hundred yards down the trail, a distraught female voice screamed: 'Hey, you've still got the car keys,' and her husband reached down into a pocket and threw them back into the snow without stopping."
    —Ian Wooldridge,
    who covered "The Last Great Race on Earth" for The London Daily Mail, *March 1977*

plan. "Especially when the gambling's for a good cause."

Regardless of all the safeguards approved for the dogs, no list of precautions proved to be perfect, however.

Butcher had invited HSUS representatives to her kennel and the organization held her up as the ultimate role model for mushers. However, when a Butcher dog died during the 1994 race, the HSUS blasted the Iditarod once more. This led to the final rupture between the Iditarod and HSUS, and soon the Iditarod booted the organization's rep off its committee and severed contact with the group.

Former Governor Steve Cowper, then an Iditarod Trail Committee board member, concluded in 1994, "We're just going to have to fight it out with them."

Officially, the Iditarod now has nothing to do with the HSUS. However, when something that displeases the group occurs during the race, the HSUS does not hesitate to submit a fresh public statement critical of the Iditarod. Despite little or no direct contact, the two groups remain at odds.

The momentum Martin Buser gained from his bold move during the storm in 1991 served him in good stead in 1992. After five consecutive top ten finishes, Buser earned the title he coveted—Iditarod champion.

And as a bonus, he became the fastest-ever Iditarod musher, breaking the eleven-day barrier with a time of 10 days, 19 hours, 17 minutes. Buser's was a truly dominating performance. His margin of victory was more than ten hours over Susan Butcher.

Buser was born in Switzerland nearly thirty-four years before his triumph, and his introduction to dog mushing came in Europe. He moved to Alaska in 1980 to learn more about the sport, planning to spend a year in the state, and worked as a handler for crafty old sprint mushing champion Earl Norris of Willow. His return to Switzerland lasted only three months before a spirit of restlessness brought him back to Alaska.

"I just couldn't hack it," said Buser. "I had grown too used to the elbow space and the freedom. Just the sheer beauty of the state."

Ultimately, Buser married, had two boys whom he named after the Iditarod checkpoints Rohn and Nikolai, and settled in Big Lake, about fifty miles north of Anchorage.

A genial man with a dry sense of humor, Buser, like most mushers, had his growing pains and struggles with weather and misfortune along the trail before his breakthrough. One of his favorite dogs died on the trail in 1989, and later he got lost in a storm.

But in 1992, everything went his way. At the finish line as Buser hugged his family, the crowd chanted, "Mar-tin! Mar-tin!"

Making it through the storm with Swenson in 1991 was an achievement that Buser did not readily understand would pay long-term dividends, but he acknowledged after his championship race that it helped a great deal.

"That was a definite confidence boost," said Buser. "Learning to win, you have to go

▲ Tomas Israelsson and team encounter a deep ravine between Cripple and Sulatna crossing in the 1992 race, a year in which the largest number of mushers started and finished in one year. Trail breakers attempted to make a tree-trunk bridge across the ravine, which worked for snowmachines, but not for dog teams.

◄ Personnel from Galena Air Force Base volunteered in the 1992 race. Among their duties as checkpoint helpers, they cleaned up used straw bedding at the Galena checkpoint.

◄ ◄ ▲ George Murphy, a former member of Iditarod's volunteer air force, soars above the Rohn checkpoint, 1992.

◄ ◄ A timed exposure shows the trails of headlamps as checkers and vets work with arriving teams at the Rohn checkpoint.

DO YOU SEE WHAT I SEE?

*When hallucinations befall
overtired mushers, the "unseen"
is a common sight.*

MUSHING ALONG the trail late at night, John Barron knew something was wrong. His dogs glowed a weird green in the dark.

Green dogs? Huskies are bred for speed and stamina for generations, but not for bright colors. Uh, oh. He'd never heard of dogs the color of a watch dial. Barron got the message. Through his dense fatigue, the Sheep Creek musher realized he was hallucinating.

"I took a break," he said. Time for a rest. Time for a nap. Time to park the dogs off the Iditarod Trail before he passed out.

Hallucinations are a hazard of the Iditarod Trail. The humans' first allegiance is to animal care, so they typically get far less sleep during the 1,100-mile race from Anchorage to Nome than the dogs. They push and push themselves, often averaging just two hours of sleep a night for the nine, ten, or eleven days of the race.

Frequently, they are woozy as they ride on the back of their sleds, holding on tight so in their weariness, running over a bump doesn't shake them loose. Other times they are so sleepy that if they're not careful, they can crack their heads on low tree branches.

Lack of sleep coupled with failure to eat enough and drink enough can lead to whoppers of hallucinations. Hardly a musher who has raced hard and long has missed out on the bizarre experience of seeing things that aren't there.

Early in his Iditarod mushing career, two-time champion Martin Buser of Big Lake was fighting off sleep on a cold night when he thought he saw something he knew couldn't be there. An X-rated scene taking place on the trail? Even in his weakened condition, it didn't sound right to him. The lady seemed very appealing at first. Until Buser realized she was a tree.

"It ended up being spruce branches," said Buser. "Just another spruce tree."

There was just a hint of regret in his voice as he said it.

Men may imagine attractive women as apparitions, but overall there seems little rhyme or reason to what the imagination conjures up when mushers are forcing themselves to stay awake.

"From the erotic to the bizarre," said Buser, summarizing the variety of hallucinations he's "seen."

"I tell people when you see cabins and you see trains, just don't go in them," he said. A reasonably sound philosophy, it would seem, since you can hardly rest or take a ride in something that's not there.

DeeDee Jonrowe of Willow has been afflicted by visions of something that she's just glimpsing. Something like a tree usually. Her instinctive reaction is to swiftly duck. And then normally she discovers there was nothing there at all.

"Over the years, the most frequent one for me is ducking or diving," said Jonrowe.

Five-time Iditarod champion Rick Swenson of Two Rivers said his best hallucinations seem to revolve around fog and pickup trucks. Another long-retired musher said he always used to see signs that read "Two miles to go." Wasilla musher Lavon Barve characterized his hallucination experiences with, "I've had some dillies."

Once Barve said he thought a light in the distance was a snowmachine looking for him, so he stopped his team and began walking toward it. No snow-machine. Another time he imagined his dogs running away from him.

Jerry Austin of St. Michael was once on a long training run with a fellow musher and became convinced he was mushing under an arched bridge with cars traversing it. In the middle of the Alaska wild.

When they mushed into a town and up to a building that his partner told him was an orphanage, Austin grabbed and hugged one of the children. He just wanted to see if the kid was real. The child was, the bridge was not. On the Iditarod Trail one can't be too sure.

It seems there is no escaping a hallucination or two if the musher is working hard enough to stay up with the pace set near the front of the pack.

Willow's Peryll Kyzer had her breakthrough race in 1994, jumping all of the way from 38th to 14th in the standings. But she also found that the fatigue that accompanies the pace can produce a world-class hallucination.

Mushing on her merry way, a bleary-eyed Kyzer watched her top-notch Iditarod dogs turn into lobsters right before her very eyes. And then the light from the head lamp of a nearby

Mushers who deny themselves enough sleep will fall victim to their own imaginations with visions right out of a science fiction novel.
A warm-up tent at Rainy Pass checkpoint becomes a dormitory in the 1994 Iditarod.

Mackey has had hallucinations that belong on movie theatre screens.

"I've seen my lead dog look like a moose," said Mackey. "I leaned on the brakes and the dog turned into himself. It's kind of a spooky business. Sometimes it's hard to coordinate your brain with your eyes."

Charging hard in the 1995 race, trying to make up ground on the front-runners, Mackey finally had to admit the need for a rest when he began hallucinating. First, he hallucinated that his handlers were leading his dog team up to the starting line. So he let go of the handlebars and stepped off the runners. Oops. Abruptly, he realized that he was on his own in the wilderness, not in downtown Anchorage, and Mackey recovered.

"Talk about scared," he said. When he began seeing his wife Patty in the couple's truck nearby and almost turned around his team to go talk to her, it dawned on him that he had no idea what he was doing and was desperate for sleep. And just to round out Mackey's hallucination history, he swears that a group of mushers once told him that they saw a spaceship on the trail.

Just maybe that was the same UFO that lit up Barron's dog team. 🐾

musher cast a strange glow which in Kyzer's mind became water so those lobsters could swim.

It was no wonder that at the finish line following her race, Kyzer's comment betrayed her exhaustion. Her dogs, she said, were fine. "They're together," she said. "I don't know if I am."

Veteran musher Rick Mackey, the 1983 champion, has been around long enough to think he's seen it all. And when he says all, he's not kidding.

A rider's view from the sled as Bill Cotter's team heads down Anchorage's Fourth Avenue from the downtown start line. For mushers, adrenaline and emotions are at their peak as thousands of spectators yell their best wishes and good luck as the race across Alaska begins.

through certain steps. It probably gave me enough courage to win."

The Iditarod usually sorts itself out in the last two hundred miles, but Buser was alone by the time he left Kaltag, more than three hundred fifty miles from Nome. He kept mushing and wondering where everyone else was. But he was just going too fast.

Buser's effort was so thorough that he had plenty of time on the mush in from White Mountain to savor his situation. He was already mentally spending his $50,000 first prize on his family, his dog lot, and vacations, and had to constantly remind himself to stay cool and not get too excited until he crossed the finish line.

The Buser victory seemed to be popular. His wife, Kathy Chapoton, had "Buser Booster Club" T-shirts available for sale and sold some three hundred of them before Buser made it to Nome.

It only took one musher to do it. Once Buser shattered the eleven-day mark, it seemed that all of a sudden, eleven-day Iditarods were slow.

In 1993, once more a new champion was crowned. Jeff King of Denali Park, a past Yukon Quest champion, out-ran perennial contender DeeDee Jonrowe of Willow, and past champion Rick Mackey of Nenana to the finish. King set a new Iditarod record, eclipsing Buser's time by just shy of two hours. And Jonrowe, who was a mere half-hour behind King, broke the year-old record, as well.

Mackey, Butcher in fourth, and Tim

Osmar in fifth, also were under eleven days. Buser had an off-race in sixth.

Mackey was the musher who seemed in control entering the final two hundred miles, but he slipped back, and the low-key King mushed hard and mushed fast. King, a family man who makes his home in the rural area near Denali National Park, stayed in the lead, but never stopped worrying about Jonrowe until he crossed the finish line.

The thirty-two minutes that separated them was the fourth closest Iditarod and closest in five years. King said he looked up at the clear sky during the race's final miles.

"I picked my star and I made my wish," said King. "As a matter of fact, it came true."

Jonrowe recorded her highest place in a year in which she wondered if she'd even be able to finish at all. She suffered from an injured knee, heavily taped, that both restricted her knee and pained her, and provoked thoughts of dropping out more than once. Instead, she also had her best time ever.

"I'm pretty thrilled," she said. Most of Alaska was, too. Not only was there a fresh face as a winner, but the pace of the race itself was so quick now that fans marveled at the change. The weather was fairly benign and that kept the trail clear, but the back-to-back record times demonstrated that neither the mushers nor dogs had maxed out.

Everyone was talking about the speed. How fast can they go?

Veteran Lavon Barve said while it's true that mushers have learned enormous

▲ ▲ Race volunteers are transported by pickup truck in McGrath during the 1993 race. McGrath is the first central hub and major town after Anchorage, so it acts as the next staging-waiting area to get volunteers farther up the trail.

▲ Trail breakers near White Mountain mark trail for the 1993 race. While the trail is actually broken in short sections by dozens of villagers who live along the trail, these volunteer trail breakers ride the entire trail a day ahead of the mushers. They'll mark the trail with the lath as well as handle any necessary trail maintenance, like building bridges or eliminating hazards.

▲ ▲ Trail breakers pack up for the trip to Nome from White Mountain in the 1993 race.

▲ In Nikolai, volunteer pilot Sam Maxwell leads dropped dogs to his plane and will fly them the short distance to the hub of McGrath. From there the dogs are loaded into flight kennels and flown to Anchorage via sponsor Northern Air Cargo. There the dropped dogs receive veterinary care, and are fed and sheltered at the Hiland Mountain Correctional Center, just outside Anchorage, until the mushers' handlers pick them up.

Susan Butcher, towing husband Dave Monson on a second sled, passes a team during the first day of the 1993 Iditarod. ITC rules state that when one team approaches within fifty feet of another, "the team behind will have immediate right of way upon demand." A team that has been passed must stay behind at least fifteen minutes before attempting to pass. Because teams begin at two-minute intervals in Anchorage, passing is a regular occurrence. For that reason the top, faster mushers who want to avoid passing like to draw a low number for their starting position.

amounts about dog care and nutrition, the single biggest factor in increased speed along the trail in the 1990s is the trail itself. Where once mushing the Iditarod was like setting off to race through a winter wonderland jungle, now the trail is often so packed down, it's closer to a highway.

"All I see is a great trail," said Barve. Indeed, teams of volunteer snowmachiners under the guidance of race manager Jack Niggemyer work long hours to make the trail slicker than merely passable. Making a good trail that is as safe as it can be and as free of pockmarks for the dogs, is a monumental operation. The trail is marked with stakes flying colored ribbons. The trail is flattened. The trail is cleared of brush. The trail is cleared of volcanic ash. Actually, when volcanoes erupt, as they occasionally do in Southcentral Alaska, the ash does tend to linger and work itself into the snow base, creating an inconvenient grit.

"Every year the trail has a set of challenges," said Niggemyer. "Next year it'll probably snow too much. Or there will be too much ice. Or a volcano will go off again."

In the weeks prior to the race start, there might be thirty snowmachiners working some stretch of trail. Once the race begins, snowmachiners motor along ahead of the leaders and trail the back-of-the-packers for safety. Markers are placed on the trail within thirty-six hours of the leaders' arrival, and as an insurance policy, just in case of a snowstorm, another team of snowmachiners remains at checkpoints, according to Niggemyer.

He can plan and plan and plan, but the weather has the final say on trail conditions. Snowfall and temperature really determine how smooth the going will be.

"You can't guarantee it," said Niggemyer. "All your well-laid plans go screwy. There are a lot of things you can't do anything about, so why lose sleep about it?"

Lavon Barve believes another factor plays a part in the improved trail—the Gold Rush Classic Iron Dog 2,000-mile snow-machine race between Anchorage and Nome. That race takes place in February, a couple of weeks before the Iditarod, and accounts for the equivalent of thousands of miles of snowmachine traffic over the same route.

"It always gives us a base," said Barve. While it may be argued that dogs are simply better-trained athletes, Barve contends the dogs always had it in them to run faster, but weren't asked to show their stuff until the trail conditions improved. What was once a trotting race for dogs became a loping race in the 1990s, he said.

"You train a dog to trot and he can go ten to twelve miles an hour," said Barve. "He's got a top speed and I don't care how good the trail is. Now you've got a loping team and maybe they're traveling ten to twelve miles an hour, but when you hit a flat stretch you think, 'What the heck, let's go fourteen miles an hour.'

"They've got the overdrive. People

▲ Volunteer HAM radio operator at Finger Lake checkpoint, 1993.

▲ ▲ Joe Garnie prepares to board his sled as it goes by at the Nikolai checkpoint, 1993.

▲ Claire Philip of France was among the international mushers who competed in the 1993 Iditarod. Crossing the finish line in a snowstorm, she placed 13th.

THE GANG OF SEVENTEEN

When the finish line looked like a scene straight from the Oklahoma land rush.

IF A SPORTING event sticks around long enough, just about everything anyone can imagine is bound to happen. But once in a while something occurs that no one could ever have dreamed up.

And that's what happened during the 1993 race when seventeen mushers finished as close to simultaneously as possible.

It's rare enough when there are two mushers coming down Front Street toward the burled arch, and three mushers within sight of the finish line at once might result in some helter-skelter action every year or two. But seventeen mushers coming lickity-split one after the other is a once-in-a-lifetime occasion.

"I couldn't even tell who they were, they were coming so fast," said former Iditarod Trail Committee President Leo Rasmussen.

The circumstances that created the unique finish that more resembled a cattle drive than a typical Iditarod scene are unlikely to be duplicated.

Winner Jeff King of Denali Park had been finished for four days. All of the top twenty money positions had been decided. The group of mushers who had been trapped in White Mountain seventy-seven miles from Nome, some for up to sixty hours because of violent snowstorms, just wanted to come on in and since there was nothing at stake except the pride of finishing, they hatched a conspiracy of cooperation.

The blizzard that unleashed nearly three feet of snow and left the route unsafe and virtually impassable paralyzed the race for the mushers still on the trail. Hunkered down in their new home, the drivers had plenty of time to talk. After resting, after eating, after playing cards, they were getting antsy to move on. Veteran mushers Jerry Austin of St. Michael and Dewey Halverson of Trapper Creek, two old buddies, hatched the scheme employing the premise of safety in numbers.

"We got everybody talked into it," said Halverson. "We thought it would be fun to caravan in, that it'd be a sight."

One of the other long-time Iditarod competitors, Terry Adkins of Sand Coulee, Montana, said it wasn't hard to see the wisdom of the plan if you'd been stuck in one spot for fifty-five hours the way he had been.

"After the storm hit and we were all out of the positions for the money, we decided to make it fun," said Adkins. "It looked foolish to go with the bad weather. We made the best of a bad situation."

And provided some entertainment for fans with stamina who climbed out of their beds and tumbled out of bars at 3 A.M. for a wagon train of mushers parading past. Usually, it's the mushers who hallucinate from fatigue on the trail. This time the spectators thought they were dreaming.

The mushers departed from White Mountain at 9 A.M. the previous day, meaning it took them eighteen hours to cover ground that normally takes ten or fewer hours. When they reached Safety,

twenty-two miles from the end, they regrouped and left single file at one-minute intervals. The theme from the old western television show "Rawhide" was actually played as they mushed out. And finally, on the outskirts of Nome at the Fort Davis Roadhouse, they lined up for the last stretch.

Generally, when a musher finishes, he gets a moment in the spotlight. Fans crowd the temporary fencing in the middle of the street and the dogs trot the final yards through a chute to the finish arch. The dogs get a few minutes rest before being taken to the dog lot at the end of the street, where they are pampered and fed. The musher's gear is checked by race officials and the finish line checker—often Rasmussen—

reads the racer's place and finish time over a loudspeaker. Then reporters interview the musher, again over the loudspeaker so the fans can hear.

This finish line ritual has been in place for years. But such meticulous, orderly protocol disappears if as many as three mushers appear together. The chute is very narrow, and the most it can accommodate comfortably is two dog teams.

The finish scene became an accelerated comedy cartoon as the seventeen teams rushed down the street, separating places twenty-two to thirty-eight by a mere six and a half minutes.

The siren that alerts fans to come out and greet the mushers was essentially useless because there was almost no gap

between mushers. The mushers' continuous approach was heralded by their headlamp beams piercing the night sky.

Dave Olesen of Yellowknife, Northwest Territories, was the first of the massive group to finish in 14 days, 17 hours, 52 minutes, 35 seconds. Austin's official time was only five seconds later. Then Laird Barron of Sheep Creek, only another fifty-eight seconds behind. Place number thirty-eight was earned by Peryll Kyzer of Willow in 14 days, 17 hours, 59 minutes, two seconds.

Officials were in a frenzy, fans were howling, and dogs were yipping. For a brief span of time it was the Iditarod circus. Olesen was the highest placer, but at the finish line he said he considered himself in a seventeen-way tie.

For once, Rasmussen, who is no shrinking violet when a microphone is placed in front of him, couldn't talk fast enough to keep up with the mushers.

"There were teams double-parked on the street everywhere," said Rasmussen, who considers the peculiar event one of the most memorable things he's ever seen in the Iditarod. "Twenty years under this arch and I've never seen anything like it."

No one had, but if you blinked you missed it. Soon after Kyzer's finish, the street was quiet again. Drinkers returned to the bars, other fans returned to their rooms, dogs were bedded down, and mushers went off either to get some rest or food.

One eyewitness to the crazy, middle-of-the-night rush hour was former champion Libby Riddles. Grinning widely, Riddles declared, "That was pretty neat."

When a stranger walked up to her and ingenuously asked, "Who all came in?" Riddles burst out laughing. Her answer: "How much time do you have?"

Strange ending to a strange night. 🐾

Traveling through weather conditions like these mushers did in the '82 race, the "Gang of Seventeen" made a memorable show at the Nome finish line.

never trained for that before because you couldn't use it."

As a by-product of increased speed, mushers no longer lingered with their fans in the villages. Where once mushers spent the night with local families and received home-cooked meals, many times now they'd rather not spend time hanging around.

And then in the early 1990s a new rule further limited contact between the mushers and residents of the checkpoint villages, removing some of the homespun nature of the event in favor of increased professionalism. Mushers no longer have the freedom to rest in a private home and share a meal, but must now stay in one common area.

The rule change, called "corraling," was passed in response to arguments that some mushers gained an unfair advantage because of their popularity. Everyone wanted a former champ in their home, but not everyone was so eager to house a back-of-the-packer, the reasoning went. Also, some sly mushers used to sneak out of town under cover of darkness to get a head start while a competitor was napping or eating.

"Corraling sped the race up," said veteran Bill Cotter, who lamented the loss of interaction with residents, but believed it was the right move for the race.

"You're right with your competitors every minute. It really changed the flavor of the race. I think the race now is very, very fair."

Speed, speed, speed. The 1994 race was notable for several reasons. The course

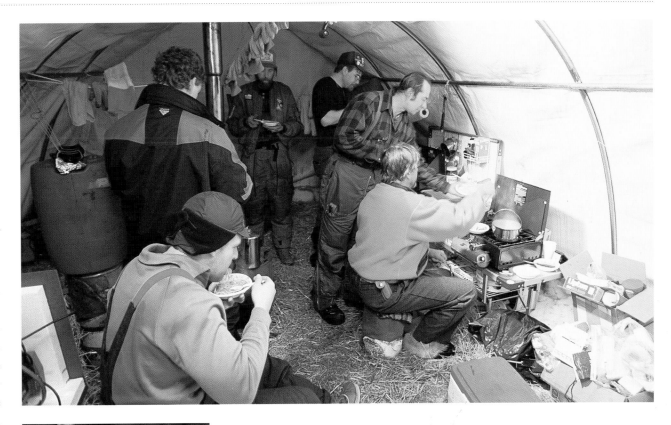

▲ Volunteers cook dinner and eat at the Dodge Lodge, Cripple checkpoint, 1994. For several years, ever since the checkpoint was moved from Ed Gurtler's cabin, the Cripple checkpoint has been a temporary establishment set up on a bend in the Innoko River.

▲ Nulato village kids pitch in to carry dog food to the checkpoint in the 1994 race. Once they arrive at a checkpoint, mushers may not accept any outside assistance in taking care of their teams.

◄ ◄ At sunrise, Rick Swenson and Bill Cotter mush uphill at Walla Walla after leaving the Elim checkpoint in 1994. Mushers dread this section of trail and often refer to it as Little McKinley because of the long uphill stretch.

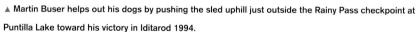

▲ Martin Buser helps out his dogs by pushing the sled uphill just outside the Rainy Pass checkpoint at Puntilla Lake toward his victory in Iditarod 1994.

► ▲ Doug Swingley heads down the longest of several dreaded switchbacks on the Happy River, 1994.

► Kate Persons is led by checker Rich Burnham to the community center as she enters Kaltag in the 1994 race. Burnham last ran the Iditarod in 1978 and has been a Kaltag checker since then.

record once again was broken, Buser became a two-time champion, joining Swenson and Butcher as the only multiple champs, and after the race, Butcher announced her retirement from Iditarod racing in order to raise a family.

Buser had a little bit tougher time claiming his second victory by about three hours over Rick Mackey and he broke King's new record by about two and a half hours, but a year after unexpected woes relegated him to sixth place, he rebounded strongly.

Once again Buser led the race from the village of Kaltag on, but he didn't have the same cushy lead he did in 1992. In this victory, he worried all the way to the finish line that he might be caught from behind, or be trapped in place by a storm and lose his lead. Nothing to fear, as it turned out. When Buser was apprised of his new record, he responded: "I think it can be done a lot faster."

Buser received the same rousing crowd cheer of "Mar-tin! Mar-tin!" that he'd experienced when he won for the first time, and he was gleeful that he got to mush all the way from White Mountain in pleasant, calm weather. Once again he had only his dogs for company.

Behind Mackey, King, the defending champ, placed third, and five-time winner Rick Swenson cruised to fourth. Butcher slipped to 10th place, and then at the post-race banquet she declared her intentions to remove herself from the race, even if she stayed in the sport of mushing.

"Life does exist beyond the Iditarod,"

D-2: MAKING HIS MARK ON THE IDITAROD

ONLY THE VERY best dogs—the lead dogs of the champion—get the chance to attend the Iditarod's post-race banquet in Nome. And rarely do those dogs get the opportunity to make a speech outside of the occasional bark or two.

But in 1994, when Martin Buser of Big Lake became the third musher to capture two Iditarod titles, his dogs made a unique statement of their own after Buser accepted his champion's trophy and the Golden Harness Award for the lead dogs who made the biggest contribution to the race.

D-2 and Dave were Buser's key leaders that year, and D-2 was in 1992 as well, when Buser won his first Iditarod. The audience of nearly a thousand people roared with shock and laughter when Buser's leaders showed their lack of self-consciousness by relieving themselves on the hardware. The easy-going Buser could do little but grin in embarrassment as the dogs showed who was really boss on the trail.

D-2 might even be called a ham. Most prominent mushers who make speeches and visit cities all around Alaska, and the rest of the country, typically have one dog with the comportment

and demeanor to travel without getting ruffled. Frequently, D-2 is Buser's companion.

In 1992, when Buser won the first time, D-2 was the first recipient of the musher's joy. At the finish line on Front Street, Buser leaned over and kissed the dog's nose.

"We were fortunate to put a good run together," said Buser. "I always stress that the dogs are the real athletes. I'm just their mouthpiece."

Even in the worst of times on the trail, Buser tries to stay unflustered and upbeat. When things get tough, he often gathers the dogs around him in a circle, and they engage in a group hug.

"Dogs are emotional sponges, and if I had had a sour disposition on the trail, they wouldn't have performed up to their potential," said Buser.

D-2 always has run up to his potential on the Iditarod. And as many witnesses would attest, it seems the husky doesn't mind performing under other circumstances, either. 🐾

said Butcher. She walked away from the Iditarod after suffering the death of a dog in the race and with a record of fifteen top-ten finishes.

However, while Butcher was firm in stating she wouldn't be racing the Iditarod again anytime soon, she did eventually hedge and say that she and husband Dave Monson might in the future return to the race that made her famous.

The obsession with going faster took on a new wrinkle for the 1995 Iditarod. A rule change transformed the downtown Anchorage beginning into a ceremonial start and made the next-day traditional Wasilla re-start the official timing start. That knocked twenty-four hours off the clock right there, virtually ensuring the first nine-day Iditarod.

And forty-year-old Doug Swingley was kind enough to oblige with a superb, out-front performance that under the category of "bound to happen someday" made him the first-ever non-Alaskan to capture the state's showcase race. Swingley, a one-time mink rancher from Simms, Montana, made an auspicious debut as Rookie of the Year in 1992 and moved up steadily in the standings from there.

Running from the front, Swingley adopted an unusual strategy of taking his mandatory twenty-four-hour rest much farther into the race than other leading mushers. He postponed the break until he'd covered more than five hundred miles of the race instead of a more typical two hundred to four hundred.

▲ Volunteer vet Mark Graves checks dogs at the Nikolai checkpoint, 1995. Veterinarians, for the love of animals and adventure, come from many parts of the United States as well as from around the world to be a part of The Last Great Race.

◄▲ Musher Rick Swenson is greeted by a few military men as he first enters Nome's Front Street in the 1995 race.

▲ Jack Berry and his jacketed dogs rest at the Nikolai checkpoint in the 1995 race.

◄◄ Kenth Fjelborg leaves Ruby to begin his one-hundred-fifty-mile run down the Yukon River in 1994. Frozen on the bank are fishwheels waiting for the summer fishing season.

▲ ▲ Volunteers in the Anchorage headquarters use computers to update the race's progress. Modern technology has nothing on the Iditarod. Most every checkpoint is connected to the race headquarters via fax or phone. The information here is uploaded into a battery of computers that send the musher status information worldwide on an hourly basis.

▲ Communications room phone notes, McGrath, 1996. Staging the Iditarod race each year is a logistical nightmare. The notes attest to that.

▶ ▶ Herring nets glisten in the eary morning sun as Vern Halter departs from Shaktoolik.

▲ ▲ In 1995, Montana resident Doug Swingley became the first non-Alaskan to win the Iditarod.

▲ Dog handlers keep Peryll Kyzer's dogs in check at the Anchorage start line for Iditarod 1995. With dogs that are ready to go, mushers usually arrange for one handler per dog in the team, as well as another four or five people to hold the sled at the start line.

Swingley had smooth going on a relatively clear, virtually storm-free Iditarod, recording a heretofore unbelievable winning time of 9 days, 2 hours, 42 minutes.

"It's innovators like Doug who change the race," fourth-place finisher DeeDee Jonrowe said of Swingley's rest break strategy.

The confident Swingley, who had verbally boosted his candidacy as a frontrunner before the other frontrunners recognized he had it in him, began dog mushing in partnership with his brother Greg only four years before his victory. Greg shared the training of the dogs and even raced them in shorter races. Together the brothers developed a definite run-to-win approach.

"We have a certain racing style," said Doug. "We don't screw around."

Swingley said he really thought it would only take a few years to conquer the Iditarod, despite the prevailing belief that those who succeed in the Iditarod do so only after putting in years of development time.

"I was impatient," said Swingley. "The dogs are the equalizer."

Some die-hard Alaskans of the gruff, wilderness persuasion seemed put out by the Iditarod title going to a musher who doesn't even live in the state, just as they were when a woman first captured the Iditarod. Swingley, who felt some coolness because of his address in the years leading up to his win, did say, "It's a moral victory for all mushers down south."

Others felt the Swingley win would actually be good for the race, spreading the

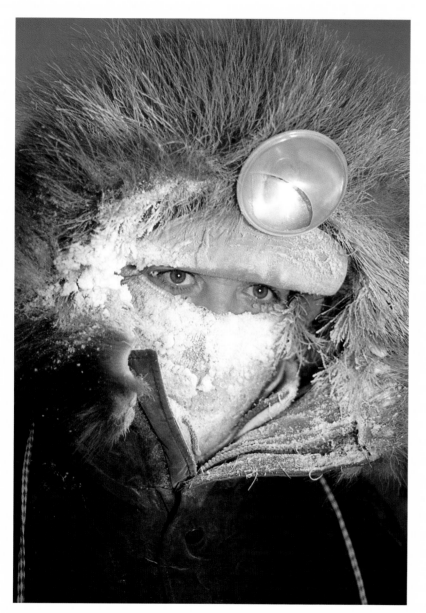

Matt Desalernos at the 1992 Ophir checkpoint, fifty below zero.

A FUNNY THING HAPPENED
ON THE WAY TO THE IDITAROD

The MOST FAMOUS poet of the far north is Robert Service. He's the guy who wrote about the strange things that happen under the midnight sun. And he never even saw the Iditarod.

Plenty of strange things happen along the Iditarod Trail, too.

Like the time veteran Nome musher Matt Desalernos got lost in a bathroom.

Desalernos, a perennial top-ten finisher and a president of the Iditarod Trail Committee, was a tired guy, mushing eight hundred miles into the 1995 race when he decided to avail himself of the facilities in an old gym in Unalakleet. In the midst of, ahem, taking care of business, the lights went out on Desalernos.

Although it seemed a trifle spooky being in complete darkness, Desalernos was confident the lights would come on again quickly. Only they didn't. He pulled up his pants, buckled his belt, and when the lights were still off realized he had a small problem.

"I was trying to remember where the door was," said Desalernos.

Feeling his way around the room, Desalernos searched hard for a way out of both the bathroom and his predicament, but couldn't do it. Hearing human activity on the other side of a wall, Desalernos was reduced to calling for help. No one answered. Perhaps he did this without the needed voice projection because he was still hoping to find his own way out, but no one heard him.

Gradually, Desalernos raised his decibel level from a low-key "help," to a pumped-up-the-volume "HELP!" and eventually a stranger heard his cries and rescued him.

"I was embarrassed," said Desalernos, who no doubt thought it would be great if he could keep his misadventure a secret. But there are few secrets on the Iditarod Trail, and when Desalernos arrived in Nome he was greeted by checker John Handeland holding a gift that would help him ward off evil spirits in the future—two flashlights.

Desalernos's mishap might have left him blushing, but it didn't cost him nearly as much in the race as the misfortune that befell Fairbanks musher Dave Dalton in the same competition. Mushing the twenty-five miles between Shageluk and Anvik well into the race, Dalton accidentally mushed sixty miles out of his way—to the village of Holy Cross. Holy Cross is a pleasant community, but not a check-point on the Iditarod. Dalton, a rookie in the 1995 Iditarod, thought he was going the right way when he turned onto what appeared to be a well-traveled trail on the outskirts of Shageluk. Discarded dog booties marked the trail and there were other signs that mushers

had recently passed by, such as sled runner tracks.

Turned out that the trail looked so inviting because it really was a dog race trail. Just not the Iditarod Trail. The recently used trail was part of the Yukon 200, another race.

Since mushers often get separated by considerable distances during the Iditarod, Dalton didn't suspect he was headed in the wrong direction until he'd mushed for about three hours without seeing any signs of other competitors.

It was dark and it was chilly and there really wasn't much for him to do, but to press on, so Dalton kept mushing hoping he was right, but worried he was wrong. He was wrong. When Dalton mushed into the next village about 10:30 P.M., all was quiet. No mushers. No checkers. No one was on the street. As he mushed through town, dogs chained outside houses jumped up and began barking, alerting their owners that someone was coming.

"I was waking up the whole neighborhood with their dogs," said Dalton.

Not that the noise got anyone curious enough to come outside and ask what the commotion was. Dalton had to park his team and go door-to-door for directions how to get back on the right

trail. Asking each resident how to get to Anvik set him up for jokes. Plenty of yucks for everyone, but not very much help for Dalton. Finally, a father and two sons guided Dalton out of town on their snowmachines.

Many awards are given to mushers for being first to a given spot on the trail, such as being the first to the Yukon River. When Desalernos heard about Dalton's plight, he joked that a new prize was bestowed on him for being the first to Holy Cross.

"I heard he got a compass," said Desalernos.

One guy who always seems to have weird experiences on the trail is veteran Dewey Halverson of Trapper Creek. He likes to joke that no one remembers second place in the Iditarod, and said he once sat in a room full of friends and quizzed them about who finished second to Libby Riddles. After a while, they all gave up.

"I think it was me," he said. Halverson also is the fellow who shot the moose that menaced Susan Butcher's team in that race and forced her to withdraw. That helpful act came to mind for him again in the 1996 race, when he earned the Sportsmanship Award for a different type of rescue.

Mushing along outside Koyuk, about one thousand miles into the race, Halverson was stunned to come upon a man terribly underdressed for the frigid temperatures walking toward him on the trail.

At this point in the race, mushers have gone without sufficient sleep for more than a week, and it would not have been out of the ordinary for Halverson to be hallucinating. But indeed he was real.

The man claimed his snowmachine had broken down, and he was walking to the closest village.

"This guy was in the middle of the tundra," said Halverson. "The middle of absolute nowhere." It also did not take much investigation for Halverson to determine that the man was distinctly drunk. "It was clear he was imbibing nature's grapes," he said.

So Halverson bundled the man into his sled, wrapped him up to protect him from the cold, and carried him ten miles down the trail to a shelter cabin.

"Hopefully, he lived happily ever after," said Halverson.

Halverson recalled his role in the moose killing of 1985 and then joked, "Am I the Red Cross or AAA of the Iditarod?" 🐾

▲ ▲ During a break at the Ruby checkpoint in the 1996 race, a weary Jerry Austin chats with his wife, Claire, back in St. Michael. The village of Ruby lies on the northern route, which is covered in years with even numbers.

▲ The children of Ruby await the 1996 mushers as they pass through the Yukon River village. The Iditarod is one of the biggest winter events in most of the villages along the trail. It is a big boost to the local economies as the mushers and press bombard the towns for a few short days.

▲ ▲ Charlie Boulding checks on his twelve-dog team seconds before countdown to the 1996 start in Anchorage.

▲ Dropped dogs receive a vet check before they're flown back to Anchorage.

▶ ▶ Teams rest on Puntilla Lake at the Rainy Pass checkpoint in 1996. Located on Puntilla Lake, the checkpoint is some twenty-five miles from the actual pass of Rainy Pass. The Rainy Pass Lodge, a hunting lodge, has been the checkpoint since the first race.

word about the Iditarod in the lower forty-eight states and perhaps enticing out-of-state mushers in greater numbers.

The 1995 Iditarod might have been more emblematic of changes the race was undergoing than any other. At the same time Swingley notched his milestone win for Outside mushers, Libby Riddles announced her retirement from the race at the finish line and was joined by Rick Swenson.

Riddles's plans came as no surprise since she said beforehand this was a nostalgic trip for her. A decade after her dynamic win, Riddles placed 33rd. In the interim she suffered a severe hip injury and underwent surgery, making it a battle to mush long distances. She said she would concentrate future racing efforts in the sprint mushing competitions, but was glad she ran the Iditarod a sixth time.

"I did enjoy going travelers' class," she said. "Sometimes it was [fun] and sometimes I thought I was crazy."

Swenson, whose 10th-place finish was his lowest in two decades, surprised listeners with his announcement. It was just time for something else, he said. He wasn't planning to retire from mushing, but wanted to compete in other major races. He might return to the Iditarod in five years.

"Back where I started," said the forty-four-year-old Swenson of his placing. "Time to quit."

As it happened, Swenson found himself in the Iditarod once more when plans to make the European Alpirod the centerpiece

▲ ▲ As Jeff King approaches open water on the Innoko River, camerman Peter Henning and helicopter pilot Tony Oney wait on the bank, ready to capture the dramatic crossing for the Outdoor Life Network in 1996.

▲ At the Rainy Pass checkpoint in 1996, Rick Swenson sought some time alone shortly after he was notified that he had been officially withdrawn. One of Swenson's dogs had died on the trail a day earlier. After the race, the withdrawal was reversed by a specially appointed appeals committee.

of his winter in 1996 fell through. The race was cancelled, and he returned to the Iditarod, renewed perhaps by the belief that he had one of the fastest teams he'd ever fielded.

But the 1996 race turned into a nightmare for Swenson when bad luck haunted him. Traveling in night-time fog on a poorly marked stretch of trail, Swenson stumbled into overflow on the Yentna River and had to lead his dog team across by foot. When he reached the other side of the crossing, about a hundred miles into the race, one of his dogs was dead in harness. Because of yet another new Iditarod rule governing the deaths of dogs along the trail, race officials decided to withdraw Swenson from the race.

In twenty years of Iditarod racing, Swenson never had had a dog die. And while no one specifically blamed him for this dog death, he was furious being tarred with the suggestion he was at fault. The removal of Swenson from the race provoked a tremendous furor. Fans wrote letters in protest and jammed Iditarod headquarters' phone lines. Fellow mushers defended him, calling Swenson the most caring of mushers who set the standard for dog care.

At a post-finish mushers' meeting, they voted him the race's Most Inspirational Musher. Bitter about his treatment, Swenson, who had not really wanted to race, anyway, said he would never compete in the Iditarod again. He ended up protesting his treatment through official channels. Weeks after the race had ended, a committee took his side saying officials were wrong to take him out of the race. Swenson was vindicated.

In what was an otherwise fairly uneventful year in terms of trials and tribulations along the way and in facing weather difficulties, Swenson's woes nearly overwhelmed the race finish.

The memorable performance turned in by Jeff King, recording his second victory in three years, refused to be overshadowed though. King joined Swenson, Butcher, and Martin Buser as one of four Iditarod multiple champions. Beyond that, King's time of 9 days, 5 hours, was within a few hours of the record.

However, what set King's triumph apart was the touching story of his early-race rider. This was the second year of the race's special Idita-Rider fund-raising program, where fans contribute a fee in order to be part of the race-day excitement at the start. King's rider was a nine-year-old boy from upstate New York named C.J. Kolbe, whose ride was arranged through the Make-A-Wish Foundation, the organization that attempts to make dreams come true for terminally ill children. It was Kolbe's dream to ride in a dog sled, and he was paired with King.

King became friends with the youngster who suffered from cancer and carried thoughts of the boy with him all the way down the trail. At the finish line, when asked what he would remember best about his second victory, King said, "I'll remember it mostly for C.J. Kolbe."

▲ Volunteer checker Kent Sheets handles the overflow of garbage at the Rohn checkpoint, 1996 Iditarod. After the race is finished, what can't be burned must be hauled out by the same planes and pilots that just weeks earlier brought it all in.

◄▲ During the 1996 Iditarod musher Jack Berry naps inside the Ruby community hall. Because of the new corraling rule, most village checkpoints are located at the community hall, where residents bring in homemade food to feed the mushers.

▲ Martin Buser finds time to drain his boots at the Cripple checkpoint in 1996. That winter's unseasonably warm weather meant many of the Innoko River crossings were covered with standing water. Mushers found themselves with wet feet, and some dogs actually swam through the water.

A THOUSAND-POUND TRAIL HAZARD

Were the mushers hallucinating from lack of sleep? A bad guess could mean someone's life. GARY SCHULTZ/ALASKA STOCK

As if sixty-below wind chill isn't bad enough, how about crossing paths with a polar bear?

POLAR BEARS? Yes, polar bears.

"I can live with moose and wolves," said musher Tomas Israelsson of Bethel, "but polar bears are going to eat you for a snack."

Wind, cold, and snow, the typical obstacles associated with the rigors of traveling 1,100 miles between

Anchorage and Nome by dog sled, seem enough to worry about. Then came mushers' claims that they saw polar bears along the trail during the 1996 race, representing an unprecedented epidemic that left fans and race officials incredulous. No one could remember another single sighting of the thousand-pound white bears, who have no fear of humans, during nearly a quarter-century of competition.

Polar bear sightings became a hot

topic in Nome during the final days of the Iditarod, but in a race where rumors travel faster than dogs, where hallucinations take the most peculiar of forms, where practical jokes are common, people were wondering if the mushers could be believed. But after mushers Israelsson, Jerry Austin, Aaron Burmeister, and Ramy Brooks all insisted they knew what they saw, it seemed possible the new Iditarod emblem could be a picture of the Alaska Zoo's dearly departed

Binky with a tennis shoe dangling from his mouth. What better symbol than Alaska's most famous polar bear who made worldwide headlines by chewing on a careless tourist's leg?

No less than three polar bears—a mother and cub several miles from the Bering Sea Coast village of Unalakleet, and still another carnivore not far from Nome, none of whom apparently ever personally knew old sneaker-toting Binky in his heyday, were spotted by mushers.

The flurry of reports from mushers through snowmachiners, pilots, and checkers drove weary race manager Jack Niggemyer slightly batty. The first sighting was reported by non-Iditarod pilots. Niggemyer was very skeptical, not only because polar bears don't usually roam in that neighborhood, but because hoaxes have been known to break out late in the race.

"I figured there was a fifty percent chance it was BS," said Niggemyer. Still, he filed away the news that they saw two bears between Unalakleet and

Shaktoolik three miles away on the offshore ice.

"I was kind of amused by it," said Niggemyer. But in his position of authority, Niggemyer also sent a fax to every Bering Sea coast checkpoint asking mushers to exercise caution.

"I thought we'd get a chuckle out of it," said Niggemyer. No laughs were forthcoming from Austin, the St. Michael musher in his 19th Iditarod, and a professional grizzly bear hunting guide. Mushing about twelve miles past Unalakleet, Austin blinked when he thought he saw a trail marker move

Race Manager Jack Niggemyer had trouble believing there was a polar bear on the trail, but he had to act as if there were.

about three hundred yards away.

"I thought, 'Maybe it's just the angle,'" he said. "I went another fifty feet and thought, 'Something's not right.'" Austin mushed on again for another thirty seconds. The bear stood up. Yep, a polar bear. It stood up to a height of about ten feet, it seemed.

Quietly, Austin tried to withdraw his .44 Magnum from his sled basket. The bear—what Austin felt was a male cub—sniffed along the ground and gazed Austin's way. His dogs barked, but the bear was unfazed. Austin stood still on his sled runners for what seemed an eternity, but was probably about four minutes. Then the bear moved about a hundred yards farther away, and Austin resumed mushing. Only as he rounded a curve in the trail he came upon a second bear. The mother, he's sure.

The bear saw him and closed to within thirty feet of his dog team. Austin mushed with his left hand holding the handlebars and his right hand gripping the pistol.

"I thought for sure I'd have to start shooting," he said. He didn't have to,

but he didn't get over the incident easily.

"I was petrified," said Austin. "I couldn't sleep a wink in Shaktoolik. I'll never go on that stretch again without a shotgun."

Several mushers did chuckle when they received Niggemyer's alert. It just seemed so unlikely to have a polar bear in the area.

Israelsson said he had serious doubts. "I thought, 'Yeah, yeah,'" he said. But when he got wind of Austin's story, he reevaluated. Israelsson, Paul Gebhardt of Kasiloff, Dewey Halverson of Trapper Creek, and Diana Moroney of Chugiak, received a snowmachine escort through the area. Israelsson saw a bear, the others did not.

Moroney was frightened, anyway. Twenty years ago she had a too-vivid dream of being eaten by a polar bear and was afraid it would now come true. She and Halverson chose to suspend racing briefly.

"Dewey and I decided 23rd, 24th, 25th place wasn't worth dying for," she said. "Maybe first or second . . ." Moroney, who finished 27th, said the trail was pock-marked with probable footprints that she knew definitely didn't belong to a moose.

"There were holes on trail all over the place," she said. "Huge ones. I wasn't

going to get off and look at them." Meanwhile, shortly before Israelsson and the others finished, Burmeister, the young Nome musher much farther back in the pack, reported seeing polar bears in the same region. Niggemyer was called by a judge in Shaktoolik giving him the word. Niggemyer felt as if he were surrounded by polar bears.

"I said, 'Did he eat the musher?'" said Niggemyer. " 'No? Good. If he didn't I don't want to hear about it.'" Straining everyone's credulity limits further, Ramy Brooks, the 11th-place finisher from Fairbanks, belatedly reported seeing a different polar bear on the final stretch coming into Nome.

Brooks didn't mention it at first because he was so tired from the race, but brought up the sighting near the Topkok shelter cabin about forty miles from Nome in the early morning. Brooks said he passed within a few hundred feet of the bear.

"You could see its head following me," said Brooks, who said he definitely was not hallucinating and knows he saw a polar bear. The mushers just hope they don't see polar bears again on the Iditarod Trail. Whether Niggemyer believes them or not.

Did they see bears? "I'm sure I did," said Brooks. "I'm sure it was." 🐾

► Jeff King, still fresh in the early stretches of the race, greets his fans at Fort Richardson near Anchorage. He would go on to take the 1996 title. Riding in King's basket is C.J. Kolbe, a boy whose dream was fulfilled through the Make-A-Wish Foundation.

► ► As dawn breaks over the Alaska Range, 1996 musher Stan Zuray pushes his sled uphill to help his fifteen-member team.

▲ Susan Butcher joins the crush of press members interviewing Jeff King following his 1996 win. After the birth of her first daughter, Butcher accepted an offer to report the race in the media. Butcher's firstborn was named Tekla, for a favorite dog.

The boy gave King a lucky coin before the race and he wore it in a pouch on a shoestring around his neck. And then after King won—and Kolbe sent a congratulatory telegram to Nome that left King misty-eyed—the musher mailed the coin back to him.

"C.J. and his family were quite an inspiration to me," said King, who said that the boy's plight put the importance of winning a dog race into perspective.

And yet King would not diminish the significance of his win, either, in edging defending champion Swingley by three hours.

"It's nice to have the trophy back in Alaska," he said.

Approaching its twenty-fifth anniversary, the Iditarod has showed it is a constantly evolving event. Mushers and dogs keep getting faster. Old dynasties fade and new dynasties emerge. It's been proven a non-Alaskan can win. The race's financial underpinnings have shifted from all in-state support to nationwide sponsorship and back to in-state backing.

At its core, though, there is one way the Iditarod has never changed.

"The Iditarod is a way of preserving the past and honoring the past," said executive director Hooley. "It's a way of standing up and saying, 'We're Alaskans and we're proud of it.'"

After twenty-five years, the Iditarod Trail Sled Dog Race remains rooted in Alaska and remains rooted in the souls of Alaskans.

MEMORABILIA

25 YEARS OF THE IDITAROD TRAIL SLED DOG RACE

COMPILED BY TRICIA BROWN

Recipe for a Runner

Emmitt Peters of Ruby, with his leader Nugget, won the 1975 Iditarod by averaging seventy-five miles a day and setting a new record at 14 days, 45 minutes, and 43 seconds. Interviewed by the *Iditarod Runner* magazine, Peters later talked about what he fed his dogs during that race:

"I cooked up green fish [frozen fish], beef tallow, and rice, put it in plastic bags and froze it. I sent twenty-five pounds of this to each checkpoint from Anchorage to Ruby, along with five pounds of commercial dog food and two pounds of honey. From Ruby on, Harold Esmailka supplied me beaver meat and beef that I cooked up with rice."

Peters said at home he builds a fire under a fifty-five-gallon drum split in half length-wise, which he fills with snow, fish, and water.

An unidentified musher in the mid-'70s demonstrates the comforts of his mobile hotel along the shores of Finger Lake. JIM BROWN

After boiling it for awhile, he adds some commercial dog food and lets it soak. When it cools, this feeds up to forty puppies and dogs in his lot.

Peters's Nugget was a leader for twelve years. She saved his life at least twice, won the Iditarod two years in a row—once for Peters and once for Carl Huntington—and raised many litters of puppies. Just ten days before the 1976 race, when Peters stopped to untangle his dogs while training in Chugiak, Nugget slipped her collar and was hit by a car. Peters later told the *Iditarod Runner*, "It took me almost one month after I lost Nugget to really feel that I belonged on a dog sled again. I felt I had lost the full control of my team. The spirit was gone, they were puzzled. I was in a daze thinking, 'Should I hang it up and retire for good?' But my folks said no, they'd help me build again."

Good thing, too. Peters went on to keep a competitive edge in the Iditarod with Nugget's son, Digger, who in 1979 won the Golden Harness Award.

Running With Purpose

Ann Mathews, who headed the membership drive in 1978, had special reason to volunteer for the Iditarod. In 1925, her mother was a baby in the village of Golovin and among those striken with diphtheria. The epidemic had swept through Nome and the surrounding area, threatening the lives of hundreds.

Through the heroic efforts of Alaska's top mushers, a life-saving antitoxin serum arrived in Nome following an incredible race against the elements and time. A six-hundred-twenty-four-mile relay of twenty mushers and teams from Nenana to Nome took less than one hundred and thirty hours, saved many lives, including that of Mathews's mother.

The men of the serum run, and the trail on which they ran, remain an essential part of the Iditarod Sled Dog Trail's history and legend.

Protecting the Trail

The late Senator Ernest Gruening first proposed the Iditarod as a national trail. But it wasn't until

A group of Ophir volunteers, including Dick Forsgren, pause for a photo before heading back to work. The stop has been an official checkpoint since 1974. JIM BROWN

early 1977 that Senator Mike Gravel introduced a bill designating the Iditarod Trail as the nation's first Historic Trail. President Jimmy Carter signed the National Historical Trail Bill, which included the Iditarod Trail, in 1978.

Today, the Iditarod is one of several National Historic Trails, among them the Oregon, Mormon, Pioneer, Lewis & Clark, Over Mountain, Victory, Nez Perce, Santa Fe, Trail of Tears, Juan Bautista, and the Pony Express Trail.

Heroes of the Serum Run

The Iditarod's bib number one was traditionally reserved to honor Leonhard Seppala, the most

famous of the mushers who transported life-saving diphtheria serum in the historic Nenana-to-Nome run of 1925.

From 1973 to 1980, Seppala was named as honorary musher. Each year since then, the ITC has chosen one or two individuals who have made a significant contribution to the sport, even if he or she is not a musher.

The first few to be recognized included the four serum runners who were still living in the early 1980s: Edgar Nollner, Edgar Kalland, Charlie Evans, and Billy McCarty.

Famed, too, were the lead dogs of the serum run, especially those of Leonhard Seppala. Togo took Seppala from Nome to Shaktoolik

The first official Iditarod Trail Committee artist was Bill Devine (left), who designed the logo that's still used to this day. With him in this 1974 photo is Iditarod veterinarian Terry Adkins.

ANCHORAGE MUSEUM OF HISTORY AND ART

to Golovin in 1925, crossing the Norton Sound through gale winds and thirty-below-zero temperatures.

However, the star of the day was Balto, who was owned by Seppala, but led Gunnar Kaasen's team and the serum into Nome. While Balto became a high-profile dog hero memorialized with a statue in New York's Central Park, Seppala long believed that Togo didn't get his due. Balto ran fifty-three miles, while Togo ran two hundred and sixty miles.

Both dogs were custom mounted after their deaths. Balto

is on display at the Cleveland Museum of Natural History; Togo's permanent home is at Iditarod headquarters in Wasilla, Alaska.

■ A Leading Lady

In 1974, Mary Shields of College, Alaska, was the first woman to complete the Iditarod Trail Race with her lead dog, Cabbage.

■ Why One Man Runs

"The Iditarod appeals to everything in me. There's some parts you'll never lose about waking up in your sled in the morning, hundreds of miles out on the trail, with eight or ten of your favorite dogs staked out around you in the snow for company, rousing yourself up to start a fire, and passing your eyes over all the incredible country stretched out to the horizon in every direction. . . .

"Maybe you pick out a pale green mountain in the distance, and warm your insides with the assurance that before you camp again, you'll be on the other side of it, looking back.

"And all the country in between—the hills and trees and rivers and valleys—well, all that country will be yours. It will belong to you in a way that no one could ever annul or diminish, because

you will have staked the only claim to it that the land itself recognizes: You will have penetrated to the heart of it—and become a part of it—and it will have become a part of you. Forever."

—*Bill Vaudrin*
1976 Iditarod Annual

■ Salute to a Veteran Musher

The 1978 Iditarod Race was dedicated to William "Sonny" Nelson, a veteran Iditarod musher from Ekwok who died in a plane crash en route to the race start.

Nelson, who was considered a serious contender for the 1978 race, had been training at Stony River. He was flying to Anchorage with his handler and team when their plane crashed due to severe turbulence near Merrill Pass. Only two dogs survived.

■ One Second Worth $4,000

In 1978, Dick Mackey took first place in a stunning one-second finish over Rick Swenson. Mackey finished in 14 days, 18 hours, 52 minutes, and 24 seconds. Swenson came in a second later, costing him $4,000 in prize money. Mackey won $12,000; Swenson, $8,000.

Arriving at 19th place, Susan Butcher that year became the first

woman musher to finish in the money. She took home $600.

Col. Norman Vaughan was the 33rd musher into Nome in a field of thirty-four. Andrew Foxie of Stebbins took the Red Lantern, crossing the finish line three seconds behind Vaughan.

■ Dollars for Dogs

The budget for the 1978 race was about $80,000. Of that, $50,000 was set aside for prize money. The balance was to be used for trail work, vet expenses, communications, and transporting checkers and other race officials along the race route. According to Von Page, president of the Iditarod Trail Committee, extensive forest fires in the Bear Creek area increased expenses in trail work.

■ Trail Wise

One month before his stunning victory in the 1978 race, Dick Mackey was the topic of this *Iditarod Runner* item:

"Dick Mackey is an institution. The man has made it to Nome every year, and was training to go again this year when he dislocated his shoulder. While driving something outrageous, like sixteen dogs, Dick stopped to untangle a pup, the hook gave way, and he

jumped on board with the pup still in tow.

"Afterwards, Dick's only comment was 'Never hop a moving freight train with baggage in the other hand.' He is healing and still plans to hit the trail."

■ What Goes In Those Sled Bags

In 1978, mushers were required to carry with them:
1. Proper cold weather sleeping bag.
2. Hand ax.
3. One pair of standard snow shoes with bindings.
4. Any promotional material that the musher has been asked by the Committee to carry to Nome.

In the 1974 race, Dick Mackey's sled got a little top-heavy with the addition of supplies delivered by the Iditarod air force. ANCHORAGE MUSEUM OF HISTORY AND ART

A volunteer HAM in the 1976 race stands by at the Iditarod Trail Committee headquarters in Nome. ANCHORAGE MUSEUM OF HISTORY AND ART

5. One day's food for each dog with a minimum of two pounds per dog.
6. One day's food ration for each musher.
7. Two sets of booties for each dog either in the sled, or in use and in the sled.

■ And a Big Thanks to My Sponsor, Bob

Before major corporate sponsors entered the picture, individual mushers looked to other Alaskans for assistance—restaurants, taverns, markets, and other Alaska businesses.

In 1978, Norman Vaughan was sponsored by a rock group called the Dr. Schultz Band. Susan

Butcher, who in the '80s and '90s became a walking billboard of corporate patches, was sponsored in the 1978 race by Bob's Homestead Cafe, Bob Jukill, and Oomingmak.

■ Golden Givers

Miners from the Manley area donated a gold nugget and earring set to the Iditarod Trail Committee for raffling at the Iditarod Banquet on March 2, 1978. The supportive miners included: Jim Mason, Livengood Creek; A.W. Pringle, Lower Shirley Bar; John A. Schilling, Slate Creek: Al Hagen, Cooney Creek: and Rick Swenson, Glenn Creek. Each miner donated a nugget, and Swenson had the set made.

■ From the HAM to the WEB

"HAM radio coverage of the 1979 Iditarod race was funded by a $3,000 grant from RCA Alaska Communications," reported the May 1979 *Iditarod Runner*. "As Alaska's only certified long-distance carrier, Alascom felt it was appropriate to support the efforts of these dedicated ham radio operators to provide the vitally needed communications for the 1,049-mile dog sled race from Anchorage to Nome. The grant paid for the operators' food, commercial airfare, and, where electricity was not available, generators and gas. The funds also provided food and other requirements for private pilots who ferried dog food and supplies to the remote race checkpoints."

By the mid-1990s, however, HAM radios were less critical to communication. Instead, telephones, faxes, and online services kept an international audience apprised of the latest race standings, bulletins, and musher biographies.

Internet Alaska provided Iditarod updates to the world via the World Wide Web. Users were directed to one of two home pages: Internet Alaska home page—http://www.alaska.net or the Iditarod home page—http://www.

iditarod.com. The Iditarod headquarters and other stations also offered race information hotlines throughout the state.

HAM radios and their operators are still among the Iditarod volunteer army, however. In Bush Alaska, when something works that well, you don't just throw it away for the newer model.

■ Care for a Sample?

Dr. Verner Stillner, M.D., conducted studies on blood and urine samples of five volunteer mushers to examine the significant changes in hematological (blood) parameters during the 1978 race.

"Participating mushers have jokingly stated that they have given everything else to the Iditarod, why not their blood and urine," Stillner told the *Iditarod Runner*.

■ Atlantic City, This Ain't

Alaska Governor Jay Hammond in 1978 vetoed a bill to establish the Iditarod Sweepstakes, which backers hoped would ensure financial security for the race.

Gov. Hammond told the Iditarod Trail Committee that he could not approve a bill that went against his moral stand on gambling. However, he encouraged the committee to follow steps to

place the bill on the ballot for a vote of the people, and offered a personal pledge to kick off the 1979 fund-raising drive.

■ A Man With Vision

Gene Leonard of Finger Lake harbored a dream of running the Iditarod since teams first pulled through his checkpoint home in 1973. Six years later, Leonard finally ran. And claimed the Red Lantern Award.

Before teams arrive at a checkpoint, the volunteers must wait. Here a volunteer veterinarian who came to Alaska from Germany passes time with a book and a flashlight inside a wall tent at the Finger Lake checkpoint during Iditarod 1996.

■ Here, There, In the Air

Larry Thompson's willingness to help got him into the volunteer business lock, stock, and airplane back in 1974. It was on the first Saturday that March, as the teams were leaving Mulcahy Stadium, that Race Marshal Dick Tozier sought out Thompson and told him there was "some food" at the airport that needed to get to Susitna Station. Could he haul it that day?

Thompson agreed and went out to the airport, where he found an overwhelming pile of sacks and boxes of dog food and supplies. As he sifted through the cargo, Thompson saw that some of the bags had "Skwentna," "Finger Lake," or "Rainy Pass" written on them. This, he thought, could be a problem. Some of the sacks had to be examined carefully to find the checkpoint destination. At that time, mushers had no instructions for labeling their goods. Thompson waded in and went to work, however. He sorted and loaded the Susitna Station food, finishing after three trips in his Cessna 180.

Back in town, Thompson was proud to report "mission accomplished" to Tozier. The race marshal said he was very grateful. Now, would Thompson mind hauling the other cargo out to Skwentna and Finger Lake?

Thompson ended up flying all day and into the night, making three trips to each of the checkpoints, most of the time while it was snowing. The next

day he flew two men out onto the trail. Later, word got to him that Tozier wondered if he could get the last of the food out to Rainy Pass. Once more, Thompson agreed and flew another three trips that day.

At the Farewell Lake FAA station he was asked, yet again, to take food back to Rohn. He ferried forward to McGrath then back to Rohn and Farewell. Thompson was having such a good time that he kept on volunteering, flying people, food, and supplies all the way to Nome.

Thompson's good times have continued. He volunteered his time and plane for about ten years,

even though, as some volunteers have found, you never get *fully* reimbursed for expenses. Thompson wasn't worried about it. He simply loved to fly and do what he could do.

That was payment enough.

■ Space-Age Dog Sled

The following item is reprinted from the December 1978 *Iditarod Runner* in which champion musher Rick Swenson sings praises to a new sled developed by Tim White.

Tim White's first designs made many people laugh, but they looked twice when his sleds proved their durability. The sled, as it is made today, is a twenty-five-pound,

In the Iditarod's early years, mushers wrestled with bulky, heavy sleds. Likewise, the dogs of the 1970s were bigger and more muscular. In 1979, Rick Swenson promoted a toboggan-style sled with a flip-down seat. Some snickered, but he won. The next year, there were forty-two sleds with flip-down seats. BILL DEVINE

durable, collapsible, plastic toboggan-style sled. Tim's background in structural engineering has enabled him to design a sled using space-age material that, with the removal of two bolts, enables it to collapse.

It will fit into a Super Cub aircraft for easy transportation to remote areas. Yet when reassembled it is capable of hauling anything and everything that can be stuffed into it or strapped onto it. This sled design is so unique and versatile that it can satisfy the needs of the trapper, novice musher, utility driver, sprint racer, or long-distance musher.

In December of 1977 at the Settler's Bay 120, I saw two of these sleds in Tim's truck and I knew I had to try one. After the race, I bought one and tried it out. I have never driven such an easy handling, tough sled. It is so easy to pull that I soon decided I would never get my dogs tough enough for the Iditarod if I used one exclusively in training. Terry Adkins and I both used one in the 1978 Iditarod and we were thoroughly pleased. We had no problems with them and plan on using them again in 1979.

A lot of other mushers have expressed interest in purchasing one of these sleds. This is the first radical design change in modern dog mushing history. This might be compared to

the first "gee-haw" leader which revolutionized dog mushing in the early 1900s or the switch from the collar harness to webbing harness.

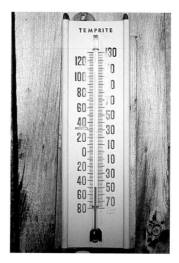

Minus fifty-one degrees at Ophir, 1992 race.

■ The Spirit of the Gold Rush

Three ghost towns lie along the Iditarod Trail: Ophir, Cripple, and Iditarod. Each was once a bustling gold mining community that saw its peak in the early part of this century. At Cripple, some $35 million in gold was mined between 1908 and 1925. Ophir was named in the Bible as a lost country, the location of King Solomon's gold mines. And Iditarod was once home to more than ten thousand people who were tied in some way to gold mining.

And It's Good Ballast, Too

Here's a recipe for a snack that veteran Bob Schlentner took along on all the Iditarods in which he mushed. His wife, Carol, sent it in to the *Iditarod Runner*, which published it in October 1978 with Carol's note: "I call it Logan Bread because it was a recipe used by a party climbing Mount Logan."

Logan Bread

1. 5 cups of dry:
   whole wheat flour
   instant milk
   wheat germ
   oatmeal
   white flour
   anything goes
   and
   1 teaspoon salt.
2. Then add chopped up
   apricots (2 cups make it tangy)
   1 cup raisins
   1 cup nuts

   Mix well. I use my hands. Then add liquid, about two-thirds cup peanut oil, 1 cup sorghum or molasses, 3 cups honey and six eggs. I grease the baking pans by hand and then mix with my hands. It should be a consistency where you press it into the pans. If too wet, add more dry.

   Cook two hours at 200° F — don't burn. I freeze it and then slice up and pack for trips. It tastes good even at forty below!
   Sincerely,
   Carol Schlentner, Fairbanks

Puppy Stampede

"I kind of live on a little peninsula. I've got creeks all around me that are big enough to stop the puppies from crossing, and I just turn the puppies loose and let them run. It gets really to be a nuisance when you have a dozen puppies running because you open the door in the morning and first thing you have all puppies hanging on you trying to tear your clothes off. This goes on until it reaches a point when you can't tolerate it anymore, and then you have got to start tying puppies up.

"Ralph Mann does it the same way, and when Ralph raises puppies, he raises twenty or thirty at a time. You pull into Ralph's place, and you step out of the car, and you got this wall of dogs coming at you down the driveway — just a wave of solid dogs — you will either be knocked flat, get in the car, or run — you got to do something!"

—*Joe May of Trapper Creek, who placed 11th in 1976, 5th in 1979, and 1st in 1980 with his trapline team*

"Father of the Iditarod" Joe Redington, Sr., at the 1988 starting line on Anchorage's Fourth Avenue.

The Big Eye

The Iditarod was on the air nationwide as well as statewide in 1982 when CBS-TV signed an exclusive contract with the Iditarod Trail Committee for coverage of the race. CBS had covered the race for their "Sports Spectacular" show in 1981.

The CBS affiliate KTVF-TV in Fairbanks was awarded the statewide rights for Iditarod 1982.

Where Dropped Dogs Go

Prisoners in a state correction facility joined the Iditarod family in the 1970s. When dogs were dropped along the trail, they were flown to Anchorage and delivered to the Eagle River Correctional Center for care.

There the dogs were fed and watered by prisoners, who also had responsibility for ensuring the dogs were returned to the right mushers.

In 1982, inmates from the Palmer Correctional Center pitched in, too. They off-loaded dog food from trucks to a refrigerated box car for storage while awaiting shipment to the smaller checkpoints between Knik and Rohn River.

Above and Beyond

Jules and Leslie Mead, who for many years owned and operated Teeland's Country Store in Wasilla, are representative of the hard-working volunteer force of the Iditarod. The Meads served at the Innoko River Lodge, the Cripple checkpoint.

"Each year at race time, they

For several years, Jules and Leslie Mead generously donated cash and food in their support of the Iditarod. Mushers often feasted on sumptuous meals such as crab dinners at the Cripple checkpoint. Jules was named Executive Director of the ITC for 1991-92.

volunteer their time, money, and a lot of effort to help the mushers at the halfway point," wrote the editors of the *Iditarod Runner* in June 1980. "They rustle up the grub—paid for out of their pocket—and chop the firewood, and help the mushers get checked in and out. It usually means working in split shifts, usually around eighteen hours each."

■ Ready . . . Set . . . Go!

The Iditarod started on Anchorage's Fourth Avenue for the first time in 1983, despite some skepticism that sixty-eight teams with more than a thousand dogs could leave "in an orderly fashion."

Each team was given a minimum of thirty feet of curb in the staging area, and a parking area was designed so dog trucks and other support crew could easily leave and meet their teams in Eagle River. Other issues that had to be worked out: electrical and telephone requirements, crowd control, press passes and public address system, street closures and parking restrictions.

And then they prayed for snow.

Thanks to the courtesy of downtown businesses, dozens of volunteers who worked the staging area and road crossings, and cooperation from the mushers, relieved race manager Jon Brobst declared the Fourth Avenue start a success: "Due to hundreds of people working together to provide a great start for the Last Great Race."

■ And a Steak for My Leader, Please

From the May/June 1982 issue of the *Iditarod Runner* came this letter submitted by musher Ernie Baumgartner's family:

"Brandy has never been run in lead position before midpoint on the '82 Iditarod. Having dropped his other leaders due to injuries, Ernie was in great turmoil whether to drop his trusty leader Chippy (on his sixth Iditarod)—simply out of compassion and respect, as the old fellow is over eight years old and was definitely not as anxious to race as in previous races. The decision was made, Chip sent home, and Brandy was in single lead for the first time! Working with him was rewarding. He's a natural!

"Early in the a.m. while Herb Nayokpuk was camped out of Shaktoolik waiting for a weather break and hoping to shoot for Koyuk—I got a message from our daughter at the radio station KSKO in McGrath, that I had a message from Ernie at Nome headquarters that was received the evening before from Shaktoolik. It went something like this: 'Have the best steak in Nome ready for Brandy at the finish line. He brought us through winds over 50 mph with snow packing his eyes shut at times.'

"Brandy had gone through that storm and on into Shaktoolik when everyone else was sitting still. The six teams camped in the last timber before Shaktoolik weren't able to follow Brandy. The stories of that day are exciting and hair-raising—Ernie hopes he never finds himself in winds like that again.

"His newly found leader definitely deserved that steak, and we're proud that the other mushers chose him out of the many deserving leaders to receive a 'Golden Harness.'"
—*Natalie Baumgartner*

■ Look, Rocky, a Message in a Bottle

When Nome resident Dan Bloom found a mysterious message in a bottle, he had a great idea for making some extra money . . . or was it the other way around?

A message signed by a "Leinad Moolb," a name as mysterious as the circumstances, "The Nome Iditarodda" was written on old parchment paper and stuffed inside a non-returnable beer bottle then thrown into the Snake River, Bloom claimed, where it became frozen in the winter ice.

Bloom said he found the bottle and its nearly illegible contents when he was ice fishing in December 1981. Since he thought the message was both timely and humorous, Bloom decided to have "The Nome Iditarodda" made into posters for sale in time for the 1982 race.

The poster begins: "Go placidly amid the snowdrifts and the wind-chill factors and remember what

Tim Osmar passes the Knik Museum, which houses the Mushers' Hall of Fame, 1995.

peace there may be in warm boots." And the message concludes: "Believe it and see you at the finish line."

■ Tragedy on the Trail

In the first major tragedy to mar the Iditarod, well-known pilot, Captain Warren "Ace" Dodson, and three members of a Spanish television film crew, died in an airplane crash twelve miles south of Shaktoolik.

The crew was filming the 1980 Iditarod for an award-winning Spanish Television program, "Man and Earth." With Dodson were Dr. Felix Rodriguez de la Fuentes, cameramen Teodoro Roa Garcia, and Alberto Mariano Huescar.

With the press corps as an audience, Larry "Cowboy" Smith enjoys Anvik's hospitality with a full-course meal in Iditarod 1983. This was the first year that a major Anchorage hotel sponsor flew in its chef to create a special meal for the first musher to the Yukon. First the Hilton, and later the Clarion and Regal Alaskan hotels participated.

Later, Alaska's Senator Ted Stevens read the following message to President Jimmy Carter and members of the U.S. Senate:

"Captain Dodson was the son of pioneer Alaskan aviator Jim Dodson. Considered by his peers to be one of the few 'natural' pilots, Dodson and his father made significant contributions to the people of Alaska and to the history of Alaskan aviation. In the days when there were few runways and less radio beacons, the senior Dodson flew the mail, pregnant mothers and sick children, gold pokes, supplies, food, and all the necessities for life on the Alaskan frontier, often risking his life to do

so. Growing up in this atmosphere, Ace Dodson did the same, flying for Northern Consolidated and then with Wien Air Alaska for over twenty years.

". . . The two weeks that the Spaniards spent in Alaska endeared them to the people of our state. Their warmth and interest in the Alaskan people was felt from Anchorage to Nome. In fact, at the news of their deaths, the people of the Indian village of Ruby composed a letter to the families of the Spaniards and people traveled from up and down the Yukon River to sign it. . . .

" . . . The people of the United States join the people of Spain in sharing this great loss."

■ As If Dog Breath Isn't Bad Enough Already

Iditarod musher Joe May, sponsored for two years by Seward Fisheries, became an advocate of fishmeal and oil in dogs' diets. May told *The Seward Phoenix Log* that the fish byproducts gave his dogs more energy, and shiny coats that shed snow and ice.

"[It] is tested for use by Alaskan dog owners, whose animals do far more than sit by the fire and chase sticks," wrote newspaper reporter Carole Jaffa.

"After the 1980 Iditarod, May, SFI plant manager Mike Meehan, and friends got down to the serious business of preparing a well-balanced complete dog food containing grain products, fishmeal and oil, vitamins and other nutrients. They intended to develop a product that would be made from Alaskan components," Jaffa wrote.

"Two different batches of the dog food are available and easily portable on the trail. May has been feeding both to his own animals with excellent results."

■ Freezer Bags in the Sled?

Rule No. 45 was a new one on the books for the 1981 race. Instituted to address the issue of mushers and moose on the trail, the rule read: "In the event that an edible game animal, i.e., moose, caribou, buffalo, is killed in defense of life or property, the musher must take measures to salvage the meat for human use and report the incident at the next checkpoint."

■ No Lack of Self-Confidence

During the 1982 race, Stan Zuray of Tanana, who would go on to win the Rookie of the Year award, wore a banner on his sled that read: "Hip Hip Zuray!"

■ The Case of the Missing Sled Dogs

How three Alaska sled dogs made front page news in the nation's capital.

When a group of Iditaroders were invited to be part of Ronald Reagan's inaugural festivities in January 1981, you can bet they started packing. But for the three famous dogs mushers—Joe Redington, Sr., Norman Vaughan, and Herbie Nayokpuk—the "luggage" would include about sixty sled dogs. After sorting out the logistics, off to Washington flew a delegation of fourteen Alaskans. The dogs boarded a different flight, however, along with the dog boxes, sleds, and other gear transported courtesy of the Flying Tigers.

Representing Alaska in the inaugural parade, Redington, Vaughan, and Nayokpuk were to mush their teams of huskies from sleds equipped with wheels. Later, the Alaskans would meet the president and other dignitaries at the inaugural ball.

But what to do with sixty dogs in the nation's capital? Walter and Nancy Hughes of Frederick, Maryland, graciously boarded their own horses so they could put up the sled dogs at their farm. Problem solved.

And yet that's also when the problems began. Returning to the Hughes farm shortly after midnight of January 18, the delegation learned that three dogs had been stolen. They included Redington's leaders, Candy and Feets, and Vaughan's leader, Joey. Although the dogs were valued at $5,000 each on paper, their personal value was immeasurable. Candy was a favorite of Redington's. She had taken him to Nome several times, and even carried him to the top of Mount McKinley.

Alaska's congressional delegation, as well as local media and police, mounted an areawide search for the dogs. The theft was a top story in the Washington paper, and a radio disc jockey called on listeners to look around for dogs that matched the descriptions of Candy, Feets, and Joey.

"The next twenty-four hours were sad ones indeed," remembered Dick Mackey, who was along on the trip. "With no sleep, having to take the teams to a demonstration on the Capitol lawn, and smile, was not easy."

Late that night came a call that the dogs had been found and that two youths had been charged with possession of stolen goods. Mackey remembered: "Most of us just whooped, some cried, and Joe just grinned the biggest of grins. Now we could truly enjoy ourselves without the dark cloud of the theft."

In the inaugural parade the next morning, each of the delegation dressed in "Alaskan best" for the trip down Constitution Avenue, and Candy, Feets, and Joey wore ribbons. Mackey recalled the hit they made.

"With the additional media coverage on the loss and return of the dogs, we were easily the most popular entry!" he said.

Preparing for the ball that night had the Alaskans in white ties, tails, and formal gowns. The sight of "a bunch of 'dog' people" so well-dressed had the group in stitches, remembered Mackey.

"In fits of laughter, we nearly succumbed to unloading the dogs and posing for a never-to-be-duplicated picture! We opted not to, as we were late as usual," he later wrote.

The Alaskans did pose for photos, sans sled dogs, and reported that rubbing elbows with dignitaries and celebrities at the ball that night was a highlight of the trip. But nothing could top the return of their beloved sled dogs.

■ The Greatest Reward

"By far, the most rewarding part of volunteering is the 'family reunion' aspect of the race. Each person has a unique story and it's fun to catch up with peoples' lives after not seeing them for a year or two. The previous years' stories are embellished, the rumor mill is always alive and well, and the current year's adventures are yet to be documented.

"It is always interesting and fun for me to see people in situations that are unlike any other they experience in day-to-day life: people who stay up all night, chase around in the freezing cold, miss a critical flight and have to bump along on a snow machine for fifty miles, people who shovel tons of 'residue,' feed fifty to one hundred Iditarod dogs but have none of their own at home, and people who contribute vacation time and any extra money they may have for a cause they love.

"It's not always easy to explain why intelligent, mature, responsible men and women do some of these crazy things, but it's all part of what we call . . . Iditarod.

— *Jim Johnson*
Scotts Valley, California
Iditarod Runner,
January 1995

A bird's-eye perspective of the Iditarod starting line along Anchorage's Fourth Avenue, 1996, with the Chugach Mountains in the background. About half of Alaska's population lives in Anchorage, the state's largest city.

■ Coming Back Strong the Alaska Way

In the aftermath of some national sponsorship withdrawals in the early 1990s, the Iditarod Trail Committee turned to Alaska-owned businesses to help make up for the financial loss in a fund-raising campaign to "Bring Iditarod Home."

In 1995, the National Bank of Alaska already had contributed $50,000 toward the winner's purse, the mushers' banquets in Anchorage and Nome, the Gold Coast Award, and the Red Lantern Trophy. The bank then made an additional cash contribution of $50,000.

GCI Inc., an Alaska-based long-distance carrier, increased its sponsorship to $150,000, and Alaska Commercial Company stepped up its commitment to more than $100,000.

Other major and supporting sponsors included Alaska Dodge Dealers, Alaska Airlines, KIMO Television, *Alaska* magazine, Regal Alaskan Hotel, Peninsula Airways, COMTEC, Inc., Stephan Fine Arts, TRF Management, Inc., City of Wasilla, Upjohn Company, SmithKline Beecham, Round Table Pizza, Alaska Industrial Hardware, Northern Air Cargo, Carr Gottstein Foods, State of Alaska, Alaska Sightseeing, Hills Brothers Coffee, Coleman Company, and AVID Microchip Technology.

The ITC goal for 1995 was to generate $500,000 by race day, seventy-five percent of which would cover the expenses of that race. The remainder would be placed in an established trust for the Iditarod Trail Race Foundation. Dividends from the trust were to provide for operational funding, and would not be used for prize moneys.

The Kindness of a Stranger

Reprinted from the April 1995 issue of the *Iditarod Runner*:

"Mrs. C.V. Whitney, a party hostess and horse racing aficionado from New York and Kentucky, and 1995 sponsor of Larry Williams, has donated money to the Iditarod Trail Committee to be used to pay the entry fees for five Iditarod mushers who did not finish in the top twenty of this year's race.

"Col. Norman D. Vaughan, a personal friend of Mrs. Whitney, and well-known adventurer, drew five names from a hat at the awards banquet in Nome following the 1995 race. The names drawn were Max Hall, Wayne Curtis, Paula Gmerek, Mark Wildermuth, and Bobby Salazar. All five mushers were rookies in the 1995 Iditarod. Each of these five mushers will have waiting for them a pre-paid entry, regardless of when they choose to run the Iditarod again."

Passing of an Era

The Canatser cabin at Eagle Island, a popular checkpoint where mushers annually feasted on moose stew, was destroyed by fire a few days after the end of Iditarod 1995.

Ralph Canatser and his late wife Helmi hosted the checkpoint there since the Iditarod first started using a southern route in 1977.

The ITC immediately began efforts to assist Ralph with funds to help rebuild the cabin, and others in the Iditarod family, including pilots and barge operators, pledged to help.

Let's Hear It for Polar Fleece

The mushers of the 1990s wear high-tech clothing made from fabrics designed to wick away body moisture and retain warmth, yet be as lightweight as possible. In 1979, the "fabric of our lives" was wool. Then two-time winner Rick Swenson offered these tips on packing for the Iditarod:

* Wool union suit. Put a cotton one under it if wool irritates you.
* Wool socks (one pair per day).
* Wool pants and shirt.
* Fiber fill vest.
* Parka, medium weight, Native-style (pullover) with a wolf or wolverine ruff.
* Snowmobile suit or quilted bib overalls.
* Shoe pacs big enough for innersole and two pairs of socks.
* Canvas mukluks for extreme cold (the white vapor barrier

The late Helmi Canatser and Martin Buser at the Eagle Island checkpoint, 1991. Helmi and her husband Ralph opened their home to the Iditarod during the odd-numbered years when the trail would go via the southern route. Helmi served great home-cooked meals, usually moose burgers and moose stew, to any musher who could make it up the fifty or more steps cut into the snow, which was the path up to their cabin from the slough where the dog teams parked.

boots formerly used by many bother some people's feet).

Just Tell Me What You Want

Sled dogs are driven not by reins, but by the spoken word. Often the musher and leader share a kind of telepathy as well. And many would rather talk to their dogs than a human any day.

The Iditarod Trail Committee offers this dictionary of common words in a musher's vocabulary:

Lead Dog or Leader: Dog who runs in front of the others. Generally must be both intelligent and fast.

Double Lead: Two dogs who lead the team side by side.

Swing Dog or Dogs: Dog that runs directly behind the leader. Further identified as right or left swing depending on which side of the tow line he's placed. His job is to help "swing" the team in the turns or curves.

Wheel Dogs or Wheelers: Dogs placed directly in front of the sled. Their job is to pull the sled out and around corners or trees.

The Real Reason For 1049 Miles of Toil
NBA's Contribution to the Iditarod: the winner's purse.
$50,000
National Bank of Alaska

National Bank of Alaska's contribution to the Iditarod is on display at the 1989 finish line: fifty thousand single dollar bills.

Joe and Norma Delia are long-time supporters and volunteers. In Skwentna nearly the entire community comes out to support the Iditarod. Kids with snowmachines begin a taxi service, ferrying spectators and others from the airport to the checkpoint for modest fares. The ladies of Skwentna, known as the Skwentna Sweeties, prepare fabulous meals for the mushers and officials. Usually the night before the race comes through, the women put on a skit at the Delia home, which has served as the official checkpoint since 1973.

Team Dog: Any dog other than those described above.

Mush! Hike! All Right! Let's Go!: All are commands to start the team.

Gee: Command for right turn.

Haw: Command for left turn.

Come Gee! Come Haw!: Commands for one hundred and eighty-degree turns in either direction.

Whoa!: Command to halt the team, accompanied by heavy pressure on the brake.

Line Out!: Command for lead dog to pull the team out straight from the sled. Used mostly while hooking dogs into team or unhooking them.

Tow Line or Gang Line: Main rope that runs forward from the sled. Generally made of polyethylene or nylon. All dogs are connected to the tow line by other lines.

Neck Line: Line that connects dog's collar to tow line and between the two collars of a double lead.

Snub Line: Rope attached to the sled that's used to tie the sled to a tree or other object.

Tether Line: A long chain with shorter pieces of chain extending from it. Used to stake out a team when stakes aren't available.

Tug Line: Line that connects dog's harness to the tow line.

Toggles: Small pieces of ivory or wood used by Eskimos to fasten tug lines to harnesses.

Trail!: Request for right-of-way on the trail.

Stake: Metal or wooden post driven into the ground to which dog is tied.

Snow Hook or Ice Hook: Heavy piece of metal attached to sled by line. The snow hook is embedded in the snow to hold the team and sled for a short time.

Stove Up: Injured, generally temporarily. Applies to both musher and dogs.

Dog in Basket: Tired or injured dog carried in the sled.

Rigging: Collection of lines to which dogs are attached. Includes tow line, tug lines, and neck lines.

Runners: The two bottom pieces of the sled that come in contact with the snow. They extend back of the basket for the driver to stand on. Runner bottoms are usually wood, covered with plastic or Teflon. This plastic or Teflon is usually replaced at least once during the race.

Booties: A type of sock worn to protect the dog's feet from small cuts and sores. These are made of various materials, such as denim, Polar Fleece, trigger cloth, etc., and usually held in place with Velcro fasteners.

Slats: Thin strips of wood that make up the bottom of a wooden sled basket. Toboggan-style sleds, however, have a sheet of plastic as the bottom for their basket.

Husky: Any northern-type dog.

Malamute: Term often used by old-timers for any sled dog. Larger husky.

Pedaling: Pushing the sled with one foot while the other remains on the runner.

Indian Dog: An Alaskan husky from an Indian village.

Siberian Husky: Medium-sized (average fifty pounds) northern breed of dog, recognized by the American Kennel Club. Siberians usually have blue eyes.

Race Manager Jack Niggemyer is perhaps more sleep-deprived than the Iditarod mushers.

■ Sleepless in Alaska

"On at least three different occasions it was the trail breakers who woke me up.

"Coming from a deep slumber to find yourself being glared at by an ice-encrusted, wind-ravaged abomination who's been on the trail for eighteen hours, beating their kidneys on wind slab, digging machines out of overflow, and putting up markers in sixty-knot winds, can create nightmares in even the crustiest of race managers."

—*Jack Niggemyer, Race Manager From "Why I Get No Sleep"* Iditarod Runner, *June 1990*

Combining sponsorship and fashion with a knack for showmanship, Norman Vaughan placed his team on the Best Dressed list for 1989. The duds-for-dogs trend remains popular.

■ A Little Parting Gift

A musher doesn't have to cross the finish line in the top twenty to get a prize. He or she may still qualify for one of these special awards:

Golden Harness Award

Hand-made harness recognizing the outstanding lead dog of the race. Presented by harness maker Lolly Medley, one of two women to run the second Iditarod in 1974.

Alaska Airlines Leonhard Seppala Humanitarian Award

To the musher who has best demonstrated outstanding care of his or her team through the race while remaining competitive. Selected by veterinary staff and race officials. Lead crystal cup on an illuminated wooden base; transportation back to Anchorage for musher and dogs; two free round-trip tickets to anywhere Alaska Airlines flies; ITC cash award of $10,000.

Rookie of the Year

To the top-placing man or woman racing his or her first Iditarod. Trophy and $1,500 prize presented by Jerry and Clara Austin.

Sportsmanship Award

Plaque for the musher who exhibits unselfishness, encouragement, or assistance in the interests of others.

Alaska Commercial Company's Sterling Achievement Award

Recognizes the most improved musher with a plaque and $500 gift certificate good at any Alaska Commercial store.

Most Inspirational Musher Award

Official finishers decide who among themselves was most inspirational on the trail. Winner receives a plaque from the IOFC.

GCI Dorothy G. Page Halfway Award

Presented at Iditarod, the halfway checkpoint in odd years when the race covers the southern route. Winners receive a trail trophy and $3,000 in gold. A perpetual trophy made of Alaskan birch and marble, and featuring a photograph of the late Dorothy G. Page, remains year-round at Iditarod headquarters in Wasilla.

Tesoro Alaska Joe Redington, Sr., Award

A drawing during the awards ceremony allows the winning musher to choose $2,500 in cash or 2,500 gallons of Tesoro gasoline. Presented in honor of the "Father of the Iditarod," Joe Redington, Sr.

National Bank of Alaska's Gold Coast Award

A trophy and $2,500 in gold nuggets goes to the first musher to arrive in Unalakleet, on the coast. A perpetual trophy commemorating the award

Volunteer checker Jasper Bond assists as chief pilot Eric Johnson loads a dropped dog onto his plane at Rohn. Next stop: McGrath.

remains year round at the Iditarod headquarters in Wasilla.

Alaska Commercial Company's Golden Pace Award

A gold nugget watch goes to the first musher to reach McGrath, the musher setting the pace for the current race.

Regal Alaskan's First Musher to the Yukon Award

A seven-course gourmet meal prepared by the Executive Chef of the Regal Alaskan Hotel awaits the first musher to the Yukon River. The winner also receives $3,500.

Fastest Time from Safety to Nome

A long-standing award presented by the Nome Kennel Club, $500 goes to the musher who finishes in the top twenty and has the fastest time from Safety to Nome.

The Alaska Dodge Dealers Official Truck Award

Keys to a fully loaded Dodge truck are handed to the winner of the Iditarod Trail Sled Dog Race at the finish line in Nome.

The National Bank of Alaska Red Lantern Award

The last musher across the finish line is presented with a Red Lantern and earns a place in Iditarod history.

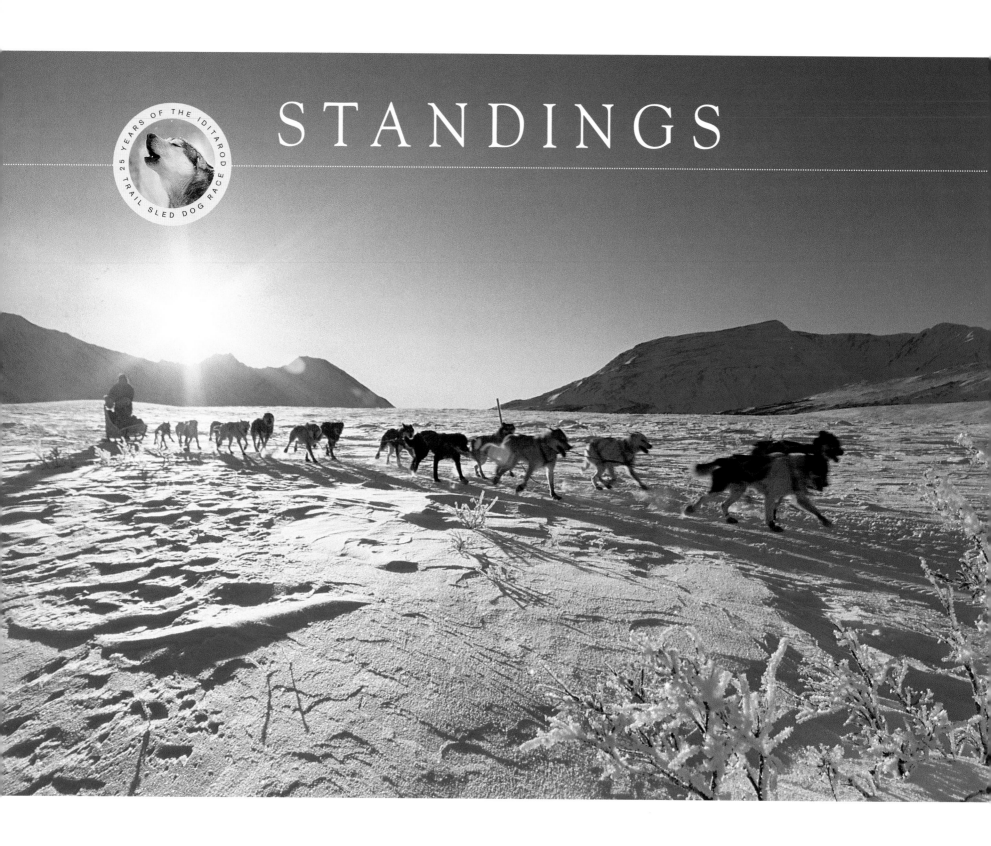

STANDINGS

THE IDITAROD CHAMPIONS

YEAR	MUSHER / HOMETOWN	DAYS	H/M/S	PRIZE
1973	Dick Wilmarth - Red Devil, AK	20	00:49:41	$12,000
1974	Carl Huntington - Galena, AK	20	15:01:07	$12,000
1975	Emmitt Peters - Ruby, AK	14	14:43:15	$15,000
1976	Jerry Riley - Nenana, AK	18	22:58:17	$ 7,200
1977	Rick Swenson - Eureka, AK	16	16:27:13	$ 9,600
1978	Dick Mackey - Wasilla, AK	14	18:52:24	$12,000
1979	Rick Swenson - Eureka, AK	15	10:37:47	$12,000
1980	Joe May - Trapper Creek, AK	14	07:11:51	$12,000
1981	Rick Swenson - Eureka, AK	12	08:45:02	$24,000
1982	Rick Swenson - Eureka, AK	16	04:40:10	$24,000
1983	Rick Mackey - Wasilla, AK	12	14:10:44	$24,000
1984	Dean Osmar - Clam Gulch, AK	12	15:07:33	$24,000
1985	Libby Riddles - Teller, AK	18	00:20:17	$50,000
1986	Susan Butcher - Manley, AK	11	15:06:00	$50,000
1987	Susan Butcher - Manley, AK	11	02:05:13	$50,000
1988	Susan Butcher - Manley, AK	11	11:41:40	$30,000
1989	Joe Runyan - Nenana, AK	11	05:24:34	$50,000
1990	Susan Butcher - Manley, AK	11	01:53:23	$50,000
1991	Rick Swenson - Two Rivers, AK	12	16:34:39	$50,000
1992	Martin Buser - Big Lake, AK	10	19:17:15	$51,600
1993	Jeff King - Denali Park, AK	10	15:38:15	$50,000
1994	Martin Buser - Big Lake, AK	10	13:02:39	$50,000
1995	Doug Swingley - Simms, MT	9	02:42:19	$50,000
1996	Jeff King - Denali Park, AK	9	05:43:13	$50,000

◄ Sunrise breaks over Rainy Pass as Stan Zuray and his team cross the Alaska Range, 1996.

1973

1. Dick Wilmarth
2. Bobby Vent
3. Dan Seavey
4. George Attla
5. Herbert Nayokpuk
6. Isaac Okleasik
7. Dick Mackey
8. John Komak
9. John Coffin
10. Ron Aldrich
11. Bill Arpino
12. Bud Smyth
13. Ken Chase
14. Ron Oviak
15. Victor Kotongan
16. Robert and Owen Ivan
17. Rod Perry
18. Tom Mercer
19. Terry Miller
20. Howard Farley
21. Bruce Mitchell
22. John Schultz

Scratched:
Dr. Hal Bartko
John Schultheis
Darrel Reynolds
Barry McAlpine
Slim Randles
Raymie Redington
John Luster
Alex Tatum
C. Killigrock
David Olson
Herbert Foster
Ford Reeves and Mike Schrieber
Casey Celusnik

1974

1. Carl Huntington
2. Warner Vent
3. Herbie Nayokpuk
4. Rudy Demoski
5. Dan Seavey
6. Ken Chase
7. Raymie Redington

8. Ron Aldrich
9. Joee Redington, Jr.
10. Dick Mackey
11. Joe Redington, Sr.
12. Tom Mercer
13. Jamie "Bud" Smith
14. Rod Perry
15. Dave Olson
16. Reuben Seetot
17. Robert Ivan
18. Victor Kotongan
19. Terry Adkins
20. Tim White
21. Desi Kanerer
22. Clifton Jackson
23. Mary Shields
24. Lolly Medley
25. Joel Kottke
26. Red Olson

Scratched:
Steve Murphy
Carl Topkok
Richard Korb
John Ace
Bernie Willis
Ward Olanna
John Luster
Don Rosevear
John Coffin
Wilbur Sampson
George Attla
Jack Schultheis
Ralph "Babe" Anderson
Jerry Riley
Bill Vaudrin
Warren Coffin
Tom Johnson
Isaac Okleasik

1975

1. Emmitt Peters
2. Jerry Riley
3. Joee Redington, Jr.
4. Herbert Nayokpuk
5. Joe Redington, Sr.
6. Henry Beatus

7. Dick Mackey
8. Ken Chase
9. Rudy Demoski
10. Eep Anderson
11. Alan Perry
12. Ray Jackson
13. Rick Mackey
14. Victor Kotongan
15. Ralph Lee
16. Robert Schlentner
17. Bill Cotter
18. Chris Camping
19. Bill Vaudrin
20. Darrell Reynolds
21. Richard Burnham
22. Jim Kershner
23. John Ace
24. Mike Sherman
25. Steve Fee

Scratched:
Col. Norman Vaughan
Edward Bosco
Hans Algottsen
Sandy Hamilton
Michael T. Holland
Ginger Burcham
Bobby Vent
Guy Blankenship
Terry McMullin
Lavon Barve
Carl Huntington
Walt Palmer
Charlie Fitka
Doug Bartko
Franklin Paniptchuk
John Komak

1976

1. Jerry Riley
2. Warner Vent
3. Harry Sutherland
4. Jamie "Bud" Smyth
5. Emmitt Peters
6. Ralph Mann
7. William "Sonny" Nelson

8. Dick Mackey
9. Tom Mercer
10. Rick Swenson
11. Joe May
12. Don Honea
13. Alan Perry
14. Ray Jackson
15. Ken Chase
16. Billy Demoski
17. Terry Adkins
18. Rudy Demoski
19. Jack Hooker
20. Ford Reeves
21. Babe Anderson
22. Lavon Barve
23. Jerry Austin
24. Ron Aldrich
25. Richard Burnham
26. Charlie Fitka
27. Steve Jones
28. Clarence Towarak
29. Alex Sheldon
30. William Solomon
31. Allan Marple
32. Peter Nelson
33. Jon Van Zyle
34. Dennis Corrington

Scratched:
Joe Redington, Sr.
Col. Norman Vaughan
Richard Hanks
Trent Long
Bob Schlentner
Peter Kakaruk
John Giannone
Lee Chamberlain
Oran Knox
Mel Fudge
Bruce Mitchell
Phillip Foxie
Steve Fee

1977

1. Rick Swenson
2. Jerry Riley
3. Warner Vent
4. Emmitt Peters

5. Joe Redington, Sr.
6. Dick Mackey
7. Don Honea
8. Robert Schlentner
9. Babe Anderson
10. Jack Hooker
11. Ken Chase
12. Alex Sheldon
13. Pete McManus
14. Terry Adkins
15. Al Crane
16. Howard Albert
17. William "Sonny" Nelson
18. Roger Nordlum
19. Rod Perry
20. Richard Burnham
21. Stein Havard Fjestad
22. Bill Cotter
23. Rick Mackey
24. Sandy Hamilton
25. Bob Chlupach
26. Charlie Harrington
27. Eep Anderson
28. Jim Smarz
29. Duane Halverson
30. Peter Kakaruk
31. Randy DeKuiper
32. Dale Swartzentruber
33. Jerry Mercer
34. Varona Thompson
35. Jim Tofflemire
36. Vasily Zamitkyn

Scratched:
Don Montgomery
Tom Mathias
Ray Jackson
Rudy Demoski
Rick McConnell
Bob Watson
Ron Gould
Franklin Paniptchuk
John Ace
Dinah Knight

Jerry Austin
John Hancock
William Solomon

1978

1. Dick Mackey
2. Rick Swenson
3. Emmitt Peters
4. Ken Chase
5. Joe Redington, Sr.
6. Eep Anderson
7. Howard Albert
8. Robert Schlentner
9. Jerry Austin
10. Alan Perry
11. Sonny Lindner
12. Ron Aldrich
13. Pete MacManus
14. Bob Chlupach
15. Ron Tucker
16. Terry Adkins
17. Harry Sutherland
18. Richard Burnham
19. Susan Butcher
20. Varona Thompson
21. Joe Garnie
22. Jerry Mercer
23. Charlie Fitka
24. Ernie Baumgartner
25. Jack Goodwin
26. Rick McConnell
27. William Solomon
28. James Brandon
29. Shelley Vandiver
30. John Wood
31. Ray Gordon
32. Gary Campen
33. Col. Norman Vaughan
34. Andrew Foxie

Scratched:
Roger Roberts
Duke Bertke
Mike Demarco
Bill Rose
Babe Anderson

1979

1. Rick Swenson
2. Emmitt Peters
3. Sonny Lindner
4. Jerry Riley
5. Joe May
6. Don Honea
7. Howard Albert
8. Rick Mackey
9. Susan Butcher
10. Joe Redington, Sr.
11. Gary Hokkanen
12. Terry Adkins
13. Dick Peterson
14. Ken Chase
15. Ernie Baumgartner
16. Melvin Adkins
17. Bob Chlupach
18. Victor Kotongan
19. Keith Jones
20. Patty Friend
21. Brian Blandford
22. John Wood
23. Ron Aldrich
24. Eep Anderson
25. Myron Angstman
26. Walter Kaso
27. Jim Rowe
28. Steve Vollertsen
29. Rick McConnell
30. Rome Gilman
31. Bud Smyth
32. Bill Rose
33. Steve Adkins
34. Cliff Sisson
35. Del Allison
37. John Barron
38. Karl Clausen
39. Jerry Lavoie
40. Gayle Nienhauser
41. Richard Burmeister
42. Jon Van Zyle
43. Jim Lanier
44. Ron Gould
45. Don Montgomery
46. Prentice Harris
47. Gene Leonard

Scratched:
Mark Couch
Isaac Okleasik
Herbie Nayokpuk
Kelly Wages
Terry McMullin
Lee Gardino
Clarence Towarak

1980

1. Joe May
2. Herbie Nayokpuk
3. Ernie Baumgartner
4. Rick Swenson
5. Susan Butcher
6. Roger Nordlum
7. Jerry Austin
8. Walter Kaso
9. Emmitt Peters
10. Donna Gentry
11. Marc Boily
12. Joe Garnie
13. Larry Smith
14. Bruce Johnson
15. Rudy Demoski
16. Dave Olson
17. Dr. Terry Adkins
18. Libby Riddles
19. Harold Ahmasuk
20. Henry Johnson
21. William Bartlett
22. Martin Buser
23. Jack Goodwin
24. DeeDee Jonrowe
25. Ken Chase
26. Bruce Denton
27. Clarence Shockley
28. John Cooper
29. Michael Harrington
30. Marjorie Ann Moore
31. Eric Poole
32. Douglas Sherrer
33. Ron Cortte
34. John Gartiez
35. Norman Vaughan
36. Barbara Moore

Scratched:
Bill Boyko
Jan Masek
Ed Craver
Eugene R. Ivey
Larry Cogdill
Robert E. Neidig
John Eckles
Steven R. Conatser
Duke Bertke
Varona Thompson
Fred Jackson
John Barron
Dick Peterson
Lee Gardino
Don Honea, Sr.
Babe Anderson
Don Eckles
Frank Sampson
Warner Vent
Sonny Lindner
Joe Redington, Sr.
Dick Mackey
Alton Walluk
Bruce Woods
Jerry Riley

1981
1. Rick Swenson
2. Sonny Lindner
3. Roger Nordlum
4. Larry Smith
5. Susan Butcher
6. Eep Anderson
7. Herbie Nayokpuk
8. Clarence Towarak
9. Rick Mackey
10. Terry Adkins
11. Duane Halverson
12. Emmitt Peters
13. Jerry Austin
14. Joe Redington, Sr.
15. Harry Sutherland
16. Joe Garnie
17. Gary Attla
18. Donna Gentry
19. Martin Buser
20. Libby Riddles
21. David Monson

22. Bruce Denton
23. John Barron
24. Gene Leonard
25. Bob Martin
26. Neil Eklund
27. Mark Freshwaters
28. Jeff King
29. Steve Flodin
30. Gary Whittemore
31. DeeDee Jonrowe
32. Sue Firmin
33. Mike Storto
34. Dan Zobrist
35. Dennis Boyer
36. Jan Masek
37. Burt Bomhoff
38. Jim Strong
Scratched:
Frank Sampson
Harold Ahmasuk
Robert Ivan
William Webb
Ernie Baumgartner
Gordon Castanza
Douglas Sherrer
Bud Smyth
Ted English
Wes McIntyre
Willie French
Clifton Jackson
Bill Thompson
Jerry Riley
Myron Angstman

1982
1. Rick Swenson
2. Susan Butcher
3. Jerry Austin
4. Emmitt Peters
5. Dave Monson
6. Ernie Baumgartner
7. Bob Chlupach
8. Don Honea, Sr.
9. Stan Zuray
10. Bruce Denton
11. Rick Mackey
12. Herbie Nayokpuk
13. Dean Osmar
14. Terry Adkins

15. Joe May
16. Marc Boily
17. Joe Redington, Sr.
18. Ed Foran
19. Guy Blankenship
20. John Stam
21. Alex Sheldon
22. Mitch Seavey
23. Glen Findlay
24. John Wood
25. Babe Anderson
26. Jim Strong
27. Ron Cortte
28. Larry Smith
29. Dean Painter
30. Ken Chase
31. Steve Gaber
32. Rose Albert
33. Jan Masek
34. Chris Deverill
35. Leroy Shank
36. Steve Flodin
37. Frank I. Brown
38. Mark "Bigfoot" Rosser
39. Bill Yankee
40. James Cole
41. Richard Burmeister
42. Rick Tarpey
43. Erick Buetow
44. Rome Gilman
45. Jack Studer
46. Ralph Bradley
Scratched:
John Barron
Michael Harrington
Steve Haver
Sue Firmin
Smokey Moff
Bill Rose
Norman Vaughan
Gary Whittemore

1983
1. Rick Mackey
2. Eep Anderson
3. Larry "Cowboy" Smith

4. Herbie Nayokpuk
5. Rick Swenson
6. Lavon Barve
7. Duane Halverson
8. Sonny Lindner
9. Susan Butcher
10. Roger Legaard
11. Joe Runyan
12. Guy Blankenship
13. Dave Monson
14. Sue Firmin
15. DeeDee Jonrowe
16. Howard Albert
17. Bruce Denton
18. Dave Olson
19. Emmitt Peters
20. John Barron
21. Neil Eklund
22. Burt Bomhoff
23. Roxy Woods
24. Walter Kaso
25. Eric Buetow
26. Jim Strong
27. Ken Hamm
28. Vern Halter
29. Shannon Poole
30. William Hayes
31. Walter Williams
32. Christine O'Gar
33. Ted English
34. Bud Smyth
35. Ron Brennan
36. Wes McIntyre
37. Ken Johnson
38. Steve Rieger
39. Connie Frerichs
40. Ray Dronenburg
41. Gary Paulsen
42. Ed Forstner
43. Mark Nordman
44. Dick Barnum
45. David Wolfe
46. Leroy Shank
47. Robert Gould
48. Fritz Kirsch
49. Steve Haver
50. Ron Gould
51. Pam Flowers
52. Norman Vaughan

53. Norm McAlpine
54. Scott Cameron
Scratched:
Terry Adkins
Eugene R. Ivey
Gene Leonard
Beverly Jerue
William Cowart
Alex Sheldon
Bob Bright
Saul Paniptchuk
Ken Chase
Clifton Cadzow
Disqualified:
Les Atherton
Dr. Hal Bartko
Doug Bartko
Jan Masek

1984
1. Dean Osmar
2. Susan Butcher
3. Joe Garnie
4. Marc Boily
5. Jerry Austin
6. Rick Swenson
7. Joe Redington, Sr.
8. Terry Adkins
9. John Cooper
10. Larry Smith
11. Vern Halter
12. Burt Bomhoff
13. Rusty Miller
14. Mark Freshwaters
15. Bob Chlupach
16. Ed Foran
17. Emmitt Peters
18. Rick Armstrong
19. Ray Gordon
20. John Barron
21. Jim Strong
22. Bob Toll
23. Eep Anderson
24. Gordon Castanza
25. Ron Cortte
26. Jerry Raychel
27. Diana Dronenburg
28. Sue Firmin

29. Rick Mackey
30. DeeDee Jonrowe
31. Dave Olson
32. Gary Whittemore
33. Eric Buetow
34. Frank Bettine
35. Kari Skogen
36. Calvin Lauwers
37. Dan Cowan
38. Francine Bennis
39. Rick Adkinson
40. Jim Lanier
41. David Sheer
42. Steve Peek
43. Fred Agree
44. Ed Borden
45. Bill Mackey
Scratched:
Ted English
James Cole
Jan Masek
Dave Aisenbrey
Gene Leonard
Ray Dronenburg
Gordon Brinker
Connie Frerichs
Don Honea, Sr.
Lolly Medley
Larry Cogdill
Brian Johnson
Miki Collins
Steve Gaber
William Thompson
Mel Adkins
Bob Sunder
Darrel Reynolds
Vern Cherneski
Ron Brennan
Disqualified:
Guy Blankenship

1985
1. Libby Riddles
2. Duane Halverson
3. John Cooper
4. Rick Swenson
5. Rick Mackey
6. Vern Halter
7. Guy Blankenship

8. Herbert Nayokpuk
9. Sonny Lindner
10. Lavon Barve
11. Tim Moerlein
12. Emmitt Peters
13. Tim Osmar
14. Jerry Austin
15. Terry Adkins
16. Roger Nordlum
17. Glen Findlay
18. John Barron
19. Raymie Redington
20. Burt Bomhoff
21. Jacques Philip
22. Bob Bright
23. Peter Fromm
24. Steve Flodin
25. Warner Vent
26. Ron Robbins
27. Kazuo Kojima
28. Nathan Underwood
29. Betsy McGuire
30. Kevin Saiki
31. Earl Norris
32. Kevin Fulton
33. John Coble
34. Alan Cheshire
35. Victor Jorge
36. Fred Agree
37. Claire Philip
38. John Ace
39. Rick Armstrong
40. Monique Bene
Scratched:
David Aisenbrey
Terry Hinesly
Susan Butcher
Ted English
Jan Masek
Joe Redington, Sr.
Fred Jackson
Victor Kotongan
Gary Paulsen
Ray Dronenburg
Joseph Maillelle, Sr.
Terry McMullin
Dennis Twarak

Ernie Baumgartner
Rudy Demoski
Norman Vaughan
Armen Khatchikian
Scott Cameron
Chuck Schaeffer
Disqualified:
Bobby Lee
Wes McIntyre

1986
1. Susan Butcher
2. Joe Garnie
3. Rick Swenson
4. Joe Runyan
5. Duane Halverson
6. John Cooper
7. Lavon Barve
8. Jerry Austin
9. Terry Adkins
10. Rune Hesthammer
11. John Barron
12. Guy Blankenship
13. Tim Moerlein
14. Bob Chlupach
15. Jerry Riley
16. Vern Halter
17. Gary Whittemore
18. Ted English
19. Nina Hotvedt
20. Rick Atkinson
21. Rusty Miller
22. Peter Sapin
23. Frank Torres
24. Paul Johnson
25. Martin Buser
26. John Wood
27. Dan MacEachen
28. Jerry Raychel
29. Raymie Redington
30. Mike Pemberton
31. David Olesen
32. Steve Bush
33. Kari Skogen
34. Gordon Brinker
35. Bobby Lee
36. Ron Robbins

37. Dave Scheer
38. Gordy Hubbard
39. Matt Desalernos
40. Alan Cheshire
41. Ray Lang
42. Roger Roberts
43. Allen Miller
44. Armen Khatchikian
45. Don McQuown
46. Mike Lawless
47. Mark Jackson
48. Joe LeFaive
49. Peter Thomann
50. Pat Danly
51. Bill Hall
52. Bill Davidson
53. Scott Cameron
54. Stan Ferguson
55. Mike Peterson

Scratched:
Abel Akpik
John Anderson
Frank Bettine
Roger Bliss
Ron Brennan
Joe Carpenter
Jim Darling
William Cowart
Ray Dronenburg
Don Honea
Fred Jackson
Rick Mackey
Jan Masek
Earl Norris
Joe Redington, Sr.
Douglas Sheldon
John Stam
Norman Vaughan

1987
1. Susan Butcher
2. Rick Swenson
3. Duane Halverson
4. Tim Osmar
5. Jerry Austin
6. Joe Runyan
7. Lavon Barve
8. Ted English

9. John Cooper
10. Martin Buser
11. Joe Garnie
12. Guy Blankenship
13. Jerry Riley
14. Diana Dronenburg
15. Stephen Adkins
16. Matt Desalernos
17. Harry Sutherland
18. Robin Jacobson
19. Bruce Johnson
20. Jacques Philip
21. Sue Firmin
22. DeeDee Jonrowe
23. Terry Adkins
24. Gary Whittemore
25. Herbie Nayokpuk
26. Claire Philip
27. Gary Guy
28. David J. Olesen
29. Dan MacEachen
30. Kazuo Kojima
31. Bruce Barton
32. Dick Mackey
33. Joe Redington, Sr.
34. Dennis J. Lozano
35. John Nels Anderson
36. John Coble
37. Michael V. Owens
38. Roger Roberts
39. Pat Danly
40. Bill Chisholm
41. Henry Horner
42. Caleb Slemons
43. Mike Lawless
44. Roy Wade
45. John T. Gourley
46. Don McQuown
47. Matt Ace
48. Brian Johnson
49. Andre Monnier
50. Rhodi Karella

Scratched:
Peter Thomann
Rick Mackey
Raymie Redington

John Barron
Burt Bomhoff
Gordy Hubbard
Libby Riddles
Gordon Brinker
Joe LeFaive
David Aisenbrey

Withdrawn:
Carolyn Muegge
Tony Burch
Norman Vaughan

1988
1. Susan Butcher
2. Rick Swenson
3. Martin Buser
4. Joe Garnie
5. Joe Redington, Sr.
6. Herbie Nayokpuk
7. Rick Mackey
8. Lavon Barve
9. DeeDee Jonrowe
10. Robin Jacobson
11. Jerry Austin
12. Jan Masek
13. Lucy Nordlum
14. Jacques Philip
15. Bill Cotter
16. Tim Osmar
17. Dan MacEachen
18. John Patten
19. Harry Sutherland
20. Matt Desalernos
21. Bill Hall
22. Darwin McLeod
23. Horst Maas
24. Ted English
25. Jerry Raychel
26. John Barron
27. Dewey Halverson
28. Peter Thomann
29. Conrad Saussele
30. Burt Bomhoff
31. Frank Teasley
32. Peryll Kyzer
33. Ken Chase
34. Babe Anderson
35. Ian MacKenzie
36. Mike Tvenge

37. Mark Merrill
38. John Suter
39. John Gourley
40. Jennifer Gourley
41. Peter Kelly
42. Tim Mowry
43. Matt Ace
44. Gordon Brinker
45. Lesley Anne Monk

Scratched:
Tim Moerlein
Terry Adkins
Joe Runyan
Brian Carver
Ray Dronenburg
Norman Vaughan

Disqualified:
Stan Ferguson

1989
1. Joe Runyan
2. Susan Butcher
3. Rick Swenson
4. DeeDee Jonrowe
5. Lavon Barve
6. Martin Buser
7. Guy Blankenship
8. Rick Mackey
9. Joe Redington, Sr.
10. Tim Osmar
11. Jacques Philip
12. Matt Desalernos
13. Bob Chlupach
14. John Barron
15. Joe Garnie
16. Libby Riddles
17. Jerry Riley
18. Bill Cotter
19. Frank Teasley
20. Terry Adkins
21. Richard Self
22. Jerry Austin
23. Mitch Brazin
24. Diana Dronenburg
25. Jamie Nelson
26. Linwood Fiedler
27. Tim Mowry

28. Bill Cavaney
29. Karin Schmidt
30. Bernie Willis
31. Pat Danly
32. Kathy Halverson
33. Kazuo Kojima
34. Frank Winkler
35. Conner Thomas
36. John Suter
37. Duane Lamberts
38. Bob Hoyte

Scratched:
Kevin Saiki
Carolyn Vaughan
Joe LeFaive
Michael Madden
Bill Chisolm
Gary Whittemore
Mike Ross
David Aisenbrey
Norman Vaughan
Roger Roberts
Jan Masek

1990
1. Susan Butcher
2. Joe Runyan
3. Lavon Barve
4. Tim Osmar
5. DeeDee Jonrowe
6. Robin Jacobson
7. Rick Swenson
8. Linwood Fiedler
9. Joe Garnie
10. Martin Buser
11. Bill Cotter
12. Rick Mackey
13. Michael Madden
14. Jacques Philip
15. Sonny Russell
16. John Barron
17. Matt Desalernos
18. John Gourley
19. Jerry Austin
20. Bill Chisholm
21. Dan MacEachen
22. Norm Stoppenbrink
23. Mike Owens

24. Terry Adkins
25. Joe Redington, Sr.
26. Mitch Brazin
27. Kevin Saiki
28. Diana Dronenburg
29. Bob Chlupach
30. Harry Sutherland
31. Don McEwen
32. Raymie Redington
33. Frank Winkler
34. Bill Hall
35. Beverly Masek
36. Malcolm Vance
37. Roy Wade
38. Roy Monk
39. Dave Breuer
40. Duane Lamberts
41. Emmitt Peters
42. Bob Hickel
43. Macgill Adams
44. Lynda Plettner
45. John Suter
46. Larry Harris
47. Greg Tibbetts
48. Bryan Moline
49. Jim Wood
50. Bert Hanson
51. Peter Kelly
52. Pecos Humphries
53. Bill Davidson
54. Lorren Weaver
55. Lars Ekstrand
56. Larry Munoz
57. John Ace
58. Paul Byrd
59. Terry Hinesly
60. Norman Vaughan
61. Steve Haver

Scratched:
Guy Blankenship
Tim Mundy
Chuck Schaeffer
Pascal Nicoud
Mike Ross
Frank Teasley
Leslie Monk
Joe LeFaive

Disqualified:
Jerry Riley

1991
1. Rick Swenson
2. Martin Buser
3. Susan Butcher
4. Tim Osmar
5. Joe Runyan
6. Frank Teasley
7. DeeDee Jonrowe
8. Matt Desalernos
9. Rick Mackey
10. Bill Cotter
11. Kate Persons
12. Jeff King
13. Jacques Philip
14. Jerry Austin
15. Michael Madden
16. Ketil Reitan
17. Lavon Barve
18. Peryll Kyzer
19. Terry Adkins
20. Bill Jack
21. Beverly Masek
22. Laird Barron
23. Joe Garnie
24. Rick Armstrong
25. Linwood Fiedler
26. Burt Bomhoff
27. Dan MacEachen
28. Dave Olesen
29. Raymie Redington
30. Dave Allen
31. Joe Redington, Sr.
32. Jerry Raychel
33. Mark Nordman
34. Malcolm Vance
35. Macgill Adams
36. Nikolai Ettyne
37. Alexander Reznyuk
38. Tony Shoogukwruk
39. Rollin Westrum
40. Brian Stafford
41. John Suter
42. Roger Roberts

43. Larry Munoz
44. Jim Cantor
45. Terry Seaman
46. Kazuo Kojima
47. Rich Bosela
48. Pat Danly
49. Dave Breuer
50. Chris Converse
51. Sepp Herrman
52. Lynda Plettner
53. Jon Terhune
54. Gunner Johnson
55. Urtha Lenharr
56. Tom Daily
57. Mark Williams
58. Catherine Mormile
59. Don Mormile
60. Brian O'Donoghue

Scratched:
David Aisenbrey
Nels Anderson
Roy Monk
Gary Moore
John Ace
Sonny Russell
Robin Jacobson
Steve Fossett
Alan Garth
Bill Peele
Barry Lee
Ken Chase
John Barron
Gary Whittemore

1992
1. Martin Buser
2. Susan Butcher
3. Tim Osmar
4. Rick Swenson
5. DeeDee Jonrowe
6. Jeff King
7. Vern Halter
8. Rick Mackey
9. Doug Swingley
10. Ketil Reitan
11. Matt Desalernos
12. Bruce Lee

13. Claire Philip
14. Ed Iten
15. Bill Cotter
16. Kate Persons
17. Lavon Barve
18. John Barron
19. Dan MacEachen
20. Joe Garnie
21. Kathy Swenson
22. Sonny Lindner
23. Beverly Masek
24. Jerry Austin
25. Linwood Fiedler
26. Dave Olesen
27. Bill Jack
28. Frank Teasley
29. Rick Armstrong
30. Terry Adkins
31. Bob Chlupach
32. Burt Bomhoff
33. Bill Hall
34. Gary Whittemore
35. Tomas Israelsson
36. Kathy Tucker
37. Susan Cantor
38. Roy Monk
39. Lynda Plettner
40. Norm Stoppenbrink
41. Joe Redington, Sr.
42. Raymie Redington
43. Charlie Boulding
44. Mike Williams
45. Nels Anderson
46. Kim Teasley
47. Steve Fossett
48. Jon Terhune
49. Bob Holder
50. Jim Oehlschlaeger
51. Cliff Roberson
52. Pete Johnson
53. Steve Christon
54. Skin Wysocki
55. Mellen Shea
56. Bill Bass
57. Bob Hickel
58. Debbie Corral
59. James Reiter
60. Loren Weaver
61. Jim Davis

62. John Peterson
63. Vern Cherneski
Scratched:
Tim Mundy
Catherine Mormile
Carolyn Muegge-
  Vaughan
Norman Vaughan
William Orazietti
Robin Jacobson
Pascal Nicoud
Emmitt Peters
Sonny Russell
Joe Runyan
Eep Anderson
Krista Maciolek
Bob Ernisse

1993
1. Jeff King
2. DeeDee Jonrowe
3. Rick Mackey
4. Susan Butcher
5. Tim Osmar
6. Martin Buser
7. Matt Desalernos
8. Doug Swingley
9. Rick Swenson
10. Bruce Lee
11. Vern Halter
12. Joe Runyan
13. Claire Philip
14. Kathy Swenson
15. John Barron
16. Joe Garnie
17. Linwood Fiedler
18. Sonny Lindner
19. Bill Cotter
20. Kate Persons
21. Dan MacEachen
22. David Olesen
23. Jerry Austin
24. Laird Barron
25. Kathy Tucker
26. Diana Dronenburg
27. Frank Teasley
28. Lynda Plettner
29. Terry Adkins
30. Dewey Halverson

31. Mike Williams
32. Mark Nordman
33. Bob Holder
34. Jason Barron
35. Keizo Funatsu
36. Ketil Reitan
37. Pecos Humphreys
38. Peryll Kyzer
39. Jim Oehlschlaeger
40. Skin Wysocki
41. Jerry Louden
42. Pat Danly
43. Stan Smith
44. Jack Goode
45. Roger Haertel
46. Paul Rupple
47. Joe Carpenter
48. Mark Chapoton
49. Kirsten Bey
50. Bert Hanson
51. Harry Caldwell
52. John Peterson
53. Spencer Thew
54. Lloyd Gilbertson
Finisher:
Beverly Masek
Scratched:
Julius Burgert
Norman Lee
Terry Hinesly
Val Aron
David Aisenbrey
Gary Moore
Robin Jacobson
Rick Townsend
Robert Morgan
Lavon Barve
John Shandelmeier
Disqualified:
Dave Branholm

1994
1. Martin Buser
2. Rick Mackey
3. Jeff King
4. Rick Swenson
5. Bill Cotter
6. Doug Swingley
7. Charlie Boulding

8. Tim Osmar
9. DeeDee Jonrowe
10. Susan Butcher
11. Matt Desalernos
12. Kate Persons
13. Vern Halter
14. Peryll Kyzer
15. Robin Jacobson
16. David Olsesen
17. Ramy Brooks
18. Linwood Fiedler
19. Diana Dronenburg
20. Kenth Fjelborg
21. Ramey Smyth
22. Jerry Austin
23. Ketil Reitan
24. Bruce Lee
25. Laird Barron
26. Frank Teasley
27. Stan Smith
28. Mike Williams
29. Lynda Plettner
30. Bill Hall
31. Bob Holder
32. Gus Guenther
33. Terry Adkins
34. Jack Berry
35. Krista Maciolek
36. Robert Somers
37. Aaron Burmeister
38. Cliff Roberson
39. Simon Kinneen
40. Bob Morgan
41. Steve Adkins
42. Dave Branholm
43. Bob Ernisse
44. Harry P. Caldwell
45. Ron Aldrich
46. Jon Terhune
47. Kazuo Kojima
48. Roger Bliss
49. Bruce Moroney
50. Mark Chapoton
Scratched:
Beth Baker
Lisa M. Moore
Lloyd Gilbertson
Mark Nordman
Jamie Nelson

Chris Converse
Rick Townsend

1995
1. Doug Swingley
2. Martin Buser
3. Bill Cotter
4. DeeDee Jonrowe
5. Charlie Boulding
6. Rick Mackey
7. Jeff King
8. Vern Halter
9. Tim Osmar
10. Rick Swenson
11. Peryll Kyzer
12. John Barron
13. Linwood Fiedler
14. Matt Desalernos
15. David Sawatzky
16. Ramy Brooks
17. Jerry Austin
18. David Olesen
19. Ramey Smith
20. Mitch Seavey
21. John Gourley
22. Mark Wildermuth
23. David Milne
24. Randy Adkins
25. Harry Caldwell
26. Jack Berry
27. Art Church
28. Cliff Roberson
29. Dave Branholm
30. Robert Salazar
31. Bob Holder
32. Kazuo Kojima
33. Libby Riddles
34. David Dalton
35. Don Lyrek
36. Nicolas Pattaroni
37. Pat Danly
38. Paula Gmerek
39. Rollin Westrum
40. Robert Bundtzen
41. Wayne Curtis
42. Jon Terhune
43. Nikolai Ettyne
44. Kjell Risung
45. Susan Whiton

46. Max Hall
47. Tim Triumph
48. Larry Williams
49. Ben Jacobson
Scratched:
Andy Sterns
Kathleen Swenson
Diana Moroney
Robert Somers
Pecos Humphreys
Barrie Raper
Lorren Weaver
Don Bowers
Keizo Funatsu

1996
1. Jeff King
2. Doug Swingley
3. Martin Buser
4. Tim Osmar
5. DeeDee Jonrowe
6. Bill Cotter
7. Charlie Boulding
8. David Sawatzky
9. Vern Haler
10. Peryll Kyzer
11. Ramy Brooks
12. David Scheer
13. Robin Jacobson
14. Lavon Barve
15. Mitch Seavey
16. John Barron
17. Linwood Fiedler
18. Cim Smyth
19. Roger Dahl
20. Sven Engholm
21. Jerry Austin
22. Johnny Baker
23. Tomas Israelsson
24. Dewey Halverson
25. Bruce Lee
26. Paul Gebhardt
27. Diana Moroney
28. Andy Willis
29. Dave Olesen
30. Nicolas Pattaroni
31. Conner Thomas
32. Steve Adkins
33. Kazuo Kojima

34. Michael Nosko
35. Harry Caldwell
36. Mike Webber
37. Jim Davis
38. Randy Romenesko
39. Susan Whiton
40. Lori Townsend
41. Bill Gallea
42. Mark Nordman
43. Aaron Burmeister
44. Rob Carss
45. Ararad Khatchikian
46. Dave Branholm
47. Lisa Moore
48. Don Bowers
49. Andy Sterns
Scratched:
Bill Hall
Roy Monk
Rich Bosela
Stan Zuray
Jack Berry
Kjell Risung
Mark Black
Withdrawn:
Rick Swenson*
Ralph Ray
Linda Joy
Bob Bright

**Decision to withdraw
Rick Swenson was
reversed by the Appeals
Board. (Page 122)*

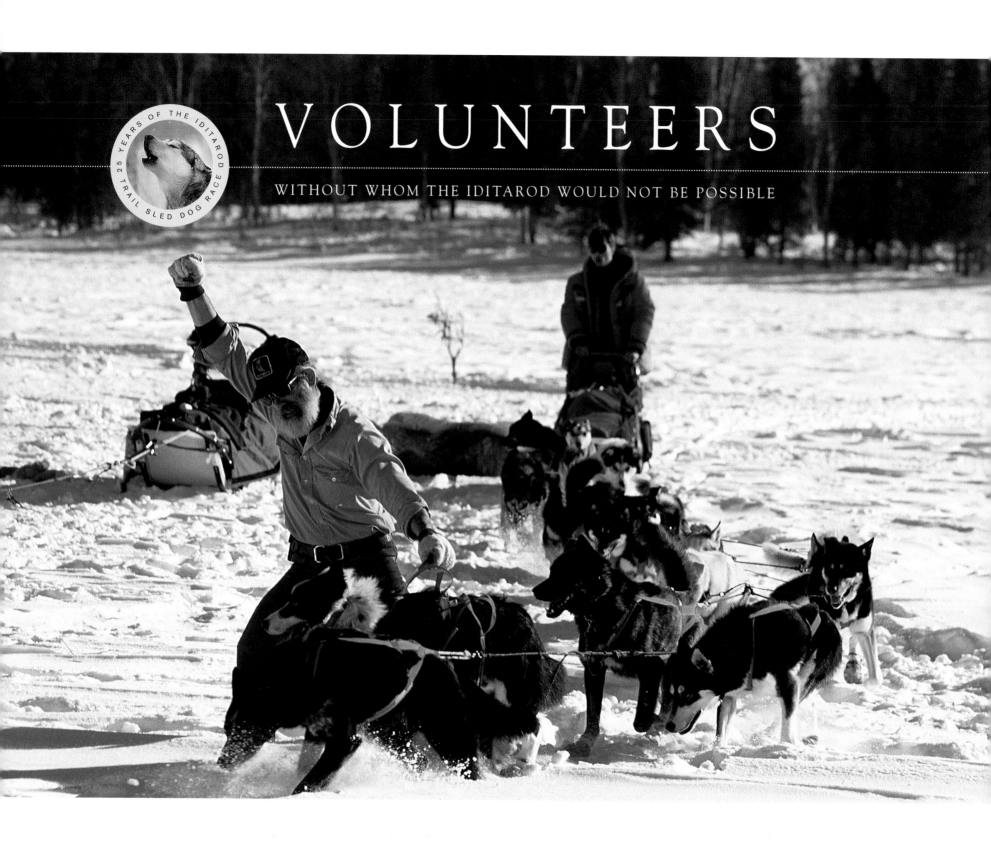

VOLUNTEERS

WITHOUT WHOM THE IDITAROD WOULD NOT BE POSSIBLE

25 YEARS OF THE IDITAROD TRAIL SLED DOG RACE

Lyn Aal	Alec Ahsoak	William Allen	Aimee Anderson	John D. Andrews	Beth Arnold	Monica Aufrecht	Cornina Baker	Paul Barker	Bob Batchelder
Eric Aanensen	Victor Ahsoak	Evelyn Allison	Alan Anderson	Tony Andrews	Don Arnold	Dan Aukon	Debbie Baker	Mary Lou Barks	John Batchelder
Jane Aanensen	Jonathan Ahwinona	Nel Alloway	Beverly Anderson	Heather Andrulli	Gayle Arnold	Marion Aukon	Eddie Baker	Kevin Barksdale	Sydney Bate
Janet Aanensen	Merle Aire	Agnes Allred	Bonnie Anderson	Al Andrus	Jean Arnold	Erick Aulabaugh	Gary Baker	Bonnie Barner	Randy Baten
Ramona Abbott	David Aisenbrey	Jackie Allred	Brian Anderson	Kenny Andrus	John Arnold	James Austin	Greg Baker	Debi Barner	Bob Bates
Sheri Abbott	Bruce Aitcheson	Linda Allschwager	C.D. Anderson	John Andrys	Kay Arnold	Marge Austin	John Baker	Dale Barnes	Patty Bates
Jerry Ableson, DVM	Nancy Aitcheson	Veronica Almaras	Charles Anderson	Jack B. Anerson	Mary Arnold	Paula Austin	Joy Baker	Dr. Barnes, DVM	Rebecca Bates
Carol Abraham	Debbie Akers	Ted Almy	Cheri Anderson	Lynette Angell	Nancy Arnold	George Austin III	Ken Baker	Jeff Barnes	Ray Battey
Nadra Abraham	Jeremy Akers	Mark Aloala	Chuck Anderson	Myron Angstman	Sandra Arnold	Don Avance	Kyle Baker	Renie Barnes	Dave Bauer
Shawn Abraham	Keith Akers	Jenny Alowa	Daisy Anderson	Jeremiah Angusuc	Susan Arnold	Ron Ax	Lester Baker	Bob Barnett	Matt Bauer
John Ace	Marty Akins	Julie Alowa	Daryl Anderson	Thomas Annayoc	Jose Arnott	Sue Ax	Marvin Baker	Denise Barnett	Tim Baughman
Brenda L. Achey	Trudy Aklin	Bill Alter	David Anderson	Paul Annette	Valerie Aron	Jill Axford	Valorie Baker	Stan Barney	David C. Baumer
Andy Achilles	Andrus Alan	Jacob Alvanna	Donna Anderson	Pete Anslem	Jack Art	Bill Aylward	Violet Baker	Ronny Barney, Jr.	Michael Baumert
Glenda Achten	Denise Albert	Andrew Alvarez	Doug Anderson	Quinn Ansted	Rich Arts	Matthew Babcock	Joseph Baldwin	Dick Barnham	George Baumgardner
Shirley Ackley	Denise Albert, DVM	Glen Alvord	Douglas Anderson	Art Anthony	Terese Ascone	Janice K. Baber	Neal Baldwin	Randal Barnhart	Dewey Baungardner
Craig Adair	Howard Albert	Jason Alward	Edward Anderson	Barbara Anthony	Eugene Aseksed	Bob Bachand	Susan Baldwin	Jolyn Baron	Charolette Baversjo
Kathy Adam	Jim Albert	Bill Alyward	Eep Anderson	Bonnie Anthony	Brenda Ashback	Everett Bachelder	Dan Bale	Martha Baron	Wendy Baxter
Mike Adama	David Alborn	Carla Alzurd	Floyd Anderson	Mike Anthony	Dave Ashback	Mina Bachelder	Bob Balern	Scotty Baron	Kurt Bayless
Barbra Adams	Mary Alborn	Deborah Aman	Frank Anderson	Tina Anthony	Greg Ashback	Debbie Bachman	Penny Balern	Adrian Barr	Keith Baystedt
Claude Adams	Jeremy Albright	Neil Amann	Fred Anderson	Tony Anthony	Ronnie Ashback	Myrt Bachman	Steward Ball	Herb Barr	Bill Beach
Dan Adams	Michelle Albright	Kzuriami Amar	Gale Anderson	J.E. Antonich	Jon Ashbrook	Dean Backen	Kristy Ballard	Mary Barr	Jerry Beach
David Adams	Shane Albright	Kuzunam Amar-Roberts	Gary Anderson	Sandy Antonich	Brandon Ashby	Sally Backes	Sandy Ballard	Marty Barrack	Joe Beach
Desiree Adams	Sue Albright	Agnes Amarok	Goog Anderson	John Antonuk	Rodger Ashcraft	Bill Bacon	Clarissa Ballot	Dan Barrett	Margee Beach
Diana Adams	Michelle Aldana	Bill Amarok	Irene Anderson	Cheryl Anzivino	Carol Ashenfelter	Bob Bacon	Christine G. Balsama	Tim Barrett	Pamela Beach
Jack Adams	Chris Alden	Bobby Amarok	Jack Anderson	Charlene Aorsi	George Ashenfelter	Bill Bacus	Gregory Balsama	Cindy Barron	Roxanne Beach
James Adams	John Alder	Debbie Amarok	Jack B. Anderson	Robert Aranow	Gerald Ashenfelter	Julie Badberg	Bill Balzarini	Cornina Barron	Lois Beachy
Jamie Adams	Steve Alder	Denny Amarok	Jessica Anderson	Art Araya	Larry Ashenfelter	Mike Badberg	George Banashefski	Jason Barron	David Beaell
John Adams	Dottie Aldrich	Dorothy Amarok	John "Andy" Anderson	Will Araya	Stanley Ashenfelter	Alfred Bagley	Patrick Banbury	Nathan Barron	Katherine Beagle
Langford Adams	Nellie Aldrich	Gary Amarok	John F. Anderson	Saeri Archebald	George Ashenfelter, Sr.	Carol Bagley	Randy Bannister	Red Barron	Mont Beal
Merry Adams	Ron Aldrich	John Amarok	Justus Anderson	L. Arcuri	John T. Asher, Jr.	David Bagley	Endo Bannon	Roxanne Barron	Bob Bean
Mike Adams	Brian Alesi	Lisa Amarok	Katie Anderson	Nikki Arguelles	Clay Askren	Julie Bagley	Steve Banse	Scotty Barron	Norm Bean
Sen. Al Adams	Nancy Alex	Mary Amarok	Larry Anderson	Dean Aring	Will Askren	Summer Bagley	Ken Baptiste	Dave Barrowcliff	Ken Beans
Sue Adams	Amy Alexander	Robert Amarok	Lyle Anderson	Margie Arlin	Julian Asplund	Kevin Bahnke	Laney Baravido	Gregory Barrowcliff	Jean Bear
Thomas Adams	Cliff Alexander	Season Amarok	Melanie Anderson	Marian Arlin	Bruce Aspray	Terry Bailard	Dee Barbaric	Bruce Barrows	Peggy Bear
Valeria Adams	Gloria Alexander	Sharasha Amarok	Mike Anderson	Pamela Armbruster	Beth Assidi	Al Bailey	Mike Barbaric	John Bartholomew	Truman B. "Bill" Bear
Eric Adamson	Jennifer Alexander	Stanley Amarok	Nancy Anderson	Monique Armendariz	Mildred Atchison	Bev Bailey	Al Barber	Michelle Bartholomew	Arlene Beard
Greg Adamson	Judie Alexander	William Amarok	Nathan Anderson	Loren Arment	Kaylene Ateberry	Christine G. Bailey	Bill Barber	Maryalice Bartholmae	Tom Beard
Terry Adkins, DVM	Judy Alexander	Mr. & Mrs. Amatoolik	Olie Anderson	James Armistead	Les Atherton	Clay Bailey	Michelle Barber	Dr. Harold Bartko	Barney Beardsley
Larae Adkins	Mark Alexander	Alan Amaya	Polly Anderson	Sheila Jo Armodt	Mark Atkins	Dick Bailey	Millette Barber	Bill Bartlett	Cindy Beardsley
Steve Adkins	Mike Alexander	Sandy Amazeen	Pudden Anderson	Barbara Armstrong	J.B. Atkinson	Elder Bailey	Ray Barber	Jillian Bartling	Dave Beardsley
Tom Adkins	Wayne Alexander	Bill Ambrose	Ralph Anderson	Connie Armstrong	Larry Atkinson	Tom Bailey, DVM	Joe Barberick	Tom Bartol	Nick Beardsley
Bertha Adsuma	Tony Alexia	Fred Ambrose	Rebecca Anderson	Glenn Armstrong	Rick Atkinson	Kathy Bailey	Glen Barbier	Betty Barve	Greg Bearidoin
Ellen Agnes	Mike Alexie	Linda Ambrose	Rick Anderson	Jack Armstrong	Tom Atkinson	Lucy Bailey	Lynda Barcome	Lance Barve	Wayne Beary
Henry Agnes	Jackie Alexie, Sr.	Kimberly Ameck	Tina Anderson	J.B. Armstrong	Joe Attatayuk	Marjory Bailey	Mary Barcot	Lavon Barve	Ed Beasley
Margaret Agnes	Victor Alexie, Sr.	Elva Amidon	Victor Anderson	Juliana Armstrong	Jack Atwater	Tammie Bailey	Rick Barengo	Randy Basaraba, DVM	John Beasley
Kathy Agoff	Dale Alford	Willie Amidon	Wayne Anderson	Mary Jane Armstrong	Bob Atwood	Don Bain	Margy Baress	Mark Bashaw	Judy Beasley
Chris Aguchak	Yvonne Alford	Bill Amos	Mishka Andreanov	Riley Armstrong	Bonnie Atwood	Pat Baird	Andy Barger	Al Basler	Peggy Beasley
Ellen Ahern	Danny Alkon	Surge Amundson	"Blueberry John" Andrews	Sandra Armstrong	Lea Atwood	Tom Baird	Robert Bargewell	Lois Basler	Dick Beattie
Sarah Ahern	Barbara Allen	Christina Anagick	DeeDee Andrews	Randy Arndt	Nicolle Atwood	Ylfelynn Baird	William Barhan	Joanna Basso	Margaret Beattie
Forence Ahnangratoguk	Dennis Allen	Gimbo Anagick	Deena Andrews	Bruce L. Arnel	Abigail Aubry	James Baisden	Anthony Barker	David A. Bastian	Linda Beatty
Lottie Ahnypkana	Jerry Allen	Terry Anarvk	Ephram Andrews	Lisa Arnel	Brenda Aubry	Abigail Baker	Bill Barker	Peggy Bastian	Larry Beauboeuf
Alec Aho	Kathy Allen	David R Anasoyuk	Jessica Andrews	W. Arnett	Dave Aubry	Anthony Baker	David A. Barker		Mark Beaudin
Sarah Aho	Scott Allen			Art Arnold	Ken Aubry	Beth Baker	Frankie Barker		Amy Beaudoin
Debbie Ahrens	Walt Allen			Barry Arnold	Ernie Aufenkamp	Bob Baker	Pam Barker		Vern Beaver

◀ At the Finger Lake checkpoint for 1996, volunteer Ray Henry parks Johnny Baker's team. Volunteers work long and hard to make the race a success for each musher.

Linda Bebe
Kami Beckman
Maurice Beckner
William Beckstine
Dave Bedell
Nikki Bedingfield
Chadwick Bedsley
John Bedsley
Peggy Bedsley
Jesse Bedsley
Joe Beech
Paul Beeman
Dennis Bege
Marge Bege
MaryAnn Begin
Bill Behnke
Mary Beiter
Jean Beiter
Kathy Belanger
Kaye Belcher
Ken Belden
Jean Belfield
Kira Belkin
Aaron Bell
Betty Bell
Brian Bell
Matthew Teayoumeak Bell
Nathan Bell
Ruth Bell
Stewart Bell
Tony Bell
Garry Beller
Joan Beller
Mariella E. Beller
Merie Beller
Merle Beller
Nancy Beller
Bob Bellmore
Donna Bellmore
Normand Bellville
Paulette Bellville
Mary Belonzi
Tim Beltz
Edward Belyea
Jeff Bemis
Bill Bemmels
Katie Bender
Linda Bender
Rick Bender
Tom Bender
Pat Bendz
Richard Beneville
Frank Benjamin

Jim Benke
Stephanie Benke
Warren Bennet
Brian Bennett
Dena Bennett
Millie Bennett
Stacy Bennett
Wayne Bennett
Willard Bennett
K.C. Benniak
Ed Benning
Francine Bennis
Joan Benoir
Bob Benson
Hobo Benson
Brian Bent
Bob Benzo
Joe Berberich
John Berdner
Sheila Berg
Trish Berg
Napolean Bergamaschi
Shawn Bergamaschi
James Bergamashi
Dennis Bergen
Charlie Berger, DVM
Kathy Bergeron
Rick Bergeron
Nick Berget
Tony Berget
Kristie Bergin
Anthony Berman
Barney Berman
JoAnn Berna
Kathleen Bernauer
Verna Berndt
Albertha Bernhardt
Mike Bernzott
Paul Berroteran
Marriner Berthole
Marriner Bertholf
Mark Berton
Kira Besh
William Bessey
Chadwick Bessinger
Jack Bessinger
Bruce Bessler
Cheryl Bessler
Lou Betera
J. Bethke
Cindy Bettine
Frank Bettine
Carolyn Bettis
Lucy Bettis

Ken Bettisworth
Jonathan Bettridge, DVM
Larry Betts
Tim Betz
Peg Bevao
Jeff Bevers
Russ Bevins
Kirsten Bey
Keith Beystedt
Mike Bianco
Gladys Bibbs
Scott Bibelhausen
Susan Bickman
Dolores Bielle
Scott Bier
Michael Bieri
John Bierman
Loren Bierman
Judy Bies
Linda Biesanz
Shane Bignell
Annie Bill
Gregory Bill
Mark Bill
Diane Billings
Jim Billingsley
Crystal Billington
Robert Billmoore
Mark Bills
Roxanne Bills
Jathan Bingham
Pearl Bingham
Johne Binkley
Kevin L. Binns
Jesse Binns
Diana Birch
David Birchfield
James Birckhouse
Charles Bird
Jeanette Birge
Erika Biringer
Jon Biringer
Josh Biringer
Louise Biringer
Luann Biringer
Robert Biringer
Bob Bishop
Bruce Bishop
Carolyn Bishop
Chris Bishop
John Bitney
Bob Bjerk, DVM
Chrissy Bjorgen

Shawn Bjorgen
June Bjornstad
Gail Bketschneider
Allen Black
John Black
Mary Black
David Blackburn
Frank L. Blackburn
Mary Blackburn
Mona Blackburn
Don Blackwell
Michael L. Blain
Jim Blair
Riley Blaire
Mike Blais
Doug Blake
Jill Blake
John Blake
Peter Blake
Cheryl Blaker
Troy Blalock
Brian Blanchard
Dexter Blanchard
Brian Blanford
Matt Blanford
Bucky Blankenship
Guy Blankenship
Jim Blanning
Troy Blaylock
Ken Bleden
Jim Blees
Dan Blevins
Alayne Blickle
Doug Bliesath
Lissa Bliesath
Bill Bliss
Jerry Bliss
Kris Bliss
Mary Ellen Bliss
Roger Bliss
Larry Blomker
Carolyn Bloom
Jack Blosser
Sarah Blue
Tracy Blue
Alma Blum
Bob Boatright
Andrew Bobby
Teddy Bobby
Tim Boddicker
Allison Bodewicz
Moreen Bodewicz
Jarret Bodfield
Nancy Bodily

Travis Bodily
Dulcy Boehle
Rachel Boekmann
Hans Boenish
Michael Boerma
David Bogart
Leslie Bogda
Kevin Boggs
Michelle Bogle
Mitchell Bogle
Karrie Bohi
Doug Bohlen
Mariella Bohlen
Joan Bohmann
Judy Bohmann
Joan Bohmark
Tom Bohn
Ed Bohnert
Jean Boiley
Marc Boiley
Anthony Boling
Carol Boling
Tammy Boling
Tony Boling
Butch Bologna
J.H. Bolt
Brad Boman
Brad Bomhoff
Burt Bomhoff
Jason Bond
Jasper Bond
Joanne Bond
Michael Bond
Orlene Bond
Mariella Bonlen
Harry Bonne
Pierre Bonnemaison, DVM
Dave Bonner
Jack Bonner
Christina Boom
Brad Boore
Kevin L Booth
Kim Booth
Pat Booth
Richard N. Booth
Robert Boothe
Ed Borden
Peggy Bordner
James Boretski
John Boretski
Igor Borissenko
Nikalai Borissenko
Kevin Bortmas

Dave Bosch
Jerry Bosch
Don Boschee
Jeanne Boschee
Ed Bosco, Jr.
Ed Bosco, Sr.
Cathy Boscoe
Rich Bosela
Edward Boston
Colleen Bostwick
Jimmy Bostwick
James Bostwick, Jr.
Grayson Bottom
Michelle Bouchard
Gabriel Bourgoin
Glenn Bovey
Roy Bow
Kassie Bowden
Bev Bowers
Bob Bowers
Don Bowers
Terry Bowle
Jeanne Bowler
John T. Bowles
Sarah Bowles
Toni Bowley
Chandra Bowley
Don Bowley
Garrett Bowley
Gary Bowley
Frank Bowlin
Amy Bowman
Art Bowman
Brad Bowman
David Bowman
Helena Bowman
Marie Bowman
Tonie Bowman
Dee Bowns
Mel Bowns
Art Bows
Eva Box
Smith Box
Bill Boyce
Julie Boyce
Robert Boyd
Cliff Boyer
Doug Boyer
Vic Boyer, DVM
Sandy Boyer
Scott Boyer
Dan Boyette
Cathy Boyington
Ralph Boyington

Maureen Boyle
Mitchell Boyle
Terry Boyle
Glen Boyles
Marvin Boyles
Clifford Boynton
Jennifer Bozarth
Tim Brabets
Bruce Braden
Sally Braden
Charlotte Bradfield
Carolyn Bradley
Fred Bradley
Miller Bradley
Nancy Bradley
Ralph Bradley
Siobhan Bradley
Nicole Braem
Tim Bragdon
Frank Bragg
Marj Bragg
Dallas Brake
Joyce Brandenburger
James Brandon
Pam Brandon
Carol Branholm
Margo Branholm
Ton Brannon III
Robert Brantley
Herb Brasseur
Peter Brautigam
Dan Breault
Karen Breck
Kenneth Breeden
Ann Brees
Christy Brendel
George J. Brendel
Judith Brendel
Betsy Brennan
Sean Brennan
Tom Brennan
Jim Brenner
Susan Brenner
Jim Brent
Kim Bressler
Ajeann Bretzke
Charlotte Breuer
Jim Breun
Joe Brewer
Megan Brewer
Bob Brickhouse
Maria Brickhouse
Chuck Bridgewater
Joyce Bridgewater

Bran Briggs
Carolyn Briggs
James Briggs
Tammy Briggs
John K Briggs II
Bob Bright
Will Bright
Debbie Brinker
Gordon Brinker
Ronald A Brinker
Jackie Briskey
James Briskey
Jackie Brisset
Bill Bristol
Dave Bristol
Liz Bristol
Peter Britches
Alex Brittain
Michelle Brittain
Earven Brittenum
Roderick Broach
Christopher T. Broadka
Christopher Brobst
Jon Brobst
Barbara Brockway
Dana Brockway
Mica Brockway
Dixie Brodigen
Dick Brogan
Lynde Brogan
Richie Brogan
Pat Brokaw
Thomas N. Brokaw
Kerryann Brokshire
Van Brollini
Kerry Bromley
Jack Bronner
Debbie Brooks
Fred Brooks
Harvey Brooks
James R. Brooks
Mary Brooks
Robert Brooks
Roger Brooks
Ronald A. Brooks
Nancy Brophy
Walt Brophy
Dan Bross
Peggy Bross
Concepci Brossard
Tamara Brossard
Corey Brothers
Boyd Brougher
Jean Brougher

Aluki Brower
Alta Brown
Blaine Brown
Bruce Brown
Carol Brown
Dave Brown
Dean Brown
Don Brown
Elder Brown
Enid Brown
Frank Brown
Glen Brown
James Brown
Jaymes Brown
Julie Brown
Kandy Brown
Lawrence E. Brown
Margo Brown
Martha Brown
Nadine L. Brown
Nancy Brown
Nick Brown
Patrick Brown
Robert Brown
Scott Brown
Sheila Brown
Sheryl Brown
Susan Brown
Vlyetta Brown
Wayne Brown
Jim Brown, Sr.
Bill Browne
Joe Browne
Richard Brownell
George Browning
Pat Brownlee
Linda Bruce
David Brucia
Theresa Brudnicki
Thomas Brudnicki
Don Brugman
Hans Brugman
Michelle Brule
Jeff Brunello
Lois Brunk
Shannon Brunlow
Ginny Bruns
Michael Brunstad
Donald Brusehaber
Susan Brusehaber
Rodney Brustuen
Thomas Brux
Frank Bryan
James R. Bryan

Joey Bryan
Martha Bryan
P.L. Bryan
Robert Bryan
John Bryant
Marcia Bryant
Tony Bryant
Bill Buchanan
Bryan Buchanan
Pat Buchanan
Susan Buchanan
Shirley Buchholz
Hans Bucholdt
Alta Buchta
Dianne Buchta
Glenn W. Buchta
Jessica Buchta
Lynda Buchta
Nick Buchta
Barbara Bucich
Vicki Buck
Mary Buckhouse
Charles Buckles
Harry Buckley
Jaymes Buckley
James Buckmiller
Jan Buckmiller
Joe Buckmiller
Theresa Buckmiller
Bill Buell
Edna Buffas
Harold Buher
Jan Buist
Pete Buist
Tom Bukowski
Dan Bull
Virgil Bullard
Ken Buller
Sherri Buller
Debbie Bullington
Brent Bunch
Billie Bundoff
Tom Bunger
David Bunjevac
Marie Bunker
Gerilynne Buonocore-Leidig
Glenn Buonocore-Leidig
Tony Burch
Michael Burchette
Suzanne Burd
Delores Burdette
Thomas Burdnicki

Ruthe Burg
Susan Burg
Steven Burgdorf
Brian Burger
Howard Burger
Bill Burgh
Doug Burgman
Dina Burk
Jim Burke
Walter Burkevich
Malinda Burkholder
Sandy Burky
Steve Burlenhoff
Aaron Burmeister
Kirsten Burmeister
Linnea Burmeister
Noah Burmeister
Rachel Burmeister
Richard Burmeister
Dorothy Burnette
Rich Burnham
Vi Burnham
Alma Burns
Don Burns
Ginny Burns
Keith Burns
P.L. Burns
Pauline Burns
Sam Burns
Sarah Burns
Steve Burris
Joey Burris
Angela Burroughs
William Burroughs, DVM
Richard Burrows, DVM
Don Burt
Lu Burton
Pete Burton
Rodger Burton
Jack Bury
Greg Busch
Julie Busch
Kathleen Busch
Steve Busch
Tom Busch
Martin Buser
Rachel Buser
Don Bush
Judy Bush
Mike Busher
Bobbie Bushue
Bridgette Bushue
Terry Bushue

Jane Busse
Ron Busse
Joella Buswell
Lewis Butch
Agnes Butcher
Carla Butcher
Helen Butcher
Susan Butcher
Lt. Col. Butler
Jeanie Button
Kevin Button
Dennis C Butts
Jean Buyze
Terry Buzzell
Bob Byars
James Byars
Velva Byars
Cary Byerly
Frank Byerly
Jane Byerly
Linda Byerly
Sgt. Byers
Don Bykonen
John Byron
Keith Bystedt
William Bystedt
Kevin Cabinboy
Michael Cabrera
Beth Cabrie
Dianne Cabrie
William Caddell
Clifton Cadzow
Bonnie Caginia
Donna Cahalane
Jessica Cahill
Ken Cahill
Stanley Cahoon
Karl Cain
Lisa Cain
Ron Calcord
Chris Calcote
Delice Calcote
Jared Calcote
Rick Calcote
Joe Caldarera
Brian Caldwell
Dr. Sharon Caldwell
Harry Caldwell
Jackie Caldwell
Santo Cali
Bob Calkins
Tommie Calkins
Rick Callaham
Connie Cameron

Kay Cameron
Scott Cameron
Angela Camos
Chris Camp
James Camp
Jan Camp
Paul Camp
Anne Campbell
Barbara Campbell
Ben Campbell
Cheryl Campbell
Dale Campbell
Jack Campbell
Pauline Campbell
Trent Campbell
Tom Canatser
Dr. Mike Canceni
Ken Canfield
Mary Beth Cangello
George Cannelos
Ann Cannon
Bill Cannon
Brian Cannon
Chris Cannon
Jean Cannon
Jim Cannon
John Cannon
Missy Cannon
Duke Canoti
Josephine Canoti
Brian Canta
Debbie Cantor
Jim Cantor
Susan Cantor
Dr. Glenn Cantor
Chris Cap
Vi Capell
John Capsul
Leroy Captain
Melvin Captain
Bill Card
Kim Cares
Claudia Carle
DeeDee Carlo
Ron Carlo
Toni Carlo
Frank Carlock
Jane Carlock
Mary Carlock
Brian Carlson
Don Carlson
Gary Carlson
Heather Carlson
Jim Carlson

Olav Carlson
Patti Carlson
Rich Carlson
Robert Carlson
Ted Carlson
Trudy Carlson
Ed Carlton
Mike Carlton
Jim Carly
Donna Carmen
Lee Carmen
Brad Carmer
Carol Carney
Denver Carney
Ed Carney
Jack Carpenter
Joe Carpenter
Sarah Carpenter
Tiffany Carpenter
Simon W. Carraway
Bob Carrick
Steve Carrick
Cary Carrigan
Tom Carrigan
Robert Carroll
Susan Carroll
Bobby Carros
Connie Carroway
Charlie Carson
Jim Carson
Art Carss
Jane Carss
Sanders Carsten
Carter B
Alison Carter
Chris Carter
Dorothy Carter
Otis D. Carter, DVM
Goldie Carter
Kim Carter
Marilyn Carter
Phyllis Carter
Ryan Carter
Russell Cartier
TSgt. Carwile
Karen Casanovas
Barbara Casebier
Markie Casebier
Coleeta Cash
Jim Cash
Bill Caspers
Lisa Casperson
Michelle Cassano
Beth Castaldi

John Castaldi
Ken Castaldi
Laura Castaldi
Gordon Castanza
Susan Casteel
Bert Castel
Phillip Castel
Randy Castel
Val Castell
Lisa Caston
Matthew Caswell
Bill Caton
Karen Cauble
Mike Cavan
Angela Caven
Mary Cavlier
Tony Cavota
Linda Cayse
Bill Cease
Charlotte Cease
George Cebula
Vaughn Center
Jim Chaddock
Patricia Chaddock
Brent Chadwick
Larry Chalifour
Alden Chamberlain
Aicen Chamberlin
Bill Chamberlin
Barb Chambers
Debbie Chambers
Jackie Chambers
Jason Chambers
Lynn Chambers
Roy Chambers
Charlie Champaine
Sara Champion
Bruce Chandler
Ethel Chandler
Jared Chandler
Jeffrey Chandler
Jim Chandler
Katy Chandler
Jon Chaney
Sullivan Chaney
Sherry Chang
Sandy Chapin
Cindy Chapman
Dan Chapman
O.J. Chapman
Angela Chapoton
Kathy Chapoton
Mark Chapoton
Debbie Chappel

Harold Charles
Wade Charles
Lonnie Charleson
A.J. Charlton
Bari Charlton
Lora Charlton
Gretchen Charon
Alecc Charron
Earl Charron
Paul Charron
Mary Charvat
Adele Chase
Art Chase
Brad Chase
Cathy Chase
Corey Chase
Don Chase
Ernie Chase
Ian Chase
Keith Chase
Ken Chase
Laura Chase
Marilyn Chase
Shannon Chase
Barbara Chasteen
Emilio Chaviano
Cheryl Cheadle
Sheri Cheadle
Ken Cheatham
Bob Check
Jackie Chephart
Penny Cherneski
Vern Cherneski
Sharon Cherrette
Larry Cheso
Ken Chick
Tricia Chick
Stefan Chieloski
Rob Childers
Steve Childers
Don Childs
John J. Chillie, Jr.
Barbara Chimiel
Bill Chisholm
Cathy Chisholm
Bob Chlupach
Sally Chlupach
Barbara Chmiel
Raymond Chmielavski
Charly Choate
Ken Choate
Sherry Choate
Tom Choate

Gabe Chokwok
Seung Chong
Ronald Choura
Chris Chrismore
Mike Chrisom
Sue Chrisom
Diane Christensen
Elder Christensen
Heather Christensen
Sue Christensen
Diane Christenson
Claudene Christian
Cathy Christiansen
Mary Christiansen
Elaine Christopherson
Dawn Adam Christy
Mike Chritsom
Maureen Chrysler
Debbie Chunn
Robert Chunn
Art Church
Elwood Church
Rosemary Church
Tammy Ciesla
Phil Cilwick
Dan Cismoski
David Clader
John Clader, DVM
Laura Clader
Alecc Clark
Angela Clark
Christie Clark
Cindy Clark
David Clark
Debbie Clark
Dennis Clark
Ella Mae Clark
Helen Clark
Jacqueline Clark
Jean Clark
Katie Clark
Kent Clark
Lorrie Clark
Robert Clark
Roger Clark
Ron Clark
Stephanie Clark
Terry Clark
Victor Clark
Vincent P. Clark
Anne Clausen
Don Clausen
Lars Clausen
Carl Clauson

Barry Clay
Hope Clay
Kacey Clayton
Murray Clayton
Stan Cleaver
Craig Clelland
Earl Clelland
Judd Clemens
Pat Clemens
Fred Clement
Skip Clements
Bruce Clemmens
John C. Cler
Nicholas Cler
Randall Cler
T. Clevengen
Aimee Clewis
Sheri Clewis
Sally Clifford
Jeremy Clifford
Linda Clifton
Doug Clinton
Susan Clore
Sherry Clouse
Troy Clouse
Kim Clowers
Dave Cloyd
Neal Cluck
Bob Clute
George Clyde
Robert Clyde
Sue Clyde
Tex Coady, DVM
Tom Coate
Minerva Cobarruvias
Linnea Cobb
Teresa Cobb
Bob Cochran
Bud Cochran
Ken Cochran
Lorraine Cochran
Roger Cochran
Colleen Cocking
Duane Cocking
James Cody
Rosemary Cody
Sandy Coelho
Evelyn Coello
Tony Coello
Tony Coffel
Dennis Coffield
Jerry Cogan
Larry Cogdill
Terry Cogdill

Don Cogger
John Coghill
Lt. Gov. Jack Coghill
Robert Coghill
VickiMarie Colacicco
Charles Colbert
Neal Colby
Neil Colby
Betsy Cole
Cheryl Cole
Dawn Cole
Ed Cole
James Cole
Janet Cole
Jeffery Cole
Jim Cole, Jr.
Jim Cole, Sr.
Beckie Coles
Barb Collier
Diane Collins
Mike Collins
Pierre Collins
Ricki Collins
Vernon Collins
Bobbie Combs
Ralph Combs
Carole Comeau
Dave Comeaux
Anne Comeaux
Tim Comfort
David Comoza
Judy Comoza
Lorraine Conary
Marta Conat
Helmi Conatser
Ralph Conatser
Steve Conatser
Travis Conatser
Tim Conay
Boyd Condon
Sylvia Condy
Bill Conklin
Gregory Conklin
Christine Conley
Jim Conley
Linda Conley
Valerie Connely
Danny Conner
Fredrick Conner
George Conner
Jennifer Conner
Renea Conner
Sara Conners
Susan Connole
Don Conrad

Diana Conrath
Peter Constable
Maurice Constandine
Joann Contini
Chris Converse
Bill Conway
James Cook
Janella Cook
Jonathon Cook
Linda Cook
Mike Cook
Phil Cook
Robert Cook
Tom Cooley, DVM
Chris Coombs
Donna Coombs
Phyl Coombs
Annie Cooper
Garret Cooper
Joe Cooper
Judy Cooper
Pat Cooper
Roger Cooper
Susannah Cooper
Brenda Coors
Bill Copeland
Mollie Copeland
Chiquita Copthron
Dorothy Corark
Martha Corbine
David Corbyn
Chuck Cordon
Dick Cordova
Linda Corelle
B.J. Cornelius
Lonnie Cornelius
Beverly Cornet
Caroll Cornett
John Cornett
Nina Cornett
Nadra Coronado
Dennis Corrington
Sue Cortee
Rebecca Lee Cory
Hal Coslin
Randall Cosper
Don Cossairt
David Costello
Pat Costello
Paul Costello
Sandra Costino
Chiquita Cothron
Bill Cotter
Jeffie Cotterman

Barbara Cotting	John Cranmer	Mary Cunningham	Cindy Dankworth	Steve Davis
Peggy Cottle	Brian Crawford	Steve Cunningham	Pat Danly	Valerie Davis
Kevin Coughlin	Clarence Crawford	Troy Cunningham	Bill Dann	Jackie Davison
Michael Couiter	Peggy Crawford	Lamont Cupp	Kathlene Dantico	Art Dawson
Jill Coulter	Chad Cray	Carol Curnell	Demi Danvig	Hank Dawson
Larry Counts	Sara Cray	James Curnell	Ilene Darby	Kathy Dawson
Nancy Courter	Kathy Crayon	Dave Curran	Barbara Darcy	Mary Dawson
Rose Courtright	Sally Creamer	Joe Currier	Will Darcy	Penny Dawson
Dr. Charles R.	Nancy Creason	Judy Currier	Peggy Dargan	Kami Day
Couvillion	Brian Creswell	Phil Currin	Don Darling	Paul Day
Mary Couvillion	Stephanie Creswell	Judy Curtis	Daryl Darnell	Terry Day
Cameron Covington	Gary Creviston	Tiffany Curtis	Lori Darnell	Yvonne Daze
Dan Cowan	Ron Crigger	Elizabeth Cusato	Pam Darnell	Paula de Jong
Dave Cowan	Craig Crippeng	Bill Cypler	Kathryn DaSilva	Bruce Deacon
Pat Cowan	Jeff Crippeng	Fohn Cyr	Pat DaSilva	Vern Deacon
Robert Cowan	Aimee Crocker	Curtis D'Aboy	Brenda Dates	Bill Deal
William Cowart	Rae Crocker	Brian D'Asaro	John Davenport	Sharon Dean
Steve Cowles	Cathy Croghan	Dianne Dabrowski	Karen David	Jo Deary-Wood
Gov. Steve Cowper	Rev. Virgil Crone	Patricia Daft	Tito David	Mr. & Mrs. Miska
Cynthia Cox	Christi Cronin	Elaine Dagget	Art Davidson	Deatphon
Dana Cox	Lucy Cronin	Lana Dahl	Bill Davidson	Tim DeBoer
Dennis Cox	Patrick T. Cronin	Cindy Dahlen	Dan Davidson	Cheryl DeBose
Diann Cox	Al Cronk	Jeremiah Dahlen	Dave Davidson	Olga DeCesare
Ginger Cox	Chuck Crosby	John M. Dahlen	Georgia Davidson	Sandy DeCesare
Kathy Cox	Don Cross	Kim Dailey	Gloria Davidson	Meredith Decker
Linda Cox	Emily Cross	Bobby Daily	Rhodi Karella	Ben Decon
Loretta Cox	Grace Cross	Darrell Daily	Davidson	Ron Dedo
Lorie Cox	Jeanette Cross	Dorothy Daily	Robert Davidson	Carol Dee
Lydia Cox	Thomas Cross	Jason Daily	Roy Davie	Justin DeFluiter
Mark Cox	Karen Crossley	Jennifer Daily	Vonnie Davie	Cathy Dehaan
Richard Cox	Barbara Crouch	John Daily	Willie Davie	Kevin Dehaan
Skip Cox	Debbie Crouch	Kimberly Daily	Christine Davies	Christina DeHart
Carl H. Coy	Steve Crouch	Theresa Daily	Lydia Davies	J.M. Deiser
Kathleen Coyle	John Crouse	Toni Daily	W. Davies	Jeff Deiser
Jay Craft	Tad Crowe	Rich Daise, DVM	Ann Davis	April Delancy
Bob Craig	Bob Crowley	Ron Dalby	Arlene Davis	John (J.D.) DeLancy
Dr. A. Morrie Craig	Neal Crozier	Dixie Dale	Betty Davis	Tonya Delancy
Dr. Leland Craig	Teddy Crump	Norv Dallin	Brian Davis	Joan Delaquito
James Craig	Carolyn Crusey	Phyllis Dallin	Chris Davis	Gail DeLeo
Larry Craig	David Crusey	Charles F. Dalton	Dave Davis	Mary Lou DeLey
Linda Craig	Ray Cuhill	Eugene Dalton	Jack Davis	Rae DeLey
Carolyn Craig-Adair	Jeremy Cummings	Mary L. Dalton	James E Davis	Christine Delia
Ginny Crain	Kevin R. Cummings	William Daly, DVM	John Davis	Joe Delia
Irene Craine	Linnea Cummings	Curt Damien	Karen Davis	Norma Delia
Patric Cramer	Margo Cummings	Marc Damien	Laura Davis	Pat Delia
Pat Crammer	Valentine B. Cummings	Lora Damon	Mary Ann Davis	Gilbert Delkittle
Ken Crampton, Jr.	Robby Cummins	Bill Dan	Mike Davis	Betsy Delp
Dianne Crandall	Annabelle	John Daniel	Pamela Davis	Brenda Delp
Gary Crandall	Cunningham	Hugh Daniell	Patti Davis	Ken Delp
Al Crane	Ben Cunningham	Danny Daniels	Paul Davis	Arben Dema
Ed Crane	Brad Cunningham	Harry Daniels	Richard Davis	Tom Demands
Jo Crane	Bud Cunningham	Roz Daniels	Scott Davis	Lori A. Demarest
Sue Crane	Dave Cunningham	Tom Daniels	Sgt. Davis	Rosa DeMelo
John Crane	Lou Cunningham	Jeanne Danison	Sherrie Davis	Bernie Dementioff

Paul Demila	Peggy Dick	Arlene Dobkowski-	Jay Dougherty	Christopher Dunbar
Paul K. Demillia	Rosanna L. Dickens	Marlar	Bob Douglas	Lance Dunbar
James Demoski	Amelia Dickenson	Mark Dobkowski-	Clara Douglas	Robert Dunbar
Nina Demoski	Doug Dickenson	Marlar	Darin Douglas	Anthony Duncan
Rudy Demoski	Janie Dickerson	Steve Dobkowski-	Donald Douglas	Christopher Duncan
Valentine B Demoski	Steve Dickerson	Marlar	Gary Douglas	Cliff Duncan
Bianca DeMoss	Chris Dickey	Allen Docter	J.R. Douglas	Jeff Duncan
D. Dendall	Marion Dickjose	Glenn Dodd	Ray Douglas	Lynne Duncan
David Denenea	Robert Dickson	Bev Dodge	Deb Douglass	Shawna Duncan
Jason Denis	Jean M. Dieden, DVM	Michele Dodge	Donald Douma	Carol Dunham
Leda Denka	Marinda Diel	Vicki Doggett	Patricia Doval	Jim Dunham
Carol Dennert	Christopher Diem	Debbie Doherty	Micaela Dover	Lloyd Dunham
Rich Dennert	Lisa Diem	Ed Doherty	Forest Dow	Harris Dunlap
Carl Dennis	Rocelle Diem	Debbie Dolan	Wendi Dow	Jerry Dunlap
John Dennis	Wrex Diem	Jerry Dolan	Jeff Dowd	Ron Dunlap
Luke Dennis	Dana Diemer	Tom Dolan	Dan Dowding	Albert Dunlevy
Nick Dennis	Hilda Dienes	Cheryl Dold	Richard Dowling	Dennis Dunlevy
Richard Dennis	Dana Dietz	Joe Dold	Carol Downey	Jean Dunlevy
Verdresia Dennis	Drew Dietz	Rita Dold	Joel Downey	Paul Dunlevy
Charlotte Dennison	Jerry Dietz	Glenn Dole	Julie Downey	Cindy Dunn
Bruce Denton	Norm Dietz	Rosey Dolenz	Michael Downs	Darlene Dunn
Donna Denton	Boxley Diggs	Scott Dolginow,	Doug Doyld	Maureen Dunn
Gavin Denton	Lunwonda Diggs	DVM	Florence Doyle	Pat Dunn
Hali Denton	Andy DiGiovanni	Kathi Dolowy	Kelly Drago	Paul Dunnington
Kelda Denton	Pat Dillard	Bob Dolphin, DVM	Marge Dragseth	Elka Dupps
Sharon Denton	Bob Dillon	Mike Dolson	Frank Drake	Bunny Durbrow
Arleen Dentz	Carol Dillon	Ken Doman	Olav Dregelid	Ann Dure
Travis DePeu	Tricia Dillon	John Dombovy	Jackie Drew	Fred Dure
Steve Deptule	Ron Diltz	Jim Donahue	Robert Driscoll	Fran Durner
Steve Dercog	Judy DiMaria	Pat Donahue	W.D. "Bill" Droke	Joyce Duss
Veronica Dercog	Toni DiMaria	Arleene Doney	Diana Dronenburg	Marcia Duss
Matt Desalernos	Dannielle Dimeglio	J.M. Donk	John Dronenburg	Dutch Dutcher
Sara Desalernos	Holly Dimeglio	Jori Donk	Muriel Dronenburg	Judy Duvall
Marcia Deschedeness	Jim Dinus	Marcie Donnetti	Jackie Dropps	Mary Duvall
Brad Desy	Kathryn Dinus	Scott Doobie	Don Drummond	Rich Duyick
Eric Desy	Lianne Dinwiddie	David Doods	John Dubek	AmyJo Dwecke
Michael Dever	Punkie Dirk	Jim Doore	Kirk Dubie	Maureen Dwyer
Bill Devine	John Dirks	John Doore	Scott Dubie	Chris Dyess
Jim Devine	Linda Dirks	Susan Doore	Terry Dubie	Jim Dyess
J. Michael Devitt	Lillian DiSalvi	Mary Lou Dordin	John Dudek	Chris Dyroff
Wanda Devlin	Linda Distad	Tom Dordin	Carol Duey	Chris Dzurovcin
Julia DeVore	Carolyn DiStasio	Frank Dorman	Harold Duff	Dean Dzurovcin
Tricia DeVries	Brett Dittlinger	Maria Dorman	Courtny Duffin	Elaine Eager
Fran Dewan	Jim Dittlinger	Mary Lou Dorman	Jim Duffy	Jim Eakin
Fred Dewey	Marge Dittlinger	Sally Dorman	Karrey Duffy	Pat Eakin
Carol DeWise	Christine Dittrich	Brandon Dorney	Stacy Duggins	Ben Eakon
Jean DeWise	Tim Dittrich	Pat Dorntrovich	Mary DuHoux	Valerie Eames
Bob Dexheimer	Steve Ditty	John Dorscher	Becky Duhr	Jesse Earl
Joe Dexter	Matt Divens	Jim Dory	Larry Duke	Mary Earl
Paul Dexter	Drew Dix	Thami Doss	Veronica Duke	Colleen Easley
Dorothy Diamond	Whitney Dix	Brenda Dotomain	Eric Dunaway	Beth Eassa
Joyce Diamond	Luther Dixon	Sean Dotomain	Howard Dunaway	Bill Eastham
Albert Dias, Jr.	Aletia Dobkowski-	Bob Doucette	Anthony Dunbar	Billy Eastham
Allan Dick	Marlar	Doug Dougherty	Cathy Dunbar	Rich Eathorne

Eugene Eaton, Jr.
Dale Ebben
Judy Ebelcurtis
Lari Eby
Lorelie Eby
John Eckels
Sue Eckels
Willa Eckenweiller
John Ecker
Dan Eckert
Patricia Eckert
Cassie Eckhardt
Rose Eckhoff
Jim Eckles
Diana Ede
Ella Ede
Julia Ede
Andy Edge
Erv Edge
Donna Edmonds
Tom Edmonds
Brenda Edmonson
Jeff Edmundson
Jo Edmunson
John Edmunson
John Edmunson, Sr.
Alex Edwards
Benny Edwards
Jason Edwards
Karl Edwards
Kelly Edwards
Tim Edwards
Laurie Egge
Jane Egger, DVM
Beth Ehrhart
Don Eickoff
Cathrine Eide
Al Eischens
John Eisenhower
Barbara Eishens
Judy Ekada
Martina Ekada
Ruth Ekern
Neil Eklund
Fran Elam
Bill Elander
Lynn Elander
Michael Eldridge
Pamela Eldridge
Laurie Elfstrom
John Elgee
Aletia Elkins
Carole Elkins
Rochelle Elkins

Susan Elkins
Donna Ellanna
Lisa Ellanna
George Elledge
Jim Ellic
Dennis Ellinger
Karen Elliot
Lynda Elliott
Mark Elliott
David Ellis
Jim Ellis
Lois Ellis
Ray Ellis
Scott Ellis
Mary Ellison
Jan Ellisworth
Candi Elmer
Denali Elmore
Jay Elmore
John Elmore
Scott Elmore
David Elson
David Elston
Speedy Elstub
Cheryl Eluska
Jennifer Eluska
George Ely
Heidi Ely
Priska Emmenegger
Lila Emmer
Carl Emmonds
Ron Emond
Virginia Emond
Katheryn Enge
Christina Engholm
Jori Engholm
Cynthia England
Kathryn Engle
Tom Englestrom
Cindy English
Connie English
Lois English
Michael English
Sandy English
Ted English
Vicki English
Bill Engstrom
Kersten Engstrom
Tom Engstrom
Amy Entwisle
Warren Enyeart
Jan Eppard
Marv Eppard
Clay Epperson

Mike Eppler
Rosanna Eppler
Zanna Eppler
Jack Epply
Dave Epstein
Holly Erb
Bruce Erickson
Cynthia Erickson
Denise Erickson
Don Erickson
Fred Erickson
Glory Erickson
Kathy Erickson
Mitch Erickson
Nancy Erickson
Richard Erickson
Rick Erickson
Vicky Erickson
Chad Ericson
Chris Ericson
Galen Ericson, DVM
Karrey Ericson
Sean Ericson
Conne Ernst
John Esai
Margaret Esai
Ted Esai
Bobby Esai, Jr.
Brunhilde Eska
Dave Eskeldson
Marge Eskeldson
Don Eskra
Dan Esler
Aggie Esmailka
Christina Esmailka
Claude Esmailka
Cynthia Esmailka
Florence Esmailka
Harold Esmailka
Howard Esmailka
Josephine Esmailka
Larry Esmailka
Randy Esmailka
Jose Esquibel
Bushra Essayad
Dennis Esslinger
George Esslinger
Steven Eteukeok
Priscilla Etherington
Al Eustice
Albert Evans
Bob Evans
Carolyn Evans
Darrel Evans

David Evans
Debbie Evans
Jack Evans
Jason Evans
Joni Evans
Julie Evans
Marcie Evans
Marge Evans
Melva Evans
Joni L Evens
Benjamin Everett
Bill Everett
Frank Everett
Ingrid Everson
Doug Ewen
Audrey Ewin
Gail Ewin
Rod Ewing
Alan Ezel
John Fabrizio
Bill Fagerholm
Kathy Fagerholm
Floyd Fagerstrom
Helen Fagerstrom
Larry Fagerstrom
Peggy Fagerstrom
Brian Fahee
Denise Faickser
Joe Fail-Kramer
Marcia Fail-Kramer
Bobby Fain
David Fair
Holly Fair
Ellen Fairbanks
Mary Fairbanks
Tony Fairbanks
Dale Falk
Ed Faller
Shaun Fallon
Susan Fallon
Michael Fanizzi
Pat Fanizzi
Susan Fanizzi
Karl Fannin
Liz Fannin
Kathy Faraci
Liz Farber
Pam Farkas
Andy Farless
Chugie Farley
Howard Farley
Jeanette Farley
Julie Farley
Missey Farley

Betty Farmer
Bill Farmer
Dave Farmer
Kyle Farmer
Paul Farmer
Rochelle Farmer
John Farnan
Travis Farnes
Sam Farney
Jean Farnham
Robbie Farnsworth
Jim Farrell
Susan Farrell
Tom Farrington
Jon Farrow
Samuel Fassig, DVM
Lynda Fast
Mary Fast
Dorothy Fatheringha
Kimsley Faulkner
Sue Faulkner
Bev Faultersack
Robert Faultersack
Tracy Faville
Richard Fawson
Jeff Fay
Jennifer Feavel
Michael Feavel
Keith Febrick
Mary Fechner
Steve Fee
Helene Feiner
Bill Fejes
Marjorie Feldberg
Christina Felker
Pam Felker
Jack Felton
Alfred Fennewald
Jeanette Fennimore
Mabel Fennimore
Mr. & Mrs. Keith
  Fenrich
David Ferguson
Diane Ferguson
Morris Ferguson
Linda Ferkenhofer
Richard Fern
Michale Fernadez
Mary Lou Ferrante
Pat Ferrari
G. Ferrell
Joanne Ferrell
John Ferri
Sister Ferrin

David Ferguson
David Fetzner
Elaine Fibranz
Connie Ficcaglia
Kevin Ficcaglia
Durinda Fields
J.R. Fields
Jerome Fields
Charlie Finch
Jeremiah Finch
Gary Fincher
Bill Fink
Joann Fink
Mayor Tom Fink
Elder Finley
Pete Finley
Pete Fiorey
Dennis J. Fiorucci
Bill Firmin
Sue Firmin
Tanya Firmin
Dennis Firucci
Judy Fischer
Deborah Fiscus
DeeDee Fish
Martha Fishback
Mel Fishback
Elder Fishbeck
Bill Fisher
Brad Fisher
Carol Fisher
Chad Fisher
David Fisher
Jay Fisher
Kael Fisher
Ken Fisher
Larry Fisher
Margo Fisher
Minnie Fisher
Olin Fisher
Rick Fisher
Phil Fisk
James Fiske
Kevin Fiske
Debbie Fison
Jerry Fitka
Heather Fitts
Mark Fitts
Dave Fitzgerald
Jeannie Fitzgerald
Kathy Fitzgerald
Kim Fitzgerald
Mary Fitzgerald
Mille Fitzgerald

Peggy Fitzgerald
Mollie Fitzsimons
Pat Fix
Dan Flaherty
Mary Flaherty
Steve Flanagan
Frank Flavin
Wayne Fleek
Bob Flegle
Harold Flegle
Helen Fleischauer
Jan Fleischer
Barbara Fleming
Bob Fleming
Dolly Fleming
Jim Fleming
Kathy Fleming
Lynn Fleming
David Fletcher
Josephine Fletcher
Ryan Fletcher
Robert Flint
Carla Flodin
Dan Flodin
Julia Flodin
Mabel Flodin
Ron Flodin
Steve Flodin
Johnny Flood
Mark A. Flower
Len Flowers
Pam Flowers
Charles Floyd
Jerry Floyd
Kazuko Floyd
Susan Floyd
Shawna Flynn
Carolyn Foelsch
Bob Folk
David Folk
Steve Folley
Bob Folz
Melvin Folz
Jeff Fondy
George Fong
Kathy Fong
Bob Foote
Kevin Foote
Ed Foran
John Forbes
Mark Forbes
Dan Ford
Don Ford
Jeron Ford

Joe Ford
Julie Ford
Karen Ford
Ken Ford
Patty Ford
Rick Ford
Warren Ford
Connie Fordham
Jeff Fore
Ellen Foreman
Judy Foreman
Pete Foresger
Kenny Forest
Bill Forman
Marge Forman
Pam Forness
Susan Forness
Liz Forrer
Wassillie Forrer
Mike Forrester
Audra Forsgren
Denise Forsgren
Dick Forsgren
Ellen E. Forsgren
Keith Forsgren
Kyle Forsgren
Christina
  Fortenberry
Curt Fortenberry
Randy Forth
Brian Fortney
Don Fortney
James Fortney
Mary Fortney
Joanne Fosdick
Brad Foss
Bart Foster
Beth Foster
Bill Foster
Carol Foster
Cindy Foster
Eric Foster
Evie Foster
Hande Foster
Jim Foster
Judith Foster
Marsi Foster
Michael Foster
Presley Foster
Rep. Richard Foster
Sherry Foster
Steve Foster, DVM
Susan Foster
Deborah Foukers

Kevin Fouts
Paul Foutz
Rae Foutz
Tom Fowler
Anne Fox
Cheryl Fox
Keith Fox
Lari Fox
Lou Fox
Pam Fox
Rob Fox
Mark Foxworthy
Jeff Foy
Deno Frakes
Terry Frakes
Josh Frame
Linda Frame
Margo Francis
Dot Frandsen
Ed Frandsen
Carolyn Frank
Diane Frank
Kevin Frank
Pam Frank
Robbie Frankevich
Al Franszman, DVM
Richard Frantz
Sheila Frantz
Gloria Frazier
Joann Frazier
Karen Frazier
Robert D. Frazier
Rusty Frazier
H.C. Fredenberg
Jim Fredenhagen
Victoria Fredenhagen
Rita Frederick
Sandee Frederick
Jackie Frederickson,
  DVM
Paul Frederickson,
  DVM
Malcolm Neal
  Fredstrom
Abby Freedman
Bill Freeman
Olen W. Freeman
Olin Freeman
Pamela Freeman
Robert Freeman
Elizabeth Freener
Kael Freese
Larry Freese
James French

Bob Frerichs
Connie Frerichs
Darla Frerichs
Lucas Frerichs
Ryan Frerichs
Sara Lynn Frerichs
Larissa Frey
Andrew Frick
Sally Frick
Sharon Frick
Lynn Fricke
Patty Friend
Kathy Frigon
Robert Frigon
Rosanne Frigon
Warren Frigon
William Frisby
Cyndy Fritts
Keegan Fritts
Rob Fritts
Zach Fritts
Carl Fritzler
Vicky Fritzler
Arlene Frost
Dennis Frost
Jack Frost
Bob Frutchay
Chrisy Fry
Becky Fryzek
John Fryzek
Mark Fuerstenau
Sara Jean Fujioka
Taro Fujita
Allen Fuller
C.T. Fuller
Fletcher Fuller
Gale Fuller
Lloyd Fuller
Mrs. Lee Fuller
Nancy Fuller
Stacey Fuller
Vicki Fuller
C. J. Fullmer
Jeron Fullmer
Betty Fulton
Judy Fulton
Tony Funk, DVM
Paul Fussey
Aaron Futhey
Dan Fvlen
Dan Gaber
Steve Gaber
Dottie Gabrielli
Ralph Gabrielli

Daniel Gabryszak
Jean Gabryszak
Jeanette Gabryszak
Joseph Gabryszak
Kimber Gabryszak
Cass Gadonski
Gerald Gadonski
Cheri Gagnon
Jeff Gagnon
Eddie Gainer
Bea Gaines
David Gaing
Steven L. Gaini
Christine Gallagher
Debbie Gallagher
Jim Gallagher
Karen Gallagher
Blaine Gallaher
Dick Gallaher
Joyce Gallaher
Dr. Bill Gallea
Brian Galleger
Gail Galleher
George Gallis
Carol Gallo
Frank Gallo
Elder Galloway
Jayson Galloway
Neil Galosich
Carlton Gamash
Pam Gamash
Kelly Gamble
Sherrie Gamechuck
Wassillie Gamechuck
Frank Ganley
Jerry Ganopole
John Gans
Ellen E. Gantly
Jimmy Gantly
Dustin Garcia
Jose Garcia
Rachelle Garcia
Sandi Garcia
Ted Garcia
Elder Gardner
Marie Gardner
Ray Gardner
Zachery Gardner
Amy Garlett
Will Garlett
Cheryl Garnder
Gary Garnder
B.J. Garner
Bonnie Garner

Cheryl Garner
Hande Garner
James Garner
Liz Garner
Monica Garner
Gloria Garnett
Joe Garnie
Diane Garrett
Mary Garrett
Pat Garrett
Paul Garrett
Tina Garrett
Joyce Garrison
Marie Garrison
Mark Garrison
Melissa Garrison
George Garten
John Gartiez
George Gartrell
Judy Gartrell
Red Garvey
Mike Gascoigne, DVM
Herman Gates
Naomi Gates
Shannon Gates
Tex Gates
Tony Gatts
Cece Gaul
Rusty Gaul
Betty Gaunt
Robert Gaunt
Mark Gausis
Myron Gavin
Mike Geedly
John Geer
Steve Gehring
Susan Geldert
Elder Gemar
Graig Gemer
Kathy Genna
Pascale Gennin
Ariana Gentile
Craig Gentile
Gerry Gentile
Nita Gentile
Bill Gentry
Darla Gentry
Donna Gentry
Larry Gentry
Pat Gentry
Robert Gentry
Sylvia Gentry
Tom George, DVM

Hank George
Linda George
Otis George
Sara Lynn George
Vito Gerante
Carole Gerard
J.B. Gerber
Linda Gerber
Phil Gerdes
Marlene Gerhart
Frank Gerjevic
Larry Gerkie
Darla Gerlach
Fred Gerlach
Rudolph "Bud" Gerling
Ron Gerton
Norma Gertson
Mark Getout
Susan Getty
Chris Geurin
Earl Geurin
Kim Geurin
Renae Geurin
Sandy Geurin
Bobbi Geyer
Steve Giani
Alice Gibbons
Ray Gibbons
Dana Gibbs
Anne Gibson
Sandy Gibson
Michele Gicault
Sara Giddings
Fr. Alfred Giebel
Delbert L. Gieber
Mary Ann Gietzen
Ellen Gigliotti
Bobbi Gilbert
Robert Gilbert, DVM
Orville Gilbert
Terry Gilbert
Bonita Gile
Howard Gile
Al Giles
Laura Gilfillan
Rosanne Gilfillan
Christine Gilgus
Todd P. Gillespi
Anita Gillespie
Debbie Gillespie
Johnny Gillespie
Anita Gillette

Scott Gilliland
Steve Gillon
Jackie Gillum
Gene Gilman
Orville Gilman
Rocelyn Gilman
Rome Gilman
Zachary Gilman
Wayne Gilmore
Hoar Gilpin
Neil Gimenes
Paula Gimerek
Mary Ginro
Meg Girard
Scott Girard
Denny Gladwin
Angie Glandien
C.J. Glasser
Sally Glasser
Bob Glassmaker
John Glavez
Dana Glavich
Lynette Glavich
Ed Glavinic
Jacqui Glavinovich
Laura Glazier
Candace Gleason
Jon Gleason
Barb Glick
Bill Glisson
Alex Glover
Dale Glover
Derek Glover
Jeff Glover
Laron Glover
Marty Glover
Sharon Glover
Tom Glover
Lisa Glynn
Paula Gmerek
Elizabeth Goad
Patricia Goard
Sylvia Goard
Ken Gober
Boyd Gochanour
Therese Gochanour
Pat Gochenauer
Madeline Gocke
Mike Godby
Gerald Goddard
Ken Goddard
Sue Godwin
Patrick Goeck
Linda Goff

Barbara Goldbaugh
Carlton Goldbaugh
Jim Golden
Dawn Goldman
Lieudell Goldsberry
Vic Goldsberry
David Goldstein
Gail Golmski
Mark Golmski
Ryan Gologergan
Galen Gologergen
Tammy Gologergen
Tim Gologergen
Gail Golomski
Mark Golomski
Agnes Gonzalez
Aubrey Gonzalez
Manny Gonzalez
Rod Gonzalez
Sherrie Gonzalez
Jimmy Good
Kirk Good
Lisa Good
Kelly Goode
Marvin Goodenough
Rhonda Goodenough
Ronnie Goodenough
Clinton Goods
Kathy Goodwin
Mike Goodwin
Valerie Goodwin
Dave Goodyear
Shirley Gordon
Anne Gore
Brad Gore
Kit Gorrell
Fred Gorsch
Gage Gorsuch
Teresa Gorsuch
Sister Gose
Kathryn Gossard
Roy Gossard
Elizabeth Gosse
Becky Gottschalk
Chuck Gottschalk
Jim Gould
Judy Gould
Phyllis Gould
Robert Gould
Ron Gould
Steve Goulette
Jennifer Gourley
John Gourley
Dan Govoni

Pamela P. Grabicki
Gretchen Grabowender
Annette Grady
Michael Graes
Charles Graham
Cory Graham
Dave Graham
Diane Graham
Ellis Graham
Gary Graham
Hal Graham
Heather Graham
Katherin Graham
Matt Graham
Mike Graham
Pamela Graham
Renne Graham
Steve Graham
Tami Graham
O. Dean Gramling
Gloria Grandaw
Dominique Grandjean, DVM
Van Grange
Barry Granlund
Darnelle Gransburg
Tracy Grant
Susan Grant-Henky
Jenny Grass
Kathy Grass
Maria Grass
Mrs. S.L. Grasse
Elder Grastiet
Jill Grastiet
Mark R. Graves, DVM
Leroy Graves
Michael Graves
Rod Graves
Roy Graves
Bernice Gray
B.J. Gray
Blythe Gray
Derek Gray
Don Gray
LaRae Gray
Monica Gray
Todd Gray
Tom Gray
Tim Grearson
Glen Greeley
Becky Green
David Green
Kenny Green

Kim Green
Lonnie Green
Marylynn Green
Mike Green
Paul Green
Rick Green
Andy Greenblatt
Fran Greene
Guy Greene
Jeanie Greene
Jody Greene
Kenny Greene
Warren Greene
Kenneth Greene, Sr.
Sue Greenly
Richard Greenwood
Tree Greenwood
David Gregg
Robert Gregg
Joaquin Gregory
Lawrence Gregory
Nadine Gregory
Katie Greim
Robert Greineisen
Marge Gresham
Max Gretzinger
Curtis Grey
Joe P. Griesa
Jens Griessl
Bob Griffin
Jack Griffin
Judy Griffin
Michael Griffin
Bill Griffith
Claudia Griffith
Phillis Griffith
Scott Griffith
Carolyn H. Griffitts, DVM
Cindy Griggs
Frank Griggs
Reba Griggs
Leon Grigoropoulos
Dan Grimes
Liz Grimes
Mona Grimes
Paul Grimes
Tanya Grimes
Michael Grimm
Mary Grisco
Dick Grissom
Cece Grives
Vincent R. Grives
Jewell Grizzle

Julie Grizzle
Connie Groat
Logan Groomer
Wayne Groomer
Leigh Anne Grooms
Kendall Grose
Dawn Groth
Amy Grout
Beverly Grout
Jason Grout
Randy Grout
Ed Grove
Maxine Grove
Pat Grove
William Grove
Tim Groves, DVM
Kelly Grubaugh
Mike Grundburg
Barry Grunlund
Christine Gual
Sharon Gudde
Clark Gudnundsen
Bill Guerry
Laurie Guerry
Alfred Guertler, Jr.
Bill Guest
Joyce Guest
Linda Guest
June Guido
Amn Aaron Guill
Cornelius Guillory
Roy Gullidge
Stephanie Gulliford
Joan Gunning
J.R. Guntler
Alfred Gurtler
Ed Gurtler, Sr.
Betty Gustafson
Ernie Gustafson
Shirley Gustafson
Mary Guthridge
Gary Guy
Carol Guzy
Clark Gwaltney
Sylvia Gwaltney
Edward Gwilym
Hanne Gwilym
Linda Gwilyn
Marsha Haas
Terra Haas
Charlie Haase
Harry Haase
Linda Haase
Lawrence Habig

Roger A.F. Habisreutinger
Stefan Habluetzel
Roger Hackett
Ted Hackman
Todd Hackman
Becky Hackney
Fred Hackney
Phyllis Hackney
Dawn Haddock
Mark Hadley
Jean Haesing
Lloyd Haessler
David Hafoka
Marsha Hagbo
Gerry Hagel
Louise Hagel
Caroline Hageland
Katy Hagen
Terry Hagen
Jane Hager
John Hager
Paul Hager
Chuck Hagerty
Jenny Haggar
Bob Haggarty
Fiona Haggett
Kari Hahn
Kavik Hahn
Ken Hahn
Laura Hahn
Pat Hahn
Roy Hahn
Amy Haigler
Sally Haigler
Tracy Hailey
Christopher Hainen
Milissa Haire
Elizabeth Halberg
Marte Halberg
Michael Halby
Debbie Hale
Jack Hale
John Hale
Ken Hale
Mitch Hale
Theresa Hale
Mitch Hale, Sr.
Rick Halford
Barbara Hall
Bill Hall
Dave Hall
F. Jean Hall
Fran Hall

Gloria Hall
Jeff Hall
Jim Hall
Jonathan Hall
Lily Hall
Linda Hall
Mary Hall
Pam Hall
Raine Hall
Tom Hall
Leo Hallgren
Vicki Hallstrom
Brad Halvensleben
Dee Halverson
Duane Halverson
Eric Halverson
Lara Halverson
Rick Halverson
Annie Hamberger
Laurie Hamberger
Ron Hamberger
Linda Hamel
Sandy Hamelton
Angie Hamill
Tom Hamill
Adolph Hamilton
Arnold Hamilton
Aubrey Hamilton
Brad Hamilton
Hamilton E. Hamilton
Hammil Hamilton
James Hamilton
Jeff Hamilton
Joe Hamilton
Rudy Hamilton
Sally Hamilton
Sandy Hamilton
Sara Hamilton
Tina Hamilton
Wani Hamilton
Wayne Hamilton
Ken Hamm
Sally Hamm
Clarence Hammer
Dianne Hammer
Gerd Hammerling, DVM
Todd Hammert
Cheryl Hammond
Don Hammond
Gov. & Mrs. Jay Hammond
Suzanne Hammond

Tammy Hanabuth	Sharon Hardin	Jason Hart	Ginny Hayes	Wayne Henderson	Bob Herrett	Josh Hill	Lisa Hodge Moser	Rocky Honea	Sarah Hotchkiss
Raymond A. Hanbeck	Dave Harding	Jim Hart	Shelia Hayes	Heide Hendrick	Nicholas R. Herrick, DVM	Kristine Hill	Ed Hodges	Don Honea, Jr.	Mark Hottmann
Dana Handeland	James Harding	Larry Hart	Brandy Haylor	F. Jean Hendricks	Michelle Herrick	Lexi Hill	Jeanne Hodges	Donald Honea, Sr.	Patti Hottmann
Ingeborg Handeland	Ben Hardwick	Lee Hartenstein	Ralph Haymond	Jim Hendricks	Helen Herriet	Linda Hill	Sandra Hodges	John Hones	Mitchell Houck
John Handeland	Todd Hardwick	Lois Harter	Susan Haymond	John Hendricks	Holly Herron	Mark Hill	Mary Hoffheimer, DVM	Patti Hong	Rae Houck
Linda Handeland	Dr. R. L. Hardy	Kelly Hartline	Randy Haynes	LaVonn Hendricks	Pat Herron	Robert Hill		Steve Honnold	Terry Houck
Del Handrath	Jamie Hardy	Michelle Hartline	Sheila Hays	Mary Hendricks	Paul Herron	Robin Hill	Buz Hoffman	Mary Honsberger	Jason Houctchins
Rosemary Handrath	Jeff Hardy	Crystal Hartman	Mary Hayward	Nancy Hendricks	Alice Hershmar	Rubin Hill	Liz Hoffman, DVM	Norm Hood	Angie Houden
Re Handren	John R. Hardy	Elaine Hartman	Brian Hayward, Jr.	Rose Ida Hendricks	Helen Herston	Susan Hill	Guy Hoffman	Stan Hoofard	Colleen Hough
Lance Hankins	Len Hardy	George Hartman	Roy Hayward, Jr.	Dave Hendrickson	Jerry Herston	Tom Hill	Lavern Hoffman	Linda Hoogendorn	Thomas Hough
Dick Hanks	Leon Hardy	Jill Hartman	Kim Heacox	Elaine Hendrickson	Joe Herte	Vern Hill	Linda Hoffman	B.J. Hoogendorn	June Houlton
Donna Hanks	Pat Hardy	Paul Hartman	Beth Head	John Hendrickson	Keith Herte	Steve Hillborn	Margaret Hoffman	Don Hook	Timothy Housand
Kirk Hannah	Terri Hardy	Butch Hartung	Laurie Head	Scott Hendrickson	Robin Herter	Bob Hiller	Martha Hoffman	Jack Hooker	Patti House
Raymond D. Hannah	Joe Harmon	Lyle Hartzell	Chuck Heath	Danny Hendrix	Jeri Hespen	Robin Hiller	Marty Hoffman, DVM	Stan Hooley	Katy Houser
Chris Hannan	Linda Harmon	Frank Harvey	Jasper Heath	Jimmie Hendrix	Chris Hess	Ron Hiller		Sally Hooper	Peg Houser
Jill Hannan	Mike Harness	Lois Harvey	Rita Heathman	Tom Henery	Fawn Hess	Bennie Hillsman	Patty Hoffman	Tom Hoosier	Tim Houssand
Betty Hannigan	Ramona Harness	Robert Harwood, DVM	Alice Hebel	Robert Henke	Mark Hess	Hank Hillsman	Stan Hoffman	Jim Hoover	Doug Houtzenhiser
Joe Hannigan	Keith Haroldsen		Jules Hebert	Charles E. Henley	Suanna Hester	Kim Hillsman	Thomas Hohl, DVM	Sally Hope	Angie Hovden
Michael Hannigan	Mona Haroldsen	Jim Hashman	Marcy Heckler	Sue Hennely	Connie Heston	Muriel Hillstrum	Michelle Hok	Carol Hopkins	Zoe Hovoa
Patty Hanrahan	Donna Harper	Brenda Hassinger	Amy Hedengeren	Steve Hennessy	Dian Heston	Lucy Hilpert	Cindy Hokkanen	J. Greg Hopkins	Elder Howard
Del Hanrath	Tommy Harrel	Chris Hassinger	Sharon Hedengeren	Kim Hennigan	Christi Heussen	Jim Hilton	Donna Holand	Lin Hopkins	Belinda Howe
Rosemary Hanrath	Merrilee Harrell	Harry Hassinger	Timothy Hedge	Brad Henning	Melanie Hewitt	Ken Hinchcliff, DVM	Linda Holbeck	Angel Hopskins	Richard Howe
Ellen Hanratty	Cornelia Harrelson	Phyllis Hassinger	Jennifer Heffele	Chris Henning	Richard Hewitt		Don Holcomb	Mike Horan	Scott Howe
Tom Hanratty	Dan Harrelson	Rubin Hassinger	Denise Hefner	Toby Henning	Al Hibbard	Dan Hinckley	John Holder	Bill Horie	Bob Howell
Bert Hansen	Benjamin Harrington	Stephanie Hassler	Fred Hefner	Dale Hennings	Paul Hibbits	Sharon Hiner	Sylvia Holder	Cassie Horie	Mapel Howell
Danny Hansen	Mike Harrington	Art Hastings	Robin Hefty	Stretch Hennings	Bob Hickel	Cari Hinesly	Timothy Holder	Mike Horn	Owen Howell
Dennis Hansen	Susan Harrington	Carol Hastings	Elizabeth Hegarty	Sue Hennley	Gov. & Mrs. Wally Hickel	Larry Hinken	Dena Holee	Shirley Horn	Ray Howell
Derek Hansen	Vincent Harrington	Kahori Hatano	Eloise Hehl	Katie Henry		Scott Hinkley, DVM	Brian Holl	Katie Horne	Louise Howerter
Elder Hansen	Debi Harriot	James Hatfield	J.P. Hehl	Raymond D. Henry	Wally Hickel, Jr.	Ed Hinson	Dustin Holl	Kay Horne	Larry Howington
Gary Hansen	Charles Harris	Jean Hatfield	Danny M. Heilemann	Rick Henry	Teri Hickman	Jo-Al Hintz	Linda Holl	Mary Horne	Angie Hoyden
Heidi Hansen	Donna Harris	Phil Hatzfeld		Robin Henry	Kathy Sarns Hickock	Joan Hintz	Brett Holland	Mike Horne	Asger Hoyem
Jack Hansen	Dora Harris	Eugene Hauck	Marte Heilemann	Gary Hensley	Carrie Hicks	Margaret Hintz	Donna Holland	Ron Horne	Bob Hoyte
Kay Hansen	Dorothy Harris	E. M. Haugen	Terry Heilser	Wes Henson	Penny Hicks	Ty Hintz	Libby Lavon Holland	Ryan Walter Horne	Anne Hreck
Lars Hansen	Elmer Harris	Elsworth Haugen	Tim Hein	Sally Henyon	Diana Hidalgo	Chris Hirons	Michelle Holland	S.M. Horne	Chris D. Hreck
Nancy Hansen	Harry Harris	Jeanne Hauser	Mark Heinrich	Christy Hepler	Benjamin Hiedman	Margaret Hirons	Brian Hollen	Toby Horne	Victor Huaco
Roger Hansen	June Harris	Katy Hauser	Betty Heinz	Jerry Hepler	Ron Hiedman	Denise Hisey	Ray Hollenbeck	Tyler Horne	Joe Hubbard
Roy Hansen	Lana Harris	Larry Hauser	Ann Heisler	Kathy Hepler	Alan Higbie	Michelle Hisey	Nils Hollensbe	Gene Horning	Phil Hubbard
Scott Hansen	Larry Harris	Rick Havard	Bridgett Heisler	Gina Herley	Heather High	Sara Hisey	Sharon Hollensbe	Howard Hornsby	Steve Hubbard
Bert Hanson	Pete Harris	Laurel Haven	Steve Heitsmith, Jr.	Chris Herman	Curtis Hightower, DVM	Del & Bunky Hiskins	Terry Hollibah	Tom Horsey II	Tom Hubbard
Blythe Hanson	Ray Harris	Joan Havenner	Bill Helem	Fred Herman		Sean Hitchcock	Theresa Holliday	Tom Horsey III	Fawn Huber
Chris Hanson	Rich Harris	Steve Haver	Theresa Helem	Kay Herman	Tom Hightower	Arnold Hitchen	Ralph Hollis	Christi Horst	Nancy Hudock
Dick Hanson	Sharon Harris	Susan Hawk	Elaine Helling	Chris D. Hermannes	Karen Higley	Glen Hitchen	Elder Hollobaugh	Karl Horst	Denise Hudsen
Glen Hanson	Sonny Harris	Barbara Hawley	Ken Helm	Dennis Hermannes	Mike Hilburn	Harold Hitchen	James Hollobaugh	Babe Horton	James Hudsen
Larry Hanson	Tanya Harris	Butch Hawley	Vickie Helm	Marilyn Hermannes	Ray Hilburn	Tony Hite	David Holmes	Coleen Horton	Ed Hudson
Marilyn Hanson	Terry Harris	Jay Hawley	Bob Helms	Petra Hermannes	Kitty Hiler	Jeff Hittson	Liz Holmes	Joe Horton	Freida Hudspath
Reb Hanson	William Harris	Lisa Hawley	Jack Helms	John Hermans	Ron Hiler	Rick Hitz	Member Holsey	Kim Horton	Larry Huff
Tara Hanson	Leona Harrison	Annie Haxsy	Mary Helms	Gary Hermes	Sarah Hiler	Teja Hlacer	Carole Holt	Ray Horton	Richard Huff
Glen Hanway	Alexander Harshbarger	John Haxsy	Robert Helms	Art Hernandez	Alan F. Hill	Gerry Hoag	Danny M. Holthe	Robert Horton	Travis Huff
Dave Harang	Clark Harshbarger	Scott Hayden	Chris Hembach	Manuel Hernandez	Alexander Hill	Jess Hoag	Lisa Holthe	Petra Horvatic, DVM	Bill Huffman
Rich Harden, DVM	Barbara Hart	Kathy Hayenga	Denise Hembach	Minnie Hernandez	Chad Hill	Ervin Hobbs	Snow Holwill		Dave Huffman
Len Harden	Betsy Hart	Barry Hayes	Erica Hembach	June Herndin	Chester Hill	Carol Hoblitzell	Lou Holzknecht	Connie Hoseid	Neil Huffman
Kenneth Hardin	Brian Hart	Bob Hayes	Joel Hembach	Knox Herndon	James Hill	Diane Hodge	Billy Honea	Linda Hotchkiss	Nell Huffman
Sam Hardin	Gary Hart	Bogie Hayes	Barbara Hems	Betty Herning	Johnnie Hill	Hurshel Hodge	Johnny Honea	Monte Hotchkiss	Sue Huffman
		Elizabeth Hayes	Janie Hendershott	Janeen Herr		Leslie Hodge	Karen Honea	Nelda Hotchkiss	Tabby Huffman

Terry Huffman
Theresa Huffman
Dian Hughes
Kelly Hughes
Leanne Hughes
Nancy Hughes
Pat Hughes
Paul Hughes
Robert Hughes
Tina Hughes
Walter Hughes
Wilson Hughes
Renette Hulce
Marie Hulke
Dan Hull
Debbie Hull
Dennis Hull
Gary Hull
Ken Hull
Vern Humble
Sue Hume
Bob Hummel
Milton Hummer
Frank Humphrey IV
Brad Humselsine
R. Hundsnursche
Mark Hunt
Paula Hunt
Allison Hunter
Bob Hunter
Chester Hunter
David Hunter
Gidgette Hunter
Jim Hunter
Leslie Hunter
Mike Hunter
Pat Hunter
Rick Hunter
Robert Hunter
Ron Hunter
Scott Hunter
Carl Huntington
Leonhard Huntington
Roger Huntington
Sidney Huntington
Charles Hunziker
George Hurd
Ann Hurley, DVM
Pat Hurren
Tabitha Hurst
Babe Hurton
Colleen Hurton
Joe Hurton

Ray Hurton
Michael Huskisson
Margaret Huston
Sandra Huston
Robert Hutchings
Greg Hutchins
Bill Hutchinson
Bruce Hutchinson
Betty Hutchison
Paula Hutchison
Albert Huthen
Cassie Hutson
Margaret Hutson
Richard Hutson
Sandra Hutson
Jay Huwley
Reuben Huyck
Linda Huynh
Billie Jo Hviid
Helen Hviid
Linda Hviid
Nils Hviid
Sheri Hyder
Ron Hykes
Kitty Hyler
Ron Hyler
Sue Iaacheri
Craig Ide
Lisa Idell
Sandy Idell
Ken Ideus
Linda Idose
Denise Ihly
George Ihly
Jerry Ilkenhons
Sandy Ilkenhons
Linda Imle
Rudi Indermuhl
Patty Ingham
Cassie Ingraham
Mary Ingraham
Ron R. Inlow
Walt Inlow
Charles Inman
Ginger Ipock
Cathy Ippolito
Joe Ippolito
Laura Ippolito
Luigi Ippolito
Marge Ireland
Robert Irmiger, DVM
Bernard Irrioo
Charles Irvin
David Irvin

Marie Irvin
Allen Isabell
James Isabell
Fred Isgrigg
Marjorie Isgrigg
Roger Isgrigg
S.M. Isgrigg
Andrea Iske
Larry Ismelka
Irv Itchoak
Ed Iten
Kathy Ito
Ellen Ivanhoff
Albert Ivanof
Burkher Ivanoff
E. Jean Ivanoff
Karen Ivanoff
Liz Ivanoff
Maurice Ivanoff
Paul Ivanoff
Ryan Walter Ivanoff
Tyler Ivanoff
Russell Ivy
Jeremy Iyapana
Rex Iyatungauk
Alica Iyatunguk
Bill Iyatunguk
Larry Iyatunguk
Cathy Jablonski
Bill Jack
Penny Jack
Roden Jack
Thurman Jack
Peggy Jacks
Becky Bear Jackson
Jerry Jackson
Jimmy Jackson
Kurt Jackson
Lydia Jackson
Sandy Jackson
Donald Jacob
Linda Jacob
Paul Jacob
Ron Jacobs
Ben Jacobson
Jami Jacobson
Jeremiah Jacobson
Josh Jacobson
Louise Jacobson
Cheri Jacobus
Kazuma Jacobus
Kenneth Jacobus
Bob Jacoby
Ersa W. Jacoby

Jill Jahnke-Leland
Deanna James
Dennis James
Ernie James
Herman James
Kathleen James
Marty James
Mike James
Patty James
Robert James
Richard Jameson
Diane Jandl
Robert Jandl
Anderson Janie
Sara Jansen
Lone Janson
Gia Janyrin
Denise Jarrett
Moe Jarrett
Marina Jarvis
Michael Jarvis
Tom Jarvis
Ben Jason
Amy Jasper
Lacy Jasper
Mike Jausoro
Terry Jausoro
Dan Jaynes
Debbie Jayo
Bonnie Jeffers
Joe Jeffers
Anne Jeffery
Steve Jeffery
Joe Jeffreys
Mr. and Mrs.
   Jemawouk
Darlene Jemewouk
Paul Jendryk
Carl Jenkins
Carol Jenkins
Heather Jenkins
Roger Jenkins
Dottie Jenks
John Jennifer
Andrea Jennings
Gary Jennings
Gayle Jennings
Jay Jennings
Joanne Jennings
Nancy Jenrette
Bill Jensen
Chris Jensen
Jim Jensen
Kathleen Jensen

Steve Jensen
Sue Jensen
Tom Jensen
Clifford Jerue
Susan Jerue
Carl Jerue, Jr.
Carl Jerue, Sr.
Pete Jeskie
Susan Jeskie
Jenny Jessup
Sue Jessup
Jim Jett
Christine Jewett
Neil Jiricek
Bernard John
Brian John
David John
Harry John
Paul John
Will John
Sammy John, Jr.
Mike Johnnie
Thomas Johnnie
Anne Johns
Debbie Johns
Fred Johns
Al Johnson
Alan Johnson
Alex Johnson
Aurora Johnson
Becky Johnson
Bernard Johnson
Betty Johnson
Billy Johnson
Blane Johnson
Bonnie Johnson
Brenda Johnson
Bruce Johnson
Burton Johnson
Carl Johnson
Cassie Johnson
Charlie Johnson
Clayton Johnson
Cookie Johnson
David Johnson
Debbie Johnson
Diane Johnson
Don Johnson
Eric Johnson
Gail Johnson
Gary Johnson
Genevieve Johnson
Gidgette Johnson
Ginny Johnson, DVM

Glenda Johnson
Gus Johnson
Henry Johnson
Hugh Johnson
Jack Johnson
James Johnson
Jan Johnson
Jeffrey Johnson
Jeremy Johnson
Jerry Johnson
Jesstine Johnson
Jewis Johnson
Jill Johnson
Jim Johnson
John Johnson
Joie Johnson
Julie Johnson
Kari Johnson
Kathy Johnson
Keith Johnson
Ken Johnson
Kim Johnson
Lenard Johnson
Leonard L Johnson
Leslie Johnson
Linda Johnson
Lisa Johnson
Marvin J Johnson
Mary Johnson
Matt Johnson
Merlen Johnson
Merry Johnson
Michelle Johnson
Miki Johnson
Monique Johnson
Myrtle Johnson
Nicole Johnson
Norma Jean Johnson
Norman Johnson
Oren Johnson
Paul Johnson
Peter Johnson
R.J. Johnson
Ray Johnson
Richard Johnson
Robert Johnson
Ron Johnson
Sandy Johnson
Saran Johnson
Scott Johnson
Shane Johnson
Sharon Johnson
Spence Johnson
Steve Johnson

Tim Johnson
Todd Johnson
Tom Johnson
Travis Johnson
Tyler Johnson
Vivian Johnson
Warren Johnson
Wayne Johnson
Harry Johnson, Jr.
Bill Johnston
Elwin Johnston
Reuben Johnston
Beverly Jollenbeck
Brandy Jolly
Alan Jones
Ali Jones
Alison Jones
Art Jones
Bill Jones
Billie Jo Jones
Bob Jones
Carol Jones
Charles S. Jones
Christi Jones
Conie Jones
Dale Jones
Dava Jones
Eva Jones
Fred Jones
Freddie Jones
Glen Jones
Greg Jones
Guy Jones
Helen Jones
Janice Jones
Janis Jones
Jarod Jones
Jerry Jones
Jim Jones
Lisa Jones
Marion Jones
Mary Jones
Melissa Jones
Michael Jones
Pat Jones
Paul Jones
Ruyedeu Jones
Seldon Chico Jones
Fred Jones, Sr.
DeeDee Jonrowe
Mike Jonrowe
Mary Jonrowe
Lee Jordan
Shawn Jorgen
Melissa Jorgensen

S. Jorgenson
Danny B. Jorgenson
Marion Dick Jose
Paul Joseph
Jackie Joshua-Robb
Steve Joyce
Buck Judkins
An Judson
Pete Juliussen
Isaac Juneby
Diane Jung
Jimmy Jurgens
Deborah Kaczmarek
Diane Kadel
Sari Kadel
Steve Kadel
Sandy Kadonada
Shirley Kadonada
Chuck Kaess
Peter Kalamarides
Mark J. Kalbus
Chris Kalerak
Kraig Kalisch
Edgar Kalland
Ken Kaltschnee
Wanda Kaltschnee
Carolyn Kalwei
Gordan Kamholy
Joe Kane
Lori Kane
Terry Kangas
John Kannegard
Ernest Karas
Elizabeth Karasch
Ken Karasch
Frank Karash
Kimberly Kardonsky
Larry Kardonsky
Mary Kardonsky
Walt Kardonsky
Rhode Karella
Marty Karow
Bill Karp
Carlene Karp
Chris Karp
David Karp
Gena Karp
Jon Karp
Mary Karp
Melani Karp
Mary Karper
Gena Karpf
Cari Karpuleon
Barbara Karthaus

Carrie Karwoski
Diana Karwoski
Walter Kaso
Doug Katchatag
Joe Katchatag
Warren Katchatag
Karen Katchatag
Fred Katchatag, Jr.
Sheldon Katchataget
David Katongan
Millie Katongan
Chief Bob Kauer
E. Jean Kaufman
Sean Kaufman
Leslie Kaul
Mike Kaupper
Jerry Kauthen
Karen Kauthen
John Kautz
John Kautzner
Jim Kavolichiglgt
Jim Kayotawape
Norm Kayton
Floyd Kazuko
Marty Keef
Guido Keel
Vicki Keele
Donald Keelick
Vernell Keelick
Gary Keen
Jack Keeny
Sharon Keeny
Ann Keffalos
Chris Keffalos
Sgt. Keggivoch
Richard Keida
Kazuma Keiko
Mary Keiko
Albert Keil
Carolyn Keil
Liz Keil
Lori Keil
Kelly Keisling
Phillip Keith
Art Keller
Jane Keller
Jean Keller
Ken Keller
Dave Kelley
Shana Kelley
Ersa W. Kelley, Jr.
Steve Kelley, Jr.
Brandon Kelliher
Eddie Kelliher

Hannelore Kelliher
Mark Kelliher
Pat Kelliher
Trudy Kelliher
Anne Kelly
Carla Kelly
Dave Kelly
Frances Kelly
Gene Kelly
James Kelly
Jean Kelly
Lisa Kelly
Mike Kelly
Ray Kelsey
Jane Kelso
Paul Kelson
Chris Kelsor
Patsy Keltka
Gary Kemmerer
Kolin Kemmerer
Vicky Kemmerer
Bill Kendall
George Kendall
Rust Kendall
Tyra Kendall
Bill Kendig
Bobby Kennedy
Bruce Kennedy
Carolyn Kennedy
John Kennedy
Meme Kenny
John Kent
Michael Kent
Becca Kenyon
Jackie Kephart
Mark Keppler
Greg Kern
Kevin Kerns
Tom Kerns
Stephen M. Kerr, DVM
Jeanne Kerr
Jeff Kersetter
Michael Kershaw
Andy Kershner
Cathy Kershner
Dennis Kershner
Eleanor Kershner
Hugh Kershner
J.J. Kershner
Jim Kershner
Katie Kershner
Nancy Kershner
Trudi Kershner
Steff Kessler

Brenda Ketchie	Ann Kinne	Jim Knopke	Jan Korner	Jane Krumlauf	Terry Lamberson	Marilyn Lapine	Bud Laws	Karin Lehmkuhl	Daisy Lewis
Ralph Kettling	Jack Kinne	Erin Knotek	Jason Korosecz	Tamaara Krumlauf	Charles "Slim"	Pete LaPlante	Mary Laws	Kristrina Lehmkuhl	Turner Lewis, DVM
Robin Kettring	James Kintz	Bruce Knowles	Laura Kosell	Gary Krupneck	Lambert	Catherine Lappo	Marcie Lawson	Ted Lehne	Drew Lewis
Lawrence Ketzler	Spencer Kirbly	Gov. Tony Knowles	Frank Koskie	Karen Krupneck	Dee Lambert	Jay B. Lappo	Mark Lawson	Chris Lehnertz	Ed Lewis
Frank Keuhn	Colleen Kirby	Jean Knowlton	Chris Koskinson	Andrew Kruse	Diana Lambert	John Lappo	Bill Laxson	Paulette Lehuizamon	Jim Lewis
R. Kevin	Dan Kirby	George Knox	Michael Koskovich	Marlene Kruse	Lee Lambert	Kay Lappo	Bob Laxson	Lonnie Leibband	Kate Lewis
Eric Khale	James Kirby	Rick Knox	Hal Koslin	Bill Kruskie	Vernell Lambert	Jeannie Largent	Chuck Layton	Lou Leibband	Lynne Lewis
Oleg Khlopotine	Connie Kirchner	Saundra Knox	Rick Koso	Mike Kryder	Gene Lamke	Trudi Largent	Steven Layton	Michelle Leibold,	Marilyn Lewis
Jan Kiach	George Kirchner	Tom Knox	Fred Kost	Allen Kubaskie	Tony Lamm	Fern Larimer	Tabitha Layton	DVM	McKenzie Lewis
Rich Kieta	Veronica Kirer	Don Knudsen	Kristine Kost	Sean Kubaskie	Ernie Lammie	Marge Larimer	C.W. Layton, Jr.	Gerilynne Leidig	Mel Lewis
Wesley A. Kiker	Robert Kirkwood	John Knudsen	Rich Kostieu	Connie Kucharski	James Lamont	Stan Larimer	Jennifer Lazrus	Glenn Leidig	Mike Lewis
David Kilgore	Friz Kirsch	Nancy Knudsen	Eric Kostiner	Travis Kudrna	Jerome Lamont	Tara Larimer	Annie Leach	Linda Leigh	Robert Lewis
Anne Kilkenny	Doris Kirschhofer	Howard Knutson	Hal Kostlin	Tom Kuffel	Sarah Lamont	Bob Larman	Jim Leach, DVM	Michael Leigh	Rose Lewis
Jeanne Killer	Karen Kirsty	Sid Knutson	Dave Kotongan	Jennifer Kuiper	Michelle	Dan LaRose	Joshua Leach	Marilyn Leland	Roy Lewis
Marge Kilpack	Jan Kisch	William Knutson	Elmer Kotongan	Mary Kulawik	Lamontagne	Bill Larsen	Matt Leach	Ryan Leley	Teresa Lewis
Chris Kilpack	Dan Kish	Cindy Koch	Judy Kotongan	Jon Kumin	Sandy Lamoreau	David Larsen	Peggy Leach	Vi Leley	Todd Lewis
Ken Kilpatrick,	Suzi Kitabijian	Glenn Koch	Ruth Kotongan	Linda Kumin	Emily Lamoreaux	Eric Larsen	Debbie Leads	Even Lemmerman	Win Lewis
DVM	Janaan Kitchen	Pat Koch	Victor Kotongan	Steve Kunert	Edward Lamphere	Leif Larsen	Morgan Leads	Gary Lemmon	Gary Lezzotte
Elder Kim	Merle Kjer	Rick Koch	Joel Kottke	Irene Kunnuk	Mary Lamphere	Lynette Larsen	Darlene Leafgren	Nancy Lemmon	Dan Libby
Paus Kimberly	Marie Klangman	Nelda Kocher	David Koutchak	Ruth Kunnuk	Anna Lampley	Michael Larsen	Ray Leafgren	Rene Lemmons	David Lichtenburg
Richard Kimmel	Carol Klapproth	Kassie Koecher	Elizabeth Koutchak	Gene Kunz	Tink Lancaster	Richard Larsen	John Leake	Demo Lemontas	David Lichtragum
Cissie Kimoktoak	Peter Klein	Wayne Koecher	Mae Koutchak	Karl Kupfer	Lois Lance	Bill Larson	Dr. Leaky	Heather Lende	Lloyd Liggett
Archie Kinch	Fred Kletka	Kimberly Koeff	Oscar Koutchak	Sharon Kupfer	Tery Lance	Don Larson	Ann Leander	George Lennon	Dixie Light
Pat Kinch	Patsy Kletka	Jan Koelzek	Drew Koutchek	Jennifer Kurka	Pamela Lanckton	Jennifer Larson	Donna Leander	Ann Lentz	Barry Lignon, DVM
Sandra Kincheloe	Gail Klewicki	Jane Koezler	Jim Kovalchick	Pat Kurtz	Tanja Lanckton	Kris Larson	Jim Leander	William Lentz	Pat Likos
Bill Kindig	Mark Klewicki	Betty Koger	Robert Kowalke	Doris Kuryius	Cathy Landfried	Lauri Larson	Mark Leander	Rita Lentzing	Tom Likos
Jim Kindseth	Hansie Kline	Bill Koger	Jerry Kowchee	Phillip Kush	Steve Landfried	Leif Larson	Marc Lebhart	Donna Leonard	Jesse Lin
Vickie Kindseth	Karen Kline	Judy Koger	Dwayne Kowder	Rhonda Kutzer	Becky Landingham	Lora L. Larson	Jim Lebiedz	Ellie Leonard	Enid Lincoln
Barbara Kineen	Don Klinefelter	Karin Koger	Sue Kozeroff	Karen Kwoluk	Michele Landis	Lynn Larson	Mark Lebiedz	Gene Leonard	Howard Lincoln
Fen Kineen	Terry Klinefelter	Jim Kohl	Bill Kramer	Pat Kyle, DVM	Anne Lane	Marcella Larson	Joe Lechorchick	June Leonard	Robert Lincoln
Simon Kineen	Bruce Kling	Melissa Kohler	Chuck Kramer	Joe Kyle	B.J. Lane	Matilda Larson	James Lecrone	Renee Leonard	Terry Lincoln
Adrienne King	Jim Kling	Ryan Kohler	Larry Kramer	Tom Kyte	Bonnie Lane	Nancy Larson	Cathy Ledbetter	Norma Lepak	Brenda Lind
C.W. King	Carol Klinnert	Andy Kohn	Matt Kramer	Peryll Kyzer	Kim Lane	Richard Larson	Zachary Ledbetter	Brenda LeRay	Marc Lind
C. King	Rich Klinnert	Dr. Helen Kohn	Phill Krauss	Stosh Labinski	Nicole Lane	Shawn Larson	Barry Lee	Lynn Lesselyoung	Sharon Lind-Camp
Christopher King	Polly Kloep	Dale Kolb	Justin Krawczyk	Larry LaBolle	Robert Lane	Shirley Larson	Bobby Lee	David Lester	Sharon Lind-Charron
James King	Lioba Kloppenburg	William Kolb	Kimberly Krawczyk	Nancy LaBolle	William Lane	Steve Larson	Goody Lee	Lois Lester	Bill Linday
Jeff King	Bob Klotz	John Kolehmainen	John Krielkamp	Mike Lacaze	Wilma Lane	Robert Lasson	Harold Lee	Herman Lestingkof	Rebecca Lindemann
John King	Joan Klotz	Karol Kolehmainen	Rita Krier	Harry Lacey	Carla Lang	Fred Lau	Kyle Lee	Ryan Letey	K. Linden
Josie King	Linda Knapp	Mary Kolowick	Terry Krier	Debbie Lacher	Mac Lang	John Lauch	Nancy Lee	Lance Lettera	Mark Lindholm
Kathleen King	Lois Knapp	Bob Koltz	Veronica Krier	Wayne Lacy	Ray Lang	Kathryn Lauch	Robert Lee	Cathy Leu	Davey Lindig
Kraig King	Pam Knapp	Joan Koltz	Christine Kriger	Jim LaFollette	Rune Innleggen	Chris Laurin	Shari Lee	Jim Leverick	Curtis Lindner
Roger King	Patrice Knebbe	Chad Komakhuk	Kim Krinke	Roger Lagaard	Langaard	Marge Laurin	Ty Lee	Linda Levishokoff	Sonny Lindner
Silvia King	Bob Knight, DVM	Samantha	Carn Kristenson	Buck LagGrew	Gordon Lange	Molly Laurin	Candi Leech	Julie Levit	Edwin Lindquist,
Svetlana King	Rebecca Knight	Komakhuk	Ellen Kristenson	Don Laird	Geoff Langer	Karl Lauterbach	Derrik Leedy, DVM	Kate Levit	DVM
Tabitha King	Tom Knight	Ron Komkoff	Eric Kristenson	Jerry Lairson	Terry Langholtz	Calvin Lauwers	Joe LeFaive	Loni Levy	Beth Lindsay
Will King	Tracey A. Knight	Henry Kondrat	Ken Kristenson	David Laity	Lila Langston	Rick Lavalle	Haran Legare	Gordon	Bill Lindsey
Oswald H. King III,	Ann Knobbe	George Konrad	Karen Kristy	Orville Lake	Carl Langton	Luc Laverdiere	Karen Legare	Lewandowski	John Line III
DVM	Mary Knobbe	Dale Koontz	Fred Kroeplin	Chuck Lakner	Gary Lanham	Bruce Laverick	Adam Legg	Jerry Lewanski	Bill Liners
Vern Kingsford	Ed Knoch	Garth Koop	Sarah Krolicki	Bruce Lalonde	Dr. Jim Lanier	James Laverick	Royatta Legg	Adron Lewis	Mat Linford
Kathy Kingston	Chris Knodel	Renee Koppenhaver	Tad Krolicki	Shirley Lalunde	Sgt. Lanier	Paul Laverty	Douglas Legge	Al Lewis	Jean Linfors
Tim Kinkead, DVM	Howie Knodel	Shirley Koppenhaver	Muriel Kronowitz	Len Lamb	Brent Lannen	Stacey Lavine	Carolyn Lehmkuhl	Bob Lewis	Jim Lingnau
Bob Kinna	Mary Knodel	Braun Kopsak	Melani Kruger	Tony Lamb	Nicki Lannen	Dan Lawrence	Frank Lehmkuhl	Butch Lewis	Laurie Lingnau
Jack Kinna	Pat Knodel	Dick Kopsak	Rick Kruger	Jerry Lamberson	Rob Lanning	Deborah Lawrence	George Lehmkuhl	Chip Lewis	Tracy Lingnau
Myrtle Kinna	Lucy Knoll	Jennifer Kormendy	Ted Kruger, Jr.	Marcheta Lamberson	Gary Lantrip	Kathy Lawrence	Judy Lehmkuhl	Chris Lewis	Arnie Link

Ian Alan McRae	Jason Merculief	S. Michall	Peter Miller	Shane Mitchell	Cameron Moore	Paula Morgan	Mike Mount	Desiree Myers	Dwight Neill
Roy McVey	Shellie Merkling	Kevin Michels	Ray Miller	Stan Mitchell	Charles Moore	Phil Morgan	Sharla Mount	Jeff Myers	Larry Neill
Chris McWilliams	John Merkouris	Mandy Michels	Rick Miller	Wingate Mitchell	Chris Moore	Tom Morgan	Kris Ann Mountain	Linda Myers	Laura Neilson
Dallas McWilliams	Paul Merkouris	Victor Micol	Rusty Miller	Dr. Von Mitton	Christy Moore	Wilse Morgano	Roy Movey	Mark Myers	Nicki Neilson
Robert Meacham	Sue Merkouris	Jeff Midaugh	Ryan Miller	Samuel Mix	Dalene Moore	Henry Mori	Connie Moylan	Reggie Myers	Benoni Nelson
George Meacock	Maleria Merrill	Molly Midaugh	Scott Miller	Herman Miyer	Dave Moore	Alberto Morillo	Pat Moylan	Carol Mymajer	Betty Nelson
Bob Mead	Mari Merrill	Neil Midaugh	Sherrill Miller	Dave Mobraten	Dottie Moore	Carol Morillo	Yvonne Mozee	Paul Nader, DVM	Bob Nelson
Chris Mead	Mark Merrill	Peggy Midaugh	Stepany Miller	Laura Mobraten	Dr. William B Moore	Kimberly Moritz	Karyn Mucklow	Sheldon Nagaruk	Corey J. Nelson
Deanna Mead	Raymond Merrill	Angie Middleton	Stephan Miller	Carol Ann Mocarski	Faye Moore	Fran Morley	Bob Mueller	Michele Naiac	Darrell Nelson
Jay Mead	Jenneth Merriman	Sandra Middleton	Susie Miller	Alice Mockerman	Gary Moore	Grant Morley	Don Muetz	Jim Nail	Dave Nelson
Jules Mead	Judy Merritt	Shirley Miessner	Terese Miller	Gene Mockerman	Gene Moore	Larry Morley	Scott Muetz	Susan Nail	Diane Nelson
Leslie Mead	Marie Merritt	Pam Mikalonis	Trevor Miller	Andy Moderow	Glen Moore	Bruce Moroney	Bryan Muktoyuk	Betty Gail Nakaahiki	Elder Nelson
Randy Meadows	David Mersereau	Toby Mikalonis	Walter Miller	Debbie Moderow	Greg Moore	Diana Moroney	Rep. Eldon Mulder	Kandi Nakaahiki	Elizabeth Nelson,
Phillip Means	Paul Mesack, DVM	Becky Milanese	Wava Miller	Hannah Moderow	Heather Moore	Jim Morran	Wendy Mulder	Vicki Nakamura	DVM
Susan Means	Roy Mescher	Marty Milanese	Wendy Miller	Mark Moderow	Jerri Moore	LeAnna Morrell	Andy Mullen	John Nakarek	Eloise Nelson
Bill Mears	Scott Messel	Joyce Miles	Zachary Miller	Sandy Modine	Lincoln Moore	Julie Morrill	Kerry Mullen	Kim Nance	Eric D. Nelson
John Mears	Robert Messenger,	Sue Miles	Fred Miller, Jr.	Mike Modryznski	Lisa Moore	Kelly Morrill	Ernest Muller	Kevin Nangle	Jack Nelson
Meri Mears	DVM	Scott Mileur	Dean Milligan	Sue Moehn	Mary Moore	Kirk Morrill	Rob Muller	Bob Nanney	Jacob Nelson
James Mechem	Thro Messer	Mike Miley	Crystal Milligrock	Mike Moerlein	Mike Moore	Larry Morrill	Arlene Muncy	Martin Nanouk	Jennifer Nelson
Sandra Medearis	Angelo Messina	Cassandra Milham	Cheryl Milline	Tim Moerlein	Sara Moore	Chris Morris	Carol Muncy	John Nash	Joanne Nelson
Lolly Medley	Bob Messinger	Kirby Milham	Vic Mills	Mae Moffat	Stephine Moore	Dean Morris	Agnew Munkholm	Marie Nash	Kathi Nelson
Bill Meehan	Norm Messinger	Tony Milionta	Ben Millstein	Dave Mograten	Tom Moore	Eric Morris	Nan Munkholm	Melinda Nash	Kristine Nelson
Roger Meehan	Cal Messmer	Nieves Miljure	Tricia Millwee	Laura Mograten	Deborah Moorhead	G. Morris	Lynn Munn	Robert Nash	Laurie Nelson
Mark Meekum	Edward Metro	Toni Mill	Tyrone Millwee	Melody Mohigh	Margaret Moorhead	Jack Morris, DVM	Anita Munson	Wendy Nashalook	Loanne Nelson
Burl Meers	Helen Metz	Doug Milland	Bimji Minard	Debbie Molbray	Steve Moorhead	Jesse Morris	Kent Murdock	Henry Nashalook, Jr.	Lori Nelson
Jan Meers	Roy Metzger	Robert Millard	Kris Minelga	Billie Jo Moline	Mike Morales	John Morris	Paul Murdock	Roger Nassuk	Lynette Nelson
Gabriele Mehnert	Chris Meusser	Nancy Milleisler	Eric Miner	Cheryl Moline	Arnie Moran	Julie Morris	Carol Murkowski	Michelle Natac	Michael Nelson
Asha Mekonian	Ann Meyer	Agnes Miller	Jim Miner	Kendra Moline	Cathy Moran	Mike Morris	A.J. Murphy	Dan Nation	Neil Nelson
Sue Mekouris	Austin Meyer	Ashley Miller	Ruth Mingo	Ann Molyneux	Cindy Moran	Randy Morris	A.S. Murphy	Mike Naumann	Pam Nelson
Sandra Melinder	Betty Meyer	Bily Miller	Marcia Minnerman	Mary-Louise	Frank Moran	Shane Morris	Alice Murphy	Kari Navjack	Peggy Nelson
Doug Melland	Carol Meyer	Carol Miller	Mary Minor	Monaghan	Jean Moran	Wayne Morris	Chris Murphy	Dan Navjokas	Richard F. Nelson
Susan Mellin	Phil Meyer, DVM	Cathy Miller	Mike Minsch	Carl Monetti, DVM	Jim Moran	Andrew Morrison	George Murphy	Vicky Navjokas	Shay Nelson
Mark Melloni	Dwight Meyer	Darlene Miller	William F. Minster	Kathy Money	Lynnett Moran	Dorothy Morrison	Jim Murphy	Jillian Nayback	Stuart Nelson, DVM
Steve Melloni	George Meyer	Dave Miller	Kathleen Minyon	Frank Moneymaker	Maggie Moran	Steve Morrison	Joe Murphy	Nicole Naylor	Thomas Nelson
Tony Melovidov	Henry Meyer	Debbie Miller	Bernie Miranda	Bill Monroe	Margaret Moran	Elaine Morrow	Mike Murphy	Herbie Nayokpuk	Edward Nentwich
Mark Melson	Herman Meyer	Denise Miller	David M. Mirneau	David Monson	Mollie Moran	Anne Morse	Rex Murphy	Walter Nayokpuk	Jim Nershak
Julia Melton	Kathi Meyer	Elder Miller	Marcia Mirneau	Sharon Montagnino	Gretchen Morava	Julie Morse	Sean Murphy	Boston Neary	Dody Nesbitt
Marsha Melton	Kent Meyer	Frank Miller	Janet Mischler	Charlene Montague	Justin Mordett	Major Morse	Una Murphy	Kathe Nedeau	David M. Netishen
Ted Melton	Larry Meyer	George Miller	Cal Misemer	Dave Montague	Will Mordett	Scott Morse	Joe Murray	Rick Nedeau	Jason Netishen
Kitty Melvin	Peggy Meyer	Glenn Miller	Al Mitchell	Allen Montanez	Judy More	Kenny Morton	John E. Murray	Martha Neeley	Mark Nettles
Bimji Menard	Scott Meyer	Jack Miller	C. Mitchell	Bob Montella	Judith Moreau	Art Mortveld	Michael Murray	Richard Neeley	Walkt Neuman
Curt Menard	Bob Meyers	Jerry Miller	Cindy Mitchell	Don Montgomery	Harold Morehart	Lisa Hodge Moser	Nathan Murray	Walter Neeley	Mike Nevel
George Menard	Gary Meyers	Jim Miller	Danny Mitchell	Jean Montgomery	Bob Morelli	Tim Mosley	Roberta Murray	Susan Neer	Chuck Newberg
Shanti Mava Menard	Jacob Meyers	Joel Miller	David Mitchell	Doug Montoya	Traci Morelli	Cathy Mossefin	Joe Murray, Jr.	Darrell Neff	Candice Newberry
John Mendenhall	Michele Meyers	K Miller	David Mitchell,	Cathi Moody	David Moreno	Dale Mossefin	Chuck Muschaney,	Kathi Negilski	Bob Newcombe
Gabriele Menhert	Scott Meyers	Krista Miller	DVM	Jim Moody	Doreen Moreno	Richard Mote	DVM	Val Negilski	Nikki Newcombe
Anne Menkews	Mary Miceli	Linda Miller	Francis Mitchell	Jon Moody	Bruce Morgan	Lori Motil	Michael Musen	Bob Neidig	Phyllis Newcombe
Betty Gail Menkews	Cliff Michael	Marc Miller	Joann Mitchell	Darryl Moon	Curt Morgan	George	Rosse Musgrove	Linda Neidig	Cindy Newman
Elaine Menzis	Sue Michael	Mariann Miller	LeAnn Mitchell	Kenn Moon	Gwen Morgan	Motischmand	Miranda Musich	Carl Neil	Derek Newman
Mary Ann Meore	Tim Michael	Mark Miller	Mark Mitchell	Lorraine Moon	Hilary Morgan	Betty Moto	Bob Mustain	Daryl Neil	George Newman
Jeanne Mercer	Elli Michaels	Marty Miller	Melissa Mitchell	Anne Moore	Jim Morgan	Henry Motoyama	Rich Mutter	Debbie Neil	Gina Newman
Jerry Mercer	Bob Michaelson	Michelle Miller	Ocie Mitchell	Barbara Moore	Leslie Morgan	Bill Mouis	Bart Mwary	Dwight Neil	Howard Newman
Richard Merchant	Nancy Michaelson	Neil Miller	Randy Mitchell	Bill Moore	Lynnete Morgan	Meri Mouis	Cyndy Myers	Gary Neil	Johnny Newman
Sue Mercoglan	Ray Michaelson	Paula Miller	Roslyn Mitchell	Bradley Moore	Marc Morgan	Larry Mouisim	Deanna Myers		Maria Newman

Jonathan Rollins
Mike Romanello
Randy Romanesko
Duane Romberg
Janet Romberg
Mary Romberg
Shawn Romberg
Rebecca Romine
Sharon Rompa
David Ronaldson
Lois Rone
Robert L Rooks, DVM
Harvey Rookus
Rocky Rooney
Dennis Roper
Darren Rorabaugh
Bess Rose
Colleen Rose
James Rose
Leighanne Rosenbaum
Susan Rosenbaum
Michelle Rosenberg
Christopher Rosenow
Rodney Rosenow
Ken Rosenstein
Hank Rosenthal
Herb Rosenthal
Don Rosevear
Terry Rosevear
William Rosier
Alexandra Ross
Carter Ross
Catherine Ross
Donald Ross
Gimmie Ross
Maggie Ross
Michael Ross
Sharon L. Ross
Shirley Ross
Ted Ross
Jackie Rossberg
Bill Rosser, DVM
Ronald Rosser
Rodney Rossnow
Jioni Roth
Peggy Roth
William Roth
Hal Rovelstad
Linda Rovelstad
Abby Rowe
Ben Rowe
Chris Rowe
Darrell Rowe
Mary Rowley

Patricia Rowley
Will Rowley
Paul Rowse
Peggy Royce
Frank J. Rozic
Anne Rozkydal
Jody Rozkydal
Mag Rozkydal
Bob Rubedeau
Mary Rubedeau
Gary Rubin
Lori Rubin
Gary Rubin, Sr.
Mel Rucker
Jeff Rudd
Susan Ruddy
Lee Rudenauer
Dick Rudy
Lincoln Rudy
Kevin Ruel
Dale Ruff
Michael Ruff
Todd Ruff
Marilyn Ruffenburg
Andrea Ruft
Carolyn Ruggles
Gayl Rumerfield
Bryce Rumery
Clay Rumph
Barry Rumple
John Rumps
Lauri Rumynner
John Runkle
Martha Runkle
Patty Runyan
Rachel Runyan
Rich Runyan
Shari Runyan
Jay Runyan, Jr.
Paul Rupple
Sam Rush
Wayne Rush
Daryl Rush II
Aline Rusnak
Jim Rusnak
Chuck Russel
A.B. Russell
Brandon Russell
Charles Russell
Craig Russell
Gari Russell
Linda Russell
Lloyd Russell
Mike Russell

Nick Russell
Reagan Russey
Tom Rutigliano
Jim Rutkowski
Sven Rutkowski
Cathy Rutman
Allison Rutter
Terrance Rutter
"Boyuk" Ryan
Charles J. Ryan
Frank Ryan
Joe Ryan
John Ryan
Julia Ryan
Kathy Ryan
Maeve Ryan
Mike Ryan
Sheldon Ryan
Mike Ryckman
Chris Ryherd
Lois Rynkiewicz
Jane Sabes
Susan Sacaloff
Joel Saccheus
Charles Saccheus, Jr.
Charles F. Saccheus, Sr.
Mike Saclamana
Cayre Saden
Beverly Sadoski
Jeanne Sage
Kim Sage
Pauline Sagnooick
George Sagoorick
Al Sahlin
Denise Saigh
Dennis Saigh
Maureen Sainy
Ben Salamone, DVM
John Salas
David Salesky
Martha Salm
Jenice Salmon
Ron Salmon
Mike Sambuco
Blythe Sampson
Bobbi Sampson
John Sampson
Sandy Sampson
Tom Sampson
Evita Samuels
Gary Samuelson
Myrna Samuelson
Jon Sander

Jimmy Sanders
Joe Sanders
Sudi Sanders
Eric Sanford
Ruth Sanford
Jim Sangl
Paul Sangl
Andres Santos
Conrad E. Santos
Ed Sao
Captain Sapayo
Jean Saperstein
Lisa Saperstein
Chuck Sappah
Kathy Sarns
Johnny Sarren
Yvonne Sarren
Brad Sathers
Robert Sato
Tae Sato
Gary Satterfield
Mona Satzgar
Mary Saugstad
Anne Saul
Janet Saul
Carl Saunders
Dottie Saunders
Karen Saunders
Mel Saunders
Conrad Saussele
Kelly Saussele
Deb Sauvageau
Sandi Sava
Katherine Savage, DVM
Mary Savage
Cole Sawdon
Gene Sawdon
Laura Sawdon
Thomas Sawdon
Frankie Sawyer
Drew Saxon
Robert Saye
Frankie Sayer
Paul Sayer
Heidi Scales
Peter Scales
Ryan Scales
Ray Scarbro
Ted Schachle
Barbara "Dog Drop" Schaefer
Toni Schafer
Janet Schaffner

Neil Schaffner
Toby Schaffner
Alvin Schalavin
Jan Schalavin
Laura Schalavin
Pam Schalavin
Jim Schanke
David Schauer
Jenny Schauer
Kirsten Schauer
Michael Schauer
Jan Schavalin
Betty Scheeler
Rick Schem
Helene Schenk
Madonna Schierholt
Linda Schild
James Schill
Joanna Schillieri
Elisa Schleifman
Mr. & Mrs. Bob Schlentner
Anita Schlief
Bruce Schmid
Debora Schmidt
Jeanne Schmidt
Karin Schmidt, DVM
Keith Schmidt
Ronna Schmidt
Sue Schmidt
Wolf Schmidt
Bill Schmidtman
Kathy Schmidtman
Wade Schmierer
Mattie Schmodt
Garrett Schnell
Larry Schockley
Marvis Schoenfeld
James Schol
Mel Scholobohm
Heidi Schoming
Shirley Schonenbach
Bill Schonenback
Dawn Schrader
Matt Schrader
Dale Schramm
Terry Schreckarghost
Carey Schreiber
Nathan Schreiner
Tom Schreiner
Carey Schrieber
Jim Schroeder
Kati Schroeder

Duane Schueller
John Schull, Sr.
Diana Schulte
Jami Schulte
Chris Schultz
Don Schultz
Hattie Schultz
Jeff Schultz
Joan Schultz
Kathy Schultz
Tony Schultz
Beverly Schupp
Leilani Schutrtpelz
Sue Schutrtpelz
Rich Schwal
Buzz Schwall
Mike Schwandt
Jim Schwanke
Von Schwanke
David Schwantes
Shane Schwark
Rick Schweim
Dale Schweum
Joe Schwieterman
Mike Schwieterman
Deanne Scillieri
Johanna Scillieri
Andy Scott
Darlene Scott
Earl Scott
Helen Scott
Hoss Scott
James Scott, DVM
John Scott
Kitty Scott
Leslie Scott
Mark Scott
Rebecca Scott
Rudy Scott
Sheila Scott
Wiley Scott
Roma Scougal
Kenneth Scruggs
Sharon Scruggs
Beverly Scrugham
Linda Scrugham
Rita Scruton
William Scull
William Seaman
Ricki Searls
William Sebulsky
Kaite Sechrist
Rose Sechrist
Harry R. Secoy

Del Seeba, DVM
Phyllis Seeba
Mark Seely
Megan Selk
Dave Sellie
Debbie Sellie
Phillip Semaken
Wilfred Semaken
Scott Semans
Darrel Semauin
Philip Semekin
Karen Sendek
Francesca Sepinski
Bob Sept, DVM
Gloria Sept
Mike Sergeant, DVM
Gil Serrano
John Serwecki
Catherine Sessions
Jack Sessions
Frank Severino
Janna Severson
Dottie Sewell
Sheila Sexton
Larry Shafer
Toni Shafer
Leo Shanahan
Neal Shanahan
Dennie Shanigan
Vina Shannon
Donna Shantz
Tommy Sharbutt
Jo Sharma
Betty Sharp
Marcia Sharp
Arnold Shavings
Barbara Shaw
Doug Shaw
Lisa Shaw
Rick Shaw
Robert Shaw
Lynn Shawback
Dodd Shay
Terri Shay
Peter P. Sheairs
Jenny Sheehy
Kent Sheets
Josephine Sheffield
T.J. Sheffield
Danny Siebert
Joyce K. Siemens
Marlene Shell
Sandra Shelley
Donna Shelton
Ed Shelton
Jimmie Shelton

John Shelton
Howard Shephard
Cindy Sherertz
Frances Sherertz
Jessica Sheridan
Jon Sheridan
Dana Sherman
Elaine Sherman
Jake Sherman
Lizzie Sherman
Steve Sherman
Tara Sherman
Doug Sherrer
Gail Sherrer
Debbie Sherwood
Colisca Shetter
Barbara Shew
Kimberly Shew
Prentice Shew
Don Shields
Barbara Shine
John Shipe
Dave Shiplett
Jim Shipman
Barbara Shive
Mary Sholton
Mike Sholton
Leo Shanahan
Neal Shanahan
Kenneth Shoogukwrk
Dennie Shanigan
Vina Shannon
Donna Shantz
Tony Shootgukwruk
Bev Short
Phillip Short
Wendy Shottenkirk
Diane Showalter
Jane Showalter
Brett Shreve
Don Shrilds
Nancy Shrum
Sandra Shuffle
John Shull
Sherry Shultz
Mike Shupe
Dodd Shuy
Shane Sibbett
Bob Sickler
Becky Sidelinger
Shawn Sidelinger
Dorothy Sidnam
Danny Siebert
Raymond Skrocke
Diane Sievenpiper
Dorothy Siewert
Doug Sikora
Ron Silas

Steve Silba
Steve Silveous
Scott Silver
Todd Silver
Jean Silvernail
John Simmons
Jolene Simmons
LoLynn Simmons
Michael Simmons
Rick Simmons
William Simmons
Aaron Simon
Carl Simon
Kim Simon
Lincoln Simon
Dale Simpson
Darrell Simpson
Judy Simpson
Scott Simpson
Bruce Sims
JoLynn Sims
Ricky Sims
Wendy Sims
Charles Sink
David Sink
Taras Sinlagavsky
Carmen Sisk
Erik Sisk
Gari Sisk
Sister Grace
Sherrie Siverson
Rich Sivets
Sandy Sivets
Harry Sjoberg
Josephine Skeete
Brenda Skelton
Richard Skelton
Matthew Skembo
Ken Skidds
Carmen Skille
Sven Skille
Beverly Skinner
Jack Skinner
Joe Skinner
Kim Skinner
Rayna Skinner
Steve Skinner
Sue Skinner
Steve Skirvin
Raymond Skrocke
Doris Skull
John Skull
Charlene Slabaugh
Daniel Slade

Judy Slanaker
Don Slate
Gwen Slater
Irene Slater
Donald C. Slater, Jr.
Denise Slauson
Ken Slauson
Carol Slavik
Evan Sledge
Caleb Slemons
Angie Slingluff
Ken Sloan
Lisa Small
Beth Smalley
Bill Smalley
Jo Smalley
Beth Smally
Jim Smarsh
Robert Smarsh
Barbara Smart
Debbie Smart
Jayson Smart
Victor Smart
Jim Smarz
Alice Smith
Angie Smith
Anne Smith
Barbara Smith
Betty Smith
Bill Smith
Bret Smith
Cole Smith
"Conrad E," Smith
Crystal Smith
Danny Smith
David Smith
Dawnell Smith
Del Smith
Denise Smith
Denzil Smith
Diane Smith
Don Smith
Donna Smith
Elizabeth Smith
Gloria Smith
Greta Smith
Harvey Smith
Hugh Smith
Jean Smith
Jeremy Smith
Jim Smith
Joe Smith
Karen Smith
Kay Smith

Kelly Smith
Kimberly Smith
Krissy Smith
Lee Smith
Liz Smith
Luke Smith
Lynda Smith
Margaret Smith
Margie Smith
Mark Smith
Mary Smith
Medfra Jack Smith
Melody Smith
Mike Smith
Nate Smith
Nikki Smith
Norm Smith
Pam Smith
Patrick Smith
Paul Smith
Pete Smith
Randall Smith
Richard Smith
Robert Smith
Sally Smith
Sam Smith
Sarah Smith
Scott Smith
Sherry Smith
Stan Smith
Steven Smith
Ted Smith
Terry Smith, DVM
Thetus Smith
Thomas Smith
Victor Smith
Wilford Smith
William Smith
Thaddeu Smitherman
Don Smithhisher
Maureen Smoot
David Smyers
Debra Smykalski
Mark Smykalski
Bud Smyth
Jim Snead
Hugh Snell
Jerry Snella
Dennis Snider
Heinie Snider
Stan Snider
Andy Snipner
Evelyn Snow
Nick Snow

Elaine Snowden
Catherine Snyder
Eve Snyder
Pam Snyder
Sharon Snyder
Stan Sobocienski
Amber Solberg
Alvin Solomon
Darrin Solomon
Debbie Soltis
Eric Somerville
Gail Somerville
Jim Somerville
Robert C. Sommer
Keith Sommers
Pam Sommers
Tom Sommerville
Hong Un Soo
Alex Sookiayak
Carol Sookiayak
Edith Sookiayak
George Sookiayak
Walter Sookiayak
Ladd Soongaruk
Lars Soosuk
Cliff Soper
Bob Soptei
Michael Soptei
Michele Soptei
Mischa Sorbo
Laura Sorenson
Abe Soria
Lilana Sotomayer
Eileen Soualik
Crystal Soule
Bill Sova
Brad Sova
Chuck Sova-Smith
Dawn Sova-Smith
Eileen Sovalik
Harold Spalding, DVM
Sherry Spangler
Shirley Spangler
Tony Spangler
Jolene Sparks
Matthew Sparks
Paul Spatzek
Tony Speaks
Jeff Spear
Judy Spear
Mia Spear
Tom Spear
Steve Spearman
David L. Spears

Jami Spears
Marie Spears
Tom Spears
Paul L. Speckmaier
Kim Speckman
John Speer
Bill Speir
James Spell
Jamie Spell
Penny Spell
Bob Spellecacy
Chris Spellecacy
Gerianne Spellecacy
Leilani Spellecacy
Christine Spencer
Justin Spencer
Kirsten Spencer
Kris Spencer
Mike Spencer
Rita Spencer
Robert Spencer
Von Spencer
Kathy Sperling
Mike Spernack
P.D. Sperry
Nancy Spielkamp
David Spirits
Kathy Spirits
John Spitsburg
Ginger Spock
Scott Sponcel
Judy Spradley
Janet Sprague
Kelley Sprague
Susie Sprague
Dawn Spreckler
Mark Sprenger
Annette Spring
Coretta Spring
Frank Spring
Don Springer
Henry Springer
Loretta Springer
Leona M. Sprinkle
Betty Sprunger
Jim Spurgeon
Marita Spurnack
Mike Spurnack
Michael St. Cross
John Staffan
Larry Stafford
Luann Stafford
Michelle Stafford
Nina Stafford

Keith Stahn
John Stamatelos
Mark Stamm
Jane Stammer
Irl Stanbaugh
Dennis Stanczuk
Rosemary Stanczuk
Donald Stand
Gerald Standeford
Laurie Standeford
Deanne Standifer
Liana Standifer
Tim Standish
Delores Standorf
Barry Stanely
Matthew Stanely
Barry Stanley
Daniell Stanley
Karleen Stanley
Kirstin Stanley
Susan Stann, DVM
Cindi K. Stanton
Deloras Stantorf
Elliot Staples
Tess Staples
Thomas Staples
Rob Stapleton
Arden Starbird
Vern Starks, DVM
Mimi Starks
Chad Starr
Kirk Starr
Nancy Starr
Stan States
Rick Stavale
John Stechman
Ann Steck
Gerald Steele
Jay Steere
Claire Steffens
Tim Steidel
Jerry Steiger
Jim Steigerwald
Bob Steiner
Doris Steiner
Linda Steiner
Sheila Steiner
Tara Steiner
Ewald Stelter
Jamie Stepetin
Ann Stephens
Joel Stephens
Linda Stephens
Wayne Stephens

Woodward
  Stephensen
Brian Stephenson
Dr. Dan Stephenson
Judy Sterling
Paul Sterling II
John Stern
Rashonda Stern
Cathy Sterner
Andy Sterns
Tass Sterns
Nancy Steuer
Andrea Stevens
Beverly Stevens
Daniel Stevens
David Stevens
Estelle Stevens
Laurel Stevens
Mary Stevens
Sid Stevens
Tjana Stevens
Deb Stevenson
Vernon Stevenson
David Stevns
Arlene Steward
Harley Steward
Robert Steward
Amber Stewart
Arlene Stewart
Blake Stewart
Bob Stewart
Darren Stewart
Eric Stewart
Harley Stewart
James Stewart
Jerry Stewart
Kathy Stewart
Keith Stewart
Kovey Stewart
Mary Stewart
Nella Stewart
Richard Stewart
Rita Stewart
Tammy Stewart
Terry Stewart
Robert Stewart, Jr.
Mickey Stickman
Mr. & Mrs. Fred
  Stickman, Jr.
Skip Stiglich
Josie Stiles
Marylou Stiles
Norm Stiles
Wendy Stiles

Dr. Vern Stillner
Brooke Stilter
Earl Stiltner
Erik Stimpfle
Josh Stimpfle
Sean Stimpfle
Stacy Stimson
Linda Stiner
Scott Stinson
Carol Stith
Heidi Stockard
Keith Stockard
Ryan Stockard
Mark Stockhowe
Esther Stockwell
Lisa Stockwell
Lynn Stockwell
Alfred Stoddard
Dr. Hannis Stoddard
Ed Stoebner
Jack Stoebner
Ed Stoikes
Terri Stoikes
Tom Stoikes
Daniel Stokes
Dora Stokes
Doris Stokes
Jeff Stokes
Ruth Stokes
John Stolman
Cindy Stolson
Jarrot Stolson
Jon Stolson
Sage Stolson
Sandy Stolson
Steve Stolson
Bob Stone
Geneva Stone
Jeremy Stone
Mr. & Mrs. Don
  Stone
Marge Stoneking
Erica Stonequist
Norm Stopinbrink
Allen Storey
Brian Storey
Ed Storey
Greg Storey
Jane Storey
Robert Storm
Larry Storry
Sue Stortz
Jim Stout
Linda Stout

Peg Stout
Steve Stout
Matt Stover
Paul Stowell
Judy Stratman
Cynthia Strau
Beverly Streba
Mike Street
Sarah Street
Ted Stretmoyer
Becky Strever
Zeke Strever
Richard Strick
Sharon Strick
John Stricklan
Kim Stricklan
Roger Stricklan
Troy Stricklan
Darrell Strickland
Tish Strickland
David Stroh
Sherrie Stroh
C. Stroll
Ken Stroney
Jim Strong
John Strong
Kenneth Strony
Fran Strother
George Strother
Jack Struder
Daniel Strukie
Mike Strunk
Pat Strunk
Jackie Struthers
Martha Stuart
Olaf Stuber
Nancy Studer
Don Stultz
Arliss Sturgulewski
Elizabeth Sturkie
Val Stuve, DVM
Jack Stuver
Cristal Suazo
Brenda Sublette
Jim Sublette
Erik Sulberg
Tony Sulberg
Evelyn Sullivan
James Sullivan
Janeen Sullivan
Maureen Sullivan
Paula Sumdum
Sherman Sumdum
Cathy Summers

Jane Summers
Kelly Summers
Sue Sumrall
Connie Sundberg
Ed Sundeen
May Sunderland
Chris Sundum
David Sunleey
Carmen Surber
Mitzi Surber
Keaton Surratt
Roy Sursa
Kristi Sustrich
John Suter
Cheryl Sutherland
Iris Sutherland
Mark Sutherland
Jim Sutter
Jane Sutton
Shirley Svoboda
David Stroh
Kathy Swaim
Paul Swalling
Rose Swan
Margaret Swanberg
Nels Swanberg
Steven Swank, DVM
Linda Swanke
Eric K. Swann
Barbara Swanson
Chip Swanson
Dino Swanson
Edward Swanson
Jerry Swanson
Linda Swanson
Rayna Swanson
Rich Swanson
Jan Swartsbacker
Carol Swartz
Jean Swearingen
Doug Sweat
Terry Sweetzer
Bruce Swenson
Kathy Swenson
Leslie Swenson
Mike Swenson
Rick Swenson
Ron Swider
M.N. Swink
Dave Sylesky
Paul Sylveira
Sandy Sylveria
Miles Symonds
Sheri Synder
Starre Szelag

Walter Szelag
Greg Tabor
Jennifer Tabor
John Tabor
Phil Tackett
Kim Taehoon
Robert Taffera
George Tagarook
Ruth Taggert
Hannah Takak
Lynn Takak, Jr.
Lynn Takak, Sr.
Maggie Takek
William Takek
Bob Talbott
Corinne Talbott
Karen Tallent
Mark Talley
Sharon Tallman
Chuck Talsky
Val Tangen
Lynda Tanner
Matt Tanner
Rocky Tanner
Susan Tanner
Frank Y. Tano
Karen Tapangco
Satch Tapangco
Dianne Tarquinia
Phil Tarr
Julie Tarrick
Pam Tarver
Barbara Tasker
George Tate
Greg Tate
Melvin Tate, Jr.
Crystal Taxac
Curms Taxac
Gilbert Taxah
Mr. & Mrs. Allan Tayl
Adam Taylor
Art Taylor
Bill Taylor
Brian Taylor
Dorthea Taylor
Elden Taylor
Gene Taylor
Geoffrey Taylor
James Taylor
Jane Taylor
Jean Taylor
Jean L Taylor
Jenny Taylor

Kevin Taylor
Mathey Taylor
Matthew Taylor
Michael Taylor
Robert Taylor
Scott Taylor
Sue Taylor
Wendy Taylor
Paul Teaford
Sarah Teaford
Joe Teeple
Nikki Teeple
Pam Teeple
Susan Teeple
Merritt Tegeler
Heather Tegoseak
Donald Telle
Michael Telles
Michael Templin
Judy Tenhoff
Lee Tenhoff
Bobby Tennis
Carolyn Terry
Floyd Terry
James Terry
Mike Terry
Robert Terry
Robin Terry
Sally Terry
Harley Tessier
Megs Testarmarta
Allan Tetis
Floyd Tetpon
Neil Thalaker
Paula Tharp
Joan Thayer
Gayle Theiman
Karen Theirer
Mandi Theirer
Margaret Theirer
Norm Theirer
Catherine Theisen,
  DVM
Dr. William Thelbold
Steve Theno
Doug D. Thibault
Alton Thibodeaux
Diane Thien
Debbie Thigpen
Jerry Thigpen
Mark Thoden
James M. Thodes
Bill Thomas
Brad Thomas

Chuck Thomas	Ann Thomson	Ed Titus	Al Townsend, DVM	Bill Turner	Maria Van Auken	John Vernon	Kasey Wakeman	Larry Walters	Becky Weaver
Conner Thomas	John Thomson	Richard Titus	William Townsend	Dane Turner	Donna Van Buren	Mike Vetsch	Jo Wald	Liz Walters	Daryl Weaver
Craig Thomas	Judy Thomson	Gene Tizel	Dick Tozier	Danielle Turner	Deanna Van Buskirk	Deena Vetwch	Jennifer Walden	Gary Waltman	Doug Weaver
Dan Thomas	Vi Thomson	Ted Tober	Brada Tracy	David Turner	John van Eijk	Vince Victorious	Michael Waldroop	Kelly Waltman	James Weaver
Darrin Thomas	Kristen Thoresen	David Tobin	Ed Tracy	Joey Turner	Karin van Eijk	David Vidmar	Mrs. Earl Waldroop	Edward Walton	Lance Weaver
Dr. Jay Thomas	John Thorn	Lew Tobin	Billy Trainer	Larry Turner	Mark Van Henter	Margaret Viera	Martin Walenga	Bob Walworth	Loren Weaver
Elder Thomas	Glenda Thorne	Liana Tobin	Julie Trainer	S. Turner	Jennifer Van Ingen	Curms Vik	Barb Walker	Elnora Wand	Mandi Weaver
Elizabeth Thomas	Marie Thorne	Mike Tobin	William Trainer	Troy Turner	Chuck Van Rossum	Peggy Vik	Carl Walker	Grant Wand	Pam Weaver
Heidi Thomas	Zeke Thornton	Thomas Tobin	Monica Trammel	Mary Ellen Tuttell	Thomas Van Straten	Jeffery Vikdal	Carol Walker	Leroy Wand	Shirley Weaver
Ilse Thomas	Cindy Thorpe	Ed Tobuk	Casey Trammell	Mike Tvenge	Matthew Van	Ed Visa	David Walker	Kaltschnee	Cheryl Webb
Ingrid Thomas	Paul Thorpe	Linda Tobuk	Peter Tranfo	Jim Tvrdy	Valkenbur	Pete Visser	Debbie Walker	Wandwade	Jerry Webb
Jane Thomas	Gerrianne Thorsness	Tara Tobuk	Paula Trapp	Randy Twarduck	Mary Van Winkle	Paul Vitek	Dwight Walker	Betty Ward	Leslie Webb
Jolene Thomas	Ward Thorsness	Tass Tobuk	Ed Trappe	Bill Tweet	Char Van Zyle	Nadezshda	Felix Walker	Gordon Ward	Wilburn Webb
Jon Thomas, DVM	Scott Thorson	Marlene Tocktoo	Mary Jane Trappe	Vickie Tweet	Jon Van Zyle	Vlassevich	Helga Walker	Jesse Ward	James Webber
Judy Thomas	Anne Thrall	Debbie Todd	Rodney Travers	Jack Twiggs	Pris Van Zyle	K. Voetmann	Jim Walker	Maynard Ward	Lisa Webber
Laura Thomas	Jeff Thrasher	Dorothy Todd	Sandy Travis	Debbie Tyger	Bryan VanAsdlan	W. Voetmann	Joany Walker	Peg Ward	Lucille Webber
Marilee Thomas	Mark Thrasher	Phil Todd	Tom Travis	Bernadette Tyler	Mitzi VanAsdlan	Carol Vogeler	Lorinda Walker	T.L. Warden	Mike Webber
Mary Thomas	Arlinda Thrun	Diane Toebe	Louis Treiber	Jeff Tyler	Donald VanAsdoll	Marie Vogeler	Matt Walker	Terry Warden	Dennis Weber
Michael Thomas	Leroy Thrun	Dianne Toebo	Barbara Trembreth	Roger Tyler	Dean Vance	Dorothy Vogelheim	Nan Walker	Tim Warden	Donne Weber
Pam Thomas	Tawnwa Thunman	Jim Tofflemire	Sage Trembreth	Tish Tyler	Tim Vance	Paul Vogelheim	Patrick Walker	Elder Ware	Jim Weber
Ron Thomas	Ernie Thurman	Beth Tokar	Goodwin Trent	Tia Tyree	Laurie Vandenberg	Dan Volberding	Paula Walker	John Ware	Maria Weber
Scott Thomas	Roxanne Thurman	Gerri Tokar	Jarrot Trexler	Hisae Uhl	Atheina Vanderpool	Larry Volker	Ray Walker	Lee Wareham	Mark Weber
Steven Thomas	Tim Thurman	Gloria Tokar	Pat Trexler	Jim Uhl	Shellie Vandiver	Terry Volkman	Robert Walker	Lew Warmen	B.J. Webster
Tracy Thomas	David Thurmer	Jerry Tokar	John F. Tribble, Jr.	Linda J. Ulak	Jerry Vanek, DVM	Jim Vonitter	Russ Walker	Jim Warner	Chuck Webster
Warren Thomas	Thurmond Family	Teri Tokar	Clint Trickett	Ben Ulen	Chris Vanghele	Roberta Vonitter	Shane Walker	Mel Warner	David Webster
Bob Thomason	Teri Tibbett	Ann Tokash	Don Trieglaff	Jim Ulh	Dino Vanghele	Daniel Vortherms	Wendy Walker	Tony Warner	Doug Webster
Robert Thomason, Jr.	Elaine Tibbetts	Estelle G. Tokash	Jon Trigg	Dick Underwood	Rachel VanHuff	Don Vortherns	Woodie Walker	Trish Warner	Nance Webster
Al Thompson	Ken Tibbetts	Robert Toll	Joanna M. Trinidad	Mike Underwood	Matt VanNortwick	Kevin Voss	Carl Walker, Sr.	Wilmot Warner	Todd Webster
Bonnie Thompson	Danny Tibbo	Ann Tolliver	Joy Triplett	Nathan Underwood	John Vanover	Chris Voth	Charles Wall	Ed Warren	Andrew Weeks
Carole Thompson	Todd Ticknok	Fred Tolliver	Peter Troesch	Sherry Underwood	Momoko Vanover	Marcey Vreeland	Barb Wallace	Henry Warren	Jacqui Weeks
Cindy Thompson	Lawrence Tideman	Mindy Tomazevic	Deby Trosper	Steve Underwood	Jason Vanwinkle	Nick Vukich	Bobby Wallace	Michael Warren	Jim Weeks
Claire Thompson	Sharon Tieman	Tom Tomazevic	Lauren Trosper	Lisa Unger	Ronald Vargas	Dustin Wacker	Heidi Wallace	Nikki Warren	Louise Weeks
Darlene Thompson	Carolyn Tierce	Carolyn Tomoroy	Sarah Trosper	Valerie Unruh	Susan Vargas	Joe Wackler	Ken Wallace	Elaine Warrick	Janet Weems
David Thompson	Gabe Tierce	Ray Tomoroy	Zeke Trosper	Aaron Unsderfer	Lisa Vargo	Lynn Waddell	Mark Wallace	Larry Warrick	Lorna Weese
Dennis Thompson, DVM	George Tierce	Gary Tone	Ovellie Trott	Tony Unsderfer	Marion Varman, DVM	Robert Waddell	Susan Wallace	Carl Warrings	Don Wegner
	Kathryn Tietz	John Tongen	Barbara Troute	Jo Ann Unsworth		Hugh Wade	Tanisha Wallace	Mr. and Mrs. Martin Wartman	Fred Wegner
Edward Thompson	Michael Tietz	Agnes P. Tony	Matt Troutfelter	Chuck Unsworth, Jr.	"Hobo Jim" Varsos	Richard A. Wade	Terry Wallace		Mary Wehatley
Helen Thompson	Bob Till	Peter Tony	Charlie Trowbridge	Chuck Unsworth, Sr.	Bob Vasey, DVM	Tonya Wade	Todd Wallace	Candace Waruch	Ada Weihart
Joanne Thompson	Marva Till	John Toomer	Mr & Mrs O. F. Troxel	John Unterberg	Craig Vassar	Wanda Wade	Lura Wallance	David Warwick	Henry Weil
John Thompson	Michael Till	Thomas Tope	John Troy	Peter Usugan	James Vatter	Dolores Waffen	Chris Waller	Judy Warwick	Dave Weimeer
Larry Thompson	Bonnie Timbers	Frank Torres	Ed Trump	John Vacek	Carolyn Muegge Vaughan	Ed Waffen	Robert Wallick	Terrell Washington	D.J. Weimer
Lee Thompson	Kirsten Timbers	Scott Torrison	Lowell Tschetter	Farrel Vail		Tony Waffen	Dick Walling	Genzo Watanabe	Dave Weimer
Loren Thompson	Rose Timbers	Kenneth Torsak	Ed Tucker	Nathan Vail	Julia E. Vaughan	Elaine Wagget	Cynthia Wallis, DVM	Bill Watkins	Sherri Weimer
Louise Thompson	John Timmerman	Steve Totten	Jeff Tucker	Tominiko Vaka	Norman D. Vaughan	Norm Waggner	William Walluk	George Watson	Mark Weinburger
Morris Thompson	Jackie Timothy	Suzan Toussaint	Karen Tucker	Sylvia Valesquez	Verona Vaughan	Sheryl Waggner	Barbra Walsh	Joseph Watson	Shari Weinburger
Nathan Thompson	Leigha Tindall	Dennis Towarak	Lacey Tucker	Jon Valette	Amy Vaughn	Dennis Wagner	John Walsh	Tom Watson	Roger Weir
Paul Thompson	Justin Tinderella	Matt Towarak	Lorraine Tucker	C.A. Valgardson	Ed Vaughn	Dick Wagner	Pearse Walsh	John Watterman	Steven Weir
Rhonda Thompson	Marilyn Tinderella	Rose Towarak	Misha Tucker	Martha Valiant	Karen Vaughn	Willie Wagner	April Walter	Barb Wattum	Ruth Weise
Roberta Thompson	Aaron Tinker	Sam Towarak	Brian Tunguenuk	Christopher Vallardson	Mary Vavick	Erling Wagner	Larry Walter	Joel Wattum	Scott Weismantel
Scott Thompson	Audrey Tinker	Tim Towarak	Liz Turinsky		Maxine Vehlow	Kathy Wainer	Carol Walters	Heather Wayman	Charles Weiss
Sue Thompson	Ira Tion	Clarence Towarak, Jr.	Rhoda Turinsky	Randy Vallee	Nancy Veitch	Daryl Waites	Charlie Walters	Marci Wayman	Mary Weiss
Vi Thompson	Doug Tipton	John Tower	Tony Turinsky	Martha Vallent	Albert Vent	Kelli Waits	Chuck Walters	John Weatherwax	Tasha Weiss
Robert Thompson, Sr.	Jana Tipton	Willie Towksjea	Andrea Turnbow	Joe Vallort	Steffen Verdin	Gleo Wakefield	Jeri Walters	Margaret Weatherwax	Joanne Welch
Cathy Thomsen	Shirley Tisdale	Robert Townley	Allen Turner	Maria Vallort	Carole Verdoia	Joe Wakefield	Jojo Walters	Randy Weatherwax	Scott Welch

Betsy Weldon
Joan Weldon
Warren Weldon
Carol Welker
Mark Well
Earl Wellen
Jennifer Welliver
Gary Wells
Ivan Wells
Kim Wells
Mark Wells
Martha Wells
Pam Wells
Doug Welsh
Jack Welsh
Jane Welsh
John Welsh
Rita Welsh
Thomas Welsh, DVM
Laura Welsher
Fred Wemark
Jim Wempe, DVM
Beth Wendel
Ed Wendt, DVM
Ron Wendt
Darrel Wentz
Kevin Wenz
C.J. Werdeo
Steven Werdeo
Don Werkema
George Werkema
Linda Werkema
Jodi Werner
Sallye Werner
Cindy Werth
Helen Werth
Hannah Wesley
Bob Wessinger
Judi Wessler
Aaron West
Jerry West
John West
Mike West
Randy West
Keith Westfall
LaDonna Westfall
Dick Westlund
Susan Westlund
Steve Weston
Rollin Westrum
Martha Westrvelt
Bryan Weyauvana
Tom Weyhing
Al Whaley

Stephanie Whaley
Lew Whalin
Rita Whalin
Barry Wharam
Bob Wheeler
Dena Wheeler
Jeff Wheeler
Kevin Wheeler
Mr. & Mrs. David
   Wheelwright
Linda Whelen
Daren D. Whitaker
Debra Ann
   Whitbeck
Rick Whitbeck
Ann Whitcock
Jay Whitcock
Cathy White
Cheryl White
Don White
Donna White
Glenda White
Ian White
Jon White
Larry White
Linda White
Lori White
Sandy White
Tim White
Virginia White
Zachary White
Benjamin Whitehead
Bonnie Whitehouse
Steve Whitehouse
Ralph Whitemore
Vince Whitington
Ann Whitlock
Darell Whitlock
Rene Whitman
Jim Whitmore
Michael Whitmore
Stan Whitmore
Ward Whitmore
Mrs. C.V. Whitney
Rich Whitney
Susan Whiton, DVM
Scott Whitson
Susan Whittemore
Helen Whittenkeller
Bonnie Whittier
Kathy Whittier
Fred Whittingham
Mike Whittington
Conrad Whyte

Marilyn Whyte
Steve C. Wical
Sorothy Wick
Steve Widmer
Dianne Widom
Ivan Widom
Mark Wienburger
Sheri Wienburger
Ronald Wierzbicki
Dawn Wiggin
Dick Wiggins
Karen Wiggins
Malcom Wiggins
Chris Wiita
Joanne Wiita
Dorothy Wik
Randy Wike
Elizabeth Wilbur
Kenneth Wilcox
Steve Wilcox
Pat Wilcoxen
Joseph Wilde
Tom Wilde
Jena Wildels
Rich Wildgrub
Eep Wilding
Thomas Wilding
Jim Wiley
Nikki Wilfong
Glynn Wilford
Smith Wilford
Wendy Wilford
Greg Wilhelmi
Linda Wilhelmi
Steve Wilhelmi
Ed Wilke
Pat Wilke
Ronnie Wilke
Mr & Mrs V.R.
   Wilkerson
Tina Wilkins
Sue Will
Wesley Willand
Dan Willequer
Peg Willett
Arthur Willetts
Amos Williams
Bill Williams
Bob Williams
Cliff Williams
Dean Williams
Dick Williams
Forrest Williams
Fran Williams

Fred Williams
Hester Williams
James Williams
Jim Williams
John Williams
June Williams
Kate Williams
Kathleen Williams
Kent Williams
Larry Williams
Liesle Williams
Linda Williams
Mara Williams
Mark Williams
Mary Williams
Milinda Williams
Penny Williams
Petra Williams
Phil Williams
R.T. (Bob) Williams
Richard Williams
Rudy Williams
Sandy Williams
Sherri Williams
Steve Williams
Sue Williams
Tiffy Williams
Tracy Williams
Van Williams
Paulette Williams-Nix
Nancy Williamson
John Willianis
Andy Willis
Ann Willis
Bernie Willis
Bill Willis
Elizabeth Willis
Jeannette Willis
Tony Willis
Willie Willis
David Willoya
Roger Willoya
Russ Wilmont
June Wilmot
S.R. Wilmot
Bill Wilson
Brad Wilson
Brada Wilson
Denise Wilson
Dick Wilson
Ellen Wilson
Greg Wilson
Jeremy Wilson
Karen Wilson

Larry Wilson
Merle Wilson
Michael Wilson
Myra Wilson
Patricia Wilson
Rich Wilson
Ted Wilson
Tom Wilson
Victor Wilson
Walter Wilson
Jan Wimberly
Ethan Windahl
Gary Windahl
Peggy Windahl
Mary Jane Windle
Norman Winelle
Hope Wing
Ed Wingard
Tom Wingard
Richard Winkleman
Anne Winkler
Frank Winkler
Barbara Winkley
Buckey Winkley
Robin Winkley
Joan Winter, DVM
Ron Winters
Jennifer Wippich
Barbara Wireman
Pat Wirschem
Ray Wirschem
Dave Wirth
Lois Wirtz
Louise Wirtz
Laura Wisbin
Tom Wisbin
Alexie Wise
Duane Wise
Joanne Wise
Rhett Wise
Richard Wise
Annie Wishon
Lauren Wishon
Larry Witaschek
Ray Witaschek
Jeff Wite
Ken Wite
Vince Withington
Helen Wittenkeller
Mary Lou Wojtalik
Al Wold
Bob Wold
Dorothy Wold
Margaret Wold

Donna Wolf
Joseph L. Wolf
Kelly Wolfbrandt
David Wolfe
Elizabeth Wolfe
Jeffrey Wolfe
Joseph Wolfe
Lee Wolfe
Roger Wollam
Lucille Wongitillin
Ann Wood
Connie Wood
Dar Wood
Iris Wood
James A. Wood
Jerel Wood
Jim Wood
John Wood
Mary Wood
Richard "Woody"
   Wood
Robert Wood
Susan Wood
Ted Wood
Leigh Ann Woodard
Lindsey Woodard
Robert Woodgeard
Johnny Woodhurst
Bernadette Woods
Bob Woods
Cass Woods
Cheryl Woods
Cornelius Woods
Gil Woods
Jim Woods
Kimberly Woods
Michael D. Woods
Susan Woods
Bob Woodward
Nell Woodward
Steve Woodward
Aaron Woody
Tom Woody
Shawna Woolard
Helen Wooley
Steve Wooliver
Chris Woosley
Len Worcester
Linda Worcester
Eric Workman
Gayle Workman
Steve Woronuk
Dave Worth
Annie Worthington

Dave Wortman
Martin Wortman
Bill Wosilius
Karen Wraith
Evelyn Wrase
Andrew Wright
Brenda Wright
Bryan Wright
Cheryl Wright
Eugene Wright
George Wright
James Wright
Janet Wright
Jason Wright
Kevin Wright
Martha A. Wright
Nancy Wright
Sandy Wright
Tom Wright
Victoria Wright
Don Wyant
Chris Wyckoff
Roger Wyckoff
Lynn Wylie
Margaret Wylie
Pete Wylie
Hazel Wyse
Linda Yacks
Jim Yagle
Nick Yaholkovsky
Ray Yakesh
Mary Ellen Yamabe
Momoko Yamabe
Arla Yancey
Ivan Yancey
Jay Yancey
Cynthia Yates
Frederick Yates
Robbie Yates
Trenton Yates
Elinor Yatlin
Johnny Yatlin
Al Yatlin, Jr.
Lisa Yeager
Norm Yeager
Rhonda Yeager
Rose Yeager
Pam Yeargan
Norman Yeaw
Steve Yedinak
Mike Yerkes
John Yerlur
Charlie Yoder
Ronald Yorgason

Tom Yorgason
Linda York
Arthur Young
Chris Young
Dan Young
David Young
Diana Young
Dick Young
Harbal Young
Harvey Young
Jennifer Young
Michael Young
Neil Young
Rep. Don Young
Richard Young
Roy Young
Sally Young
Theresa Young
Tom Young
Betsy Yount
Myra Yount
Bob Zachel
Tina Zacher
Liza Zahler
Kent Zakzensik
Kent Zakzeu
Kendra Zamzow
Igor Zandeur
Lisa Zanetti
Cynthia Zappala
Harold Zarr
John Zeller
Lorena Zeller
Paul Zeller
Cordy Zepada
Jack Zerbel
Robin Zerbel
A. Sasha Zermanek
Clare Zickuhr
Andy Ziegler
Linda Ziesmer
Kevin Zilco
Buster Zimmer
Lori Zollum-Boots
Dave Zuggsberger
David Zukowski
JoAnn Zukowski
Johnny Zutz

AND

all the people of Skwentna, Nikolai, McGrath, Ruby, Galena, Nulato, Kaltag, Unalakleet, Shageluk, Anvik, Grayling, Golovin, Shaktooklik, Koyuk, Elim, White Mountain, Solomon, and Nome. Organizers put it best in the April/May 1978 issue of the *Iditarod Runner*: "Without your enthusiasm and support, there could be no race. Thanks for taking the mushers into your homes. Thanks for taking in the aviators, race marshals, wives and friends, media personnel, and race officials. Thank you for sharing your wood, your fuel, your beds, coffee, and the many, many good meals. Most of all, thank you for being there to welcome the drivers as they arrive in your village."

If you volunteered for the Iditarod Trail Sled Dog Race any time during its twenty-five-year history, but don't find your name here, we want to include you in future editions. Write: Epicenter Press, Iditarod Volunteers, P.O. Box 82368, Kenmore, Washington 98028; or fax (206) 481-8253.